ARCHAEOLOGY BELOW THE CLIFF

CARIBBEAN ARCHAEOLOGY AND ETHNOHISTORY

L. Antonio Curet, Series Editor

ARCHAEOLOGY BELOW THE CLIFF

Race, Class, and Redlegs in
Barbadian Sugar Society

MATTHEW C. REILLY

THE UNIVERSITY OF ALABAMA PRESS
TUSCALOOSA

The University of Alabama Press
Tuscaloosa, Alabama 35487-0380
uapress.ua.edu

Typeface: Adobe Garamond Pro and Trajan Pro

Cover image: Annalee Davis, Saccharum officinarum *and Queen Anne's
Lace*, detail, latex on dry wall, 70″ × 88″, 2014; courtesy of Annalee Davis
Cover design: David Nees

Cataloging-in-Publication data is available from the Library of Congress.
ISBN: 978-0-8173-2028-7
E-ISBN: 978-0-8173-9242-0

To my parents, for everything

CONTENTS

ILLUSTRATIONS

Figures

Table

PREFACE

Books of history are often responsive to the dangers of the moments in which
they appear, but they cannot be called into being in those moments.

—David Roediger (2017:51)

Scholarly work is often affected by a particular political moment or climate.
This book is no exception. Much of the research that led to the publication
of this book was undertaken between 2012 and 2015. During my time in Barbados, it was regularly explained to me that I happened to begin this project
at the right time. There was a growing awareness of the story of the Redlegs,
and many people on the island who claim Redleg ancestry or are ascribed with
the label of *Redleg* or *poor white* were far more willing to discuss the historical
and social baggage of these terms than in generations past. This is of course
advantageous from the perspective of a researcher, but this openness is not
without its caveats. Why, all of a sudden, in the early decades of the twenty-
first century, had the story of the Redlegs become easier or less taboo to talk
about? What was the catalyst for a degree of comfort in discussing the historical particulars of a seemingly anomalous population on a Caribbean island
that was for so long defined by race-based plantation slavery?

There are positive and productive reasons for this sudden growth of interest
in the story of the Redlegs. Despite centuries of vicious stereotypes that have
been leveled against this population said to have descended from seventeenth-
century indentured servants from Europe, a more publicly pronounced sense
of pride came to be associated with Redleg identity and ancestry. As genealogical research and heritage tourism continue to expand, kinship networks
that span the globe traced genealogical webs that converged in rural corners
of the southeasterly Caribbean island of Barbados. Additionally, those who
are today associated with the pejoratives *Redleg* and *poor white* promote a
story of resilience and perseverance. As this book describes, life for those living on the margins of the plantation landscape, regardless of racial identity
or genealogy, was often difficult. While Barbadian poor whites were not the
victims of the brutalization and dehumanization of African chattel slavery,
theirs is nonetheless a story of economic hardship and placemaking. In the
chapters that follow, I illustrate how the Redlegs became an intricate part of
Barbadian society. In this sense, there are elements of this story that should
be celebrated and promoted as an essential component of Barbados's rich and
vibrant heritage.

The story of the Redlegs, however, must not eclipse the larger narrative of

Barbadian and Caribbean modern history. Barbados was one of England's first grossly successful overseas colonies in terms of profit extract. In no uncertain terms, the wealth derived from Barbados and its neighboring colonial territories in the centuries to come was produced by the blood, sweat, and tears of enslaved Africans. This dark and criminal history is palpable in most, if not all, facets of Barbadian life; it can be experienced on the landscape, in the architecture, in the political infrastructure, in monuments and memorials, in economic distribution and inequality, in kinship patterns, in local food and flavor, and in daily social interactions. This living history manifests in new permutations and formations that are linked to imperial pasts.

The Redlegs of Barbados, for better or for worse, are very much part of this history. Unlike many of the historical accounts and scholarly perspectives cited throughout this book, the findings presented here refuse to sever the story of the Redlegs from the composite whole of the Barbadian social fabric and the trajectory of Atlantic-world modernity. There are certainly elements of this narrative that are precarious and unique within the annals of Caribbean history, but to dismiss the Redlegs as simply marginal, exceptional, or anomalous avoids the complicated ways in which histories and material signatures of race, class, colonialism, and capitalism become intertwined on the Barbadian plantation landscape. The idiosyncrasies of race and class, the main analytics of this study, were of major consequence for all those who lived, worked, and died in an exploitative, colonial system, including the Redlegs. Their experiences were often drastically different from those of enslaved and free Africans and Afro-Barbadians, and I am therefore careful not to conflate the two. At the same time, nonelites similarly had to navigate the turbulent waters of plantation life. Part of that process included interactions and relationships across racial lines that spanned the good, the bad, and the ugly. Relevant to any archaeological study, the quotidian, material dimensions of plantation life are revelatory of the effects that colonial, capitalistic, and racialized structures had on poor whites and Afro-Barbadians.

Through my telling of the story of Barbadian Redlegs in public and in print, I have been encouraged and humbled by positive receptions and feedback concerning some of the research presented here, but those who hold a radically different perspective on the history of the Redlegs have raucously made their positions heard. Many believe that the Redlegs are the descendants of the first slaves to work in the Americas and in Barbados, specifically. Proclaiming the historical fact of white slavery, more radical segments of the transatlantic public that subscribe to this narrative reduce the history of poor whites to an unsubstantiated myth of slavery. A quick Google search for stories about white or Irish slavery will reveal an assortment of memes and factually inaccurate stories dedicated to honoring the slaves whom history forgot, or, more specifically, the slaves whom the liberal academy refuses to acknowledge.

Much of this pseudohistory, which ultimately falls apart under the slightest bit of scrutiny, serves to justify steadfast denials of racial inequality or injustice. "My [or our] ancestors were slaves, but I [or we] just got over it"—or so it goes. Some who are more familiar with the historical literature will suggest that the distinction between slavery and indentured servitude was one of semantics, thus overlooking the experiential implications that those distinctions had and the monumental consequences that they *would* have in centuries to come. Now entering the mainstream, white nationalist ideology, rooted in gross manipulations of history and despicable racist attitudes, has made its presence known on social media, in the streets, and in public office. The belief that whites or the Irish were the first slaves in places like Barbados, and the use of this distorted history in support of pernicious political attitudes, is just a minute example of why these histories matter. These are some of the politics that weighed heavily while the process of writing this book was closing.

Of course, not every person who believes that the Irish were slaves in the Caribbean is a supporter of alt-right movements harboring racist beliefs, and it would be dangerous and unfair to assume so. Debates about the nature of slavery, unfreedom, bound labor, and race are critical for the advancement of our knowledge of these subjects. In fact, I have had the good fortune to discuss and debate these issues with open-minded scholars, colleagues, and friends who appreciate the productive power in applying critical thought to historical questions that have sociopolitical relevance in the present. If these conversations result in greater insight into the inner workings of colonial and capitalistic formulations of race and class, perhaps such insights can be useful in dismembering the exploitative and oppressive foundations of these systems.

The most distressing and frightening aspect of the growth of the white slavery narrative is the stunning degree to which racism is fueled by and fuels imagined histories. Another resulting tragedy of the rise of this pernicious myth has been the sidestepping of the realities, horrors, and criminal violence characterizing African chattel slavery and systemic racism. To return to the Redlegs, however, there is another consequence of this white or Irish slave mythology that more directly relates to the study at hand. As the Redlegs continue to be understood through a lens of perceived seventeenth-century enslavement, their nuanced identities and histories have become sidelined; plights of economic hardship among segments of the population serve as evidence confirming an ancestry of slavery, bypassing over three hundred years of life on the plantation landscape. The Redlegs, therefore, become frozen in place and time, passive and often voiceless regarding how they perceive their own place in Barbadian history and society.

This book is an attempt to rectify this myopia. Although I briefly engage with the issues surrounding the distinction between seventeenth-century indentured servitude and slavery, most of the book focuses on a community at the margins of a large sugar plantation in which poor white families once lived. I was fortunate enough to meet Barbadians of diverse racial ancestries who still reside in the area of this now-abandoned community. They generously shared their stories with me, and, for that, I am forever in their debt. I have the utmost respect for those Barbadians who opened their homes and histories to me, and I hope that respect seeps through these pages. This story, after all, is theirs. Those expecting to find a story about the white slaves of Barbados should look elsewhere. Instead, I offer an archaeological approach to the story of a small plantation community spawned by modern, racialized logics of colonialism—a community that nonetheless offers lessons concerning the vulnerability of colonial systems, and it is my hope that these lessons inspire those committed to the dismantling of those systemic forms that stubbornly persist.

ACKNOWLEDGMENTS

When I first went to college, I never thought that I would study archaeology, let alone write a book about it. This book can very much be attributed to that windy path of discovery that ultimately led me to a rather unexpected career and Barbados, which I now warmly consider somewhat of a second home. Every word in this book is owed to the people who made that journey possible and welcomed me as one of their own in my adopted home.

I have greatly benefited from academic mentors who continue to inspire me and push me to be a better scholar and person. This journey began at the University of Maryland and eventually took me to the University of Chicago, Syracuse University, Brown University, and now the City College of New York. I am only here today with my academic mentors' support. Thank you to Stephen Brighton, Mark Leone, Paul Shackel, Shannon Dawdy, Francois Richard, Chris DeCorse, Theresa Singleton, Shannon Novak, Lars Rodseth, the late Bill Kelleher, Sue Alcock, Tony Bogues, John Cherry, Peter van Dommelen, and my new colleagues at City College, especially Lotti Silber. Two mentors, in particular, put in tremendous amounts of time and effort to make sure I did not fall flat on my face throughout this process. I have gotten into dicey situations with Doug Armstrong on more than one occasion, but he has remained a mentor, teacher, leader, collaborator, and advocate. Many thanks for your patience, time, and support. Even after the countless headaches that I am no doubt responsible for, Jerry Handler is still an incredibly generous mentor. His knowledge of Barbados is unparalleled, and I am incredibly grateful that he shared his time, wisdom, notes, suggestions, and occasional pessimism with me.

Whether they know it or not, friends and colleagues shaped the ideas presented in this book through conversations in the classroom, at conferences, in the field, and, more often than not, in the bar. I have the utmost respect for the work that you do and value our friendships. Many thanks to Adela Amaral, Lynsey Bates, Zach Beier, Jess Bowes, Kate Brunson, Sarah Craft, Declan Cullen, Eve Dewan, Müge Durusu, Kristen Fellows, Adrienne Frie, Kevin Garstki, Liza Gijanto, Geneviève Godbout, Linda Gosner, Ryan Gray, Liam Hogan, the late Rachel Horlings, Lauren Hosek, Steve Karasic, Brett Kaufman, Sarah Kautz, Steve Lenik, Laura McAtackney, Fran McCormick, Sophie Moore, Miriam Müller, James Osborne, Kwame Otu, Tate Paulette, Sean Reid, Miriam Rothenberg, Krysta Ryzewski, Dwayne Scheid, Alex Due Smith, Fred Smith, Parker VanValkenburgh, Diane Wallman, and Alanna Warner.

Several students, volunteers, and friends braved a sometimes-treacherous walk through the woods to help me excavate in the community of Below Cliff. Thank you for your time, bucket-lifting abilities, insights, collegiality, good humor, patience, and dedication: Alan Armstrong, O-Dizzle Klein, Amber Lewis, Heidi Murray, Phil Nanton, Megan Porter, Dan Reilly, Ashley Silverstein, Lauren Silverstein, Eric Siedow, Michael Stoner, Rachel Susio, and Yevgeniy Zborovskiy.

Good luck to anyone who wants to convince me that there is a better place to work and live than Barbados. The beauty of the island is matched only by the people who inhabit this small corner of the Caribbean. Barbados is also home to some of the most gifted and dedicated scholars in the world. What can be overwhelming, however, is that just about everyone, in one way or another, is a scholar of the island in his or her own right. I learned a tremendous amount from all of those who offered slices of their endless wisdom. More importantly, you all treated me like family when I was far from my own. I count myself extremely lucky to consider you all colleagues, collaborators, and friends. Thank you to William Burton, Annalee Davis, Kevin Farmer, Ayesha Gibson, Richard Goddard, Newlands and Denyse Greenidge, Msgr. Vincent Harcourt-Blackett, Tara Inniss-Gibbs, Lynda Lewis, Diann Blades, John Knox, Marie-Claire Lyder, Evelyn O'Callaghan and Phil Kingston, Harriet Pierce, the Ward family, and Karl Watson. My deepest debt is owed to the extraordinary people who make up what I refer to in the book as the Below Cliff community. You welcomed me into your homes and trusted me with your stories. Some surnames appear in the pages that follow, but I provide them here to acknowledge my deep respect and gratitude. Thank you to members of the Norris, Gibson, Fenty, and Watson families who welcomed me into their community and homes. I especially want to single out the Norris family. Your kindness, generosity, and warmth resulted in a friendship that I will always cherish.

The actual research was made possible with the support of grants and institutions that welcomed me. The Fulbright IIE, a truly wonderful program that is in danger of losing funding, allowed me to reside in Barbados and complete the bulk of this research. Additionally, I received support and encouragement from the Maxwell School at Syracuse University and from the Joukowsky Institute for Archaeology and the Ancient World and the Center for the Study of Slavery and Justice at Brown University. In Barbados, I was warmly welcomed by the Barbados Museum and Historical Society, the University of the West Indies, and the Barbados National Trust. The writing process was facilitated by a very patient editor, Wendi Schnaufer. I greatly appreciate your dedication to this project and all of your advice throughout this process. I am also grateful to Antonio Curet for including this book is such a reputable Caribbean archaeology series.

The members of my family have provided me with unwavering support, for which they will have to settle for this book. You keep me grounded, loved, distracted (in a good way), and human. I hope my grandmother sees some of her late husband, my grandfather, in these pages; our family history was of course a source of inspiration for this project. My sister, Rebecca, was understandably more interested in Barbados's beaches than what the woods had to offer, but she continues to support me. She makes it easy for an older brother to look up to a younger sister. My brother, Dan, will likely disagree with many of the points being made in this book, but he still sweat his way through the woods to help me excavate and put up with what seemed like endless boxes of books in multiple moves around the country. The next pint is on me.

My parents, to whom this book is dedicated, have provided me with more love and support than I thought possible. My father, who cursed me with being a Vikings fan, provided me with nothing but encouragement in an endeavor so far removed from anything with which he was even remotely familiar. That, to me, is the definition of parental love. My mother has read more of my work than anyone else, from elementary school books about professional wrestling to academic journal articles. I continue to value her feedback, even if it is often filled with mom-isms. You both have been incredible advocates and even better parents. All of the good I have in my life I owe to you. I love you both.

INTRODUCTION

When you see de "ecky-bekky"
Man yuh so surprise, cause dey look funny:
Yellow hair, speckly-face an' dey feet brick-red.
Is fo' dat we does call dem de Redlegs.
> —From traditional Barbadian folk song "Backra
> Johnnies—Da Redleg Song" (Marshall et al. 1981)

A 4 × 4 Jeep bearing the logo Island Safari, with its doors painted to mimic the stripes of a zebra, slowly winds down the steep road leading from the village of Church View to the rough waters of Martin's Bay along the rugged east coast of Barbados. Visitors staying on the island and cruise ship passengers who elect to take a break from the island's beautiful beaches are treated to breathtaking views of the island's rocky coastline. These tourists fill the padded seats in the back of the Jeep as their local guide points out flora and fauna of interest. On this safari, however, spectators will not find giraffes, rhinos, large reptiles, or other exotic beasts. Rather, passengers encounter the natural beauty of the limestone island while simultaneously witnessing the still-visible plantation landscape and its inhabitants. Agricultural fields, rolling hills, the ruins of rustic windmills, and Barbadians calmly operating on "island time" provide visitors with a quaint impression of rural life in the former English colony. This brief tour across the island introduces passengers to a landscape that, while transformed over time, has dominated Barbadian society, economics, politics, and geography for nearly four centuries.

The safari experience introduces visitors to the history of the sugar industry, an industry that is slowly crumbling on the island but that has left an enduring and palpable legacy across the Caribbean region (see Thompson 2002; Henry 2004). The Jeep roams the countryside passing large, often-gated plantation great houses, the ruins of windmills, and derelict plantation works that were once used for the boiling and curing of sugarcane. As it passes the meticulously planted rows of cane, passengers then encounter plantation tenantries. These communities, often bearing the name of the plantation, were largely established following emancipation in 1834 when the villages for enslaved Afro-Barbadian laborers were demolished and plowed for the cultivation of cane. As a result, the plantation laborers took up residence in these newly established tenantries at the peripheries of plantation lands, renting small parcels from the very planters who had previously owned their bodies.

While traditional architectural techniques and styles are continually being replaced by more modern homes made of concrete, chattel houses, the architectural staple for which Barbados is known, can still be spotted in plantation tenantries. These historic boarded structures are rectangular in shape and rest atop large limestone blocks known as groundsels and can be easily disassembled and reassembled if moving is necessary—a convenient characteristic for residents who own their home but not the land on which the structure is situated. Passengers on the island tour can catch a glimpse of rural Barbadians as they wash and hang clothes to dry, cultivate small household gardens, repair or paint their homes, feed chickens, walk along the side of the narrow road to the bus stop, socialize with friends and neighbors, and play dominos at the local rum shop. Most of the individuals the tourists encounter are predominantly of African descent—a very direct reminder, even if overlooked by some island visitors, of the legacies of slavery and the realities of a colonial and industrial system that has indelibly linked Africans and Afro-Barbadians to the plantation landscape for generations.

Each year, thousands of tourists flock to the southeasterly Caribbean island of Barbados (Figure I.1) for the sun, beaches, sweet rum drinks, all-inclusive resorts, and all the frills associated with a Caribbean getaway. While the island is certainly a global destination, the largest numbers arrive by plane or cruise ship from the United Kingdom, Canada, and the United States (Barbados Hotel and Tourism Association 2014). Additionally, the majority of such island visitors are white, meaning of European descent. On an island where roughly 92.4% of the population self-identifies as black, racial politics weigh heavily in how local communities understand and promote their own heritage in a tourism-driven economy (Gmelch 2012; Battle-Baptiste 2017).[1] Those who forego a day at the beach for an excursion around the island may marvel at the natural beauty of the island and even appreciate the brief introduction to Barbadian history and culture. Do they, however, feel a direct connection with those that lived or labored on this southeasterly Caribbean island? As short-term visitors to an island nation independent since 1966, and legally free of slavery since 1834, how do tourists experience, if at all, the local history of colonialism and chattel slavery? These questions are admittedly abstract, but they speak to the messy entanglements that bind people, places, and things throughout the Atlantic world in the past and present—a temporal and postcolonial messiness that too often goes unacknowledged. How we think about those connections and how they are experienced locally in a place like Barbados are important themes throughout this book. The population which takes center stage in this study, however, adds complicated dimensions to understandings of Barbadian and Caribbean history and society.

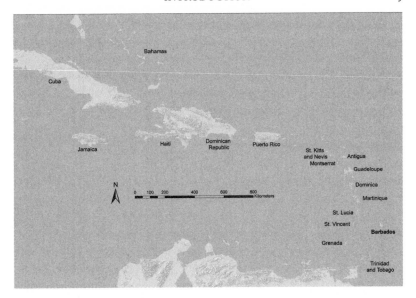

Figure I.1. Map of the Caribbean region with Barbados highlighted in bold in the southeast. (Matthew C. Reilly)

As the Jeep makes its way past the small village of Church View, a postemancipation tenantry on the periphery of Clifton Hall Plantation, tour guides often inform passengers of a rather unique aspect of Barbadian history that is now most visible in this small corner of the island. In addition to spotting Afro-Barbadian residents whose homes line the meandering road from Church View to Newcastle to Martin's Bay, the safari adventurers catch a glimpse of light-skinned community residents. These are the so-called Redlegs or poor whites of Barbados. After hearing descriptions of this population that link them to seventeenth-century European indentured servants, the passersby may find the presence of these individuals perplexing. If the history of Barbados is largely defined by a sugar and slavery system, what are we to make of the presence and persistence of a nonelite, European-descendant population in these small villages at the margins of sugar plantations? The very sight of such individuals along the rural roads of the parish of St. John connotes a population out of place and out of time. For those who encounter the Redlegs or their story, like countless tourists who visit the island each year, the presence of an impoverished white population in a prototypical slave society (Berlin 1998) has sparked quizzical interest as well as a pointed politicization of Barbadian history.

Over the last two decades, the rise of popular literature (McCafferty 2002;

Kelleher 2001; Plummer 2012; Dolan 2012), works of nonfiction (Hoffman 1993; O'Callaghan 2000; Jordan and Walsh 2008; Akamatsu 2010), television and radio documentaries, and music concerning the Redlegs of Barbados suggests that at least some of the individuals who have directly encountered the Redlegs, or at least their history, have connected to their story. In 2009, two television documentaries produced by an Irish documentary company, Moondance Productions, aired on Ireland's TG4 and BBC Scotland, portraying the present-day Redlegs of St. John as the direct descendants of the "Cromwellian slaves" originally sent across the Atlantic from Ireland, Scotland, England, and Wales in the 1650s to suffer the hardships of laboring on the island's burgeoning sugar plantations. The general popularity of these films suggests that the documentaries were particularly successful at tugging at the heartstrings of Irish, Scottish, English, Canadian, American, and even Caribbean viewers who sympathized with the plight of the Redlegs, or the descendants of the island's first "slaves," who were interviewed and featured throughout the films.

Despite the select popularity of such productions and publications, the story of the Barbadian poor whites is still a relatively unknown aspect of Barbadian, Caribbean, and Atlantic-world history. The preceding discussion serves to demonstrate that when acknowledged or encountered, the narrative of the Barbadian poor whites has been particularly enticing to individuals eager to learn about the island's "white slaves" (Handler and Reilly 2017; Hogan et al. 2016) with whom some transatlantic audiences feel an ancestral connection. Greatly lacking, however, is a comprehensive analysis of the place of Barbadian poor whites in island history and society that directly seeks to understand their daily experiences on the plantation landscape, including how they interacted with those around them (for the most substantive, locally situated discussions to date, see Davis 1978; Jones 2007; Lambert 2005; Rosenberg 1962; Sheppard 1977; Watson 1970, 2000b). Additionally, the tourist experience and works discussed above have largely been from the perspective of or produced for audiences outside the Caribbean. How did Barbadian Redlegs of centuries past live their daily lives in a sugar and slavery society? Furthermore, how do individuals who would today be labeled as Redlegs understand their own identity, history, ancestry, and place in Barbados?

Presenting answers to these broad questions is one of the primary considerations of this book. In addressing these questions, it is essential to ponder the conceptual implications of the Redleg presence on the island. Redlegs' very existence as largely poor and ostensibly white puts them at odds with the broader narrative of an Atlantic-world social, political, and economic hierarchy that was, and is, laden with racial attitudes that legitimized the white over black mentality and reality (Jordan 1968; Mills 1997).[2] This book presents a new approach to interpreting the lives of the poor whites in the past and present. Using historical archaeological methods, data presented illuminate the realities poor white community members faced. Additionally, through an exploration of the historical record, it is possible to reveal how Barbadian and colonial elites developed particular attitudes toward the poor whites that shaped how they were, and are, perceived by outsiders. Through a case study of the poor white tenantry of Below Cliff, this analysis highlights a friction between the perception of the poor whites and what occurred at the local level in these communities. This friction contests static conceptualizations of plantation infrastructure and the ways in which laborers experienced the hyperindustrialized sugar landscape and its diverse inhabitants.

WHO ARE THE REDLEGS?

The poor whites, Redlegs, Ecky-Beckies, or Buckra Johnnies, as they are pejoratively referred to, have inhabited the island for nearly four centuries. Thousands arrived in the seventeenth century as indentured servants or small farmers. In the wake of the mid-seventeenth-century sugar revolution, however, the white underclass was soon prodded to the margins of the plantation landscape as English planters met increasing labor demands with a more aggressive involvement in the African slave trade (Beckles 1985, 1989; Dunn 2000 [1972]; Menard 2006; Newman 2013). While indentured servitude and its permutations (such as apprenticeship) would persist well into the postemancipation period, the majority of this poor white demographic—whose numbers consistently hovered between 8,000 and 12,000 from the eighteenth to the twentieth century (see Sheppard 1977)—sought refuge on the "rab" lands of the island, or those parcels deemed unworthy of sugar production. In addition to urban neighborhoods in the Bridgetown area in which many poor whites found employment, it was, and still is, here in these rural communities that the Redlegs have made a living on the edges of the plantation landscape.

This historical archaeological investigation seeks to address the lived realities of the white underclass of Barbados from their arrival as indentured servants and small farmers to their inhabitation of village tenantries. Despite the existence of several known poor white tenantries around the island, Below Cliff was selected as the primary focus of investigation. Thus I have incorporated archaeological and historical data from this now-abandoned community in the parish of St. John (Figure I.2). Now hidden by dense forest overgrowth, Below Cliff sits directly underneath Hackleton's Cliff along the island's east coast and was once the site of dozens of households. Archaeological and

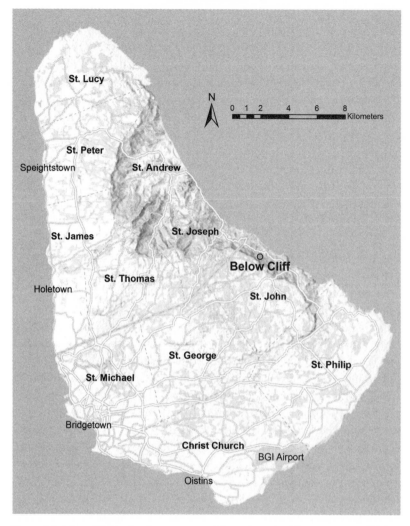

Figure I.2. Map of Barbados depicting parish boundaries and larger towns. The location of Below Cliff is marked in the easterly parish of St. John. (Matthew C. Reilly)

historical data confirm the occupation of the tenantry from at least the mid-eighteenth, and possibly mid-seventeenth, century to the early 1960s.

This is the first archaeological investigation of the poor whites of Barbados. Although a small number of anthropological case studies have investigated the lives of those living in poor white communities in St. John from the 1960s to the 1970s (Davis 1978; Rosenberg 1962; Simmons 1976; Watson 1970), many attempts to address the poor whites have succumbed to the perpetuation of stereotypes (see, for example, O'Callaghan 2000; Keagy 1972, 1975; Price 1957; see also Reilly 2013). While this project owes a debt of gratitude to these early historical and anthropological works, it is also a noticeable departure from approaches that treated the poor whites or Redlegs as a distinct, bounded, and socioeconomically isolated group. Each of these works illustrates some degree of interaction and cultural similarities among the Redlegs and the Afro-Barbadian population (see especially Watson 1970, 2000b), but sentiments of poor white isolation are still ingrained in island histories. As such, this study situates the story of the Redlegs *within* island history and society; in other words, this analysis privileges inclusion and embeddedness over exclusion and isolation.

An introduction to the Redlegs in general, and to the archaeological site of examination more specifically, has been provided, now the central terminology of this study needs clarification. *Poor white* and *Redleg* are pejoratives that carry baggage. These monikers can be used in derogatory ways, but they remain the only terms available to adequately refer to this seemingly exceptional and distinct population. In general terms, the label poor white refers to impoverished peoples with pale complexions who are typically found on the island's east coast and throughout the rugged northeasterly region known as the Scotland District. Other pejoratives, such Ecky-Beckie and Buckra Johnny, are equally derisive. Of critical importance is the fact that the adjectives in the label poor white are the very subjects of inquiry in this study. Arguments concerning the instability of racial boundaries and categories question the implied purity of the term "white" (see Monahan 2011; Jones 2007). Additionally, despite the ubiquitous usage of the term "poor white" in the historical record and contemporary Barbadian society, uncritical usage of the moniker allows the group's economic circumstances to be a defining attribute of their identity. In essence, although quotation marks will not be used around the colloquial terms (as they are in several of my publications), my reliance on these terms simultaneously recognizes their social currency and challenges the assumptions, discrimination, and politics that are laden within such epithets.

But why use such terms at all if they are so negatively charged? Sociologist Matt Wray addresses similar terms that reference poor whites in the United States like poor white trash, lubber, and cracker. He argues that these labels are stigmatypes, "stigmatizing boundary terms that simultaneously denote and enact cultural and cognitive divides between in-groups and out-groups, between acceptable and unacceptable identities, between proper and improper behaviors" (Wray 2006:23). The boundary work done by stigmatypes, one of the focuses of Wray's analysis, is similarly important to a study of the poor whites of Barbados. In his critique of scholars who have eschewed terms like white trash, hillbilly, or redneck because of their negative connotations, John Hartigan provides a similar defense for the use of these terms, arguing that "if images of poor whites in popular cultural forms were reduced to a generic, neutral form of reference, the rhetorical identity of white trash as a function of a discourse of difference would be rendered unintelligible, though hardly inoperable" (Hartigan 2005:113). In other words, the terms carry historical weight that can be cutting, but their social power demands attention to the ways that they rhetorically mark boundaries and operate in local vernacular. Presented as a question, what do terms like Redleg say about the racial and class status of those inscribed with this identity, and how are group boundaries established, maintained, contested, or permeated?

Etymologically, the origins of the term Redleg and its earliest uses are imprecise. David Lambert suggests connections between Redshanks, a term used for Scottish Highlanders in the seventeenth century, and its Redleg derivative. It was not until the late eighteenth century, however, that the term Redlegs came to "describe the poor whites in general" (Lambert 2005:100). Associated with the Scottish connection, it has been suggested that Redleg came to replace "Redshank" as it came to refer to the sunburn from which seventeenth-century European indentured servants suffered as they toiled under the unforgiving tropical sun (Sheppard 1977:2–3). While there is no explicit use of the term in primary sources from the seventeenth century, it may very well have been a colloquial label, particularly when the population of indentured laborers on the island was considerable. The earliest known written appearance of the term is found in Dr. John Williamson's account of his time on the island in 1798: "A ridge of hills, in the adjacent country, about the middle of the island, is called Scotland, where a few of the descendants of a race of people transported in the time of Cromwell still live, called Redlegs" (Williamson 1817:27). Etymologies aside, Redleg, Buckra, Ecky-Beckie, and poor white, among others, came to represent impoverished Barbadians of European descent in rural and urban contexts.

In the ensuing chapters, I address the construction of the discourse that engendered notions of poor white exceptionalism and exclusion. This discourse would eventually lend itself to historical and public understandings of the poor whites. It is against this backdrop that I present archaeological data, insights from archival sources, and oral histories to provide a more inclusive interpretation of the poor whites. The research undertaken for this book sparked significant questions concerning the entanglements of race and class. What did it mean to be labeled white and poor in Barbados? Did Redlegs struggle to the same degree as enslaved and free Afro-Barbadians? If not a quantifiable phenomenon, how can we comparatively measure economic status and the experience of hardship? How porous were the boundaries between white and black, and what was done to patrol or maintain these physical and conceptual boundaries? How does the material record of the poor whites lend itself to an interpretation of daily life? How does the material record of the poor whites compare with that of contemporaneous Afro-Barbadians? In what follows, I address such questions, among others, in a study that navigates the history of the poor whites from English settlement of the island in 1627 to the present.

The research questions enumerated here were in part developed prior to and during initial research trips to Barbados beginning in 2011. They were, however, substantially expanded and altered as the project commenced and congealed. Methodological difficulties and realizations reached during the course of research affected the questions that were being asked and how and where research was conducted. These transformations were also significantly influenced by my interactions with Barbadians who offered unique and personal insights about their experiences and knowledge of the local area and its history. The metamorphosis of this research project can best be described as organic in that it was based on happenstance in the field, making research objectives amenable to frequent and considerable change. In many ways, anthropological archaeological fieldwork is a serendipitous project (Rivoal and Salazar 2013). The ability to allow local experiences to shape research design should not be understated, as it is instrumental in forging new investigative directions. By way of brief narrative, a description of the reshaping of this project speaks to how contingencies can reveal the shortcomings of research design and the ability of consequential themes and issues to present themselves throughout the research process.

RESEARCH REIMAGINED

When a research project in Barbados was first envisioned, the intended goal was to study the Irish presence on the island. Several thousand Irish voluntarily and involuntarily arrived in Barbados throughout the seventeenth century, typically laboring under terms of indentured servitude (discussed in more detail in chapter 2). Most indentured servants, regardless of ethnic origins, experienced harsh treatment, but it was the Irish who occupied a particularly low socioeconomic status in seventeenth-century Barbadian and Caribbean society, in large part due to colonial frictions and antecedents in Ireland, English discrimination against the Catholic faith, and a general belief that the Irish constituted a "riotous and unruly lot" (Beckles 1990; see also Handler and Reilly 2015; Reilly 2015a; Block and Shaw 2011; Welch

2012; Shaw 2013). Inspired by a burgeoning archaeology of the Irish diaspora (Brighton 2009), I sought to locate sites on plantations and in inconspicuous locales where the Irish would have lived as laborers, subsisted as small farmers in villages, or discreetly congregated outside the gaze of their English masters.

Methodological difficulties hindered efforts to successfully establish an archaeological investigation of the Irish. Signatures of an Irish presence on the island can still be gleaned from toponyms and surnames (see Reilly 2015a), but determining spaces that were inhabited or used by the Irish in centuries past was nearly impossible. Plantations for which lists of indentured servants existed would occasionally include the use of Irish servants but failed to provide any indication of where on the landscape such individuals would have resided. Additionally, while material culture had previously been uncovered in inconspicuous spaces such as caves (for the precolumbian period, see Lange and Handler 1980; for the colonial era, see Smith 2008:104–133; Armstrong 2015), associating archaeological assemblages to a particular ethnic group such as the Irish remained a dubious endeavor, especially given the multiethnic nature of the indentured servant and enslaved population (see Welch 2012). Laborer contexts from the earliest dates of English settlement have been identified on the island (Armstrong and Reilly 2014), but assigning an ethnic identity to those associated with such assemblages poses historical and archaeological challenges.

Despite frustrations, the initial process of developing a research strategy for the study of the Irish proved fruitful. Through a consideration of the complex world that the Irish would have experienced in seventeenth-century Barbados (see Shaw 2013), questions and goals were reimagined to more comprehensively understand the cosmopolitan nature of island society despite its agrarian economic structure. In exploring the island, surveying plantations, participating in hikes, visiting historical sites, and meeting local residents it became evident that on a relatively small and densely populated island (even by seventeenth-century standards) significant interaction would have been taking place between servants and the enslaved, despite historical literature that had largely treated them as disparate populations. Generating a dialogue between the narratives and experiences of servants and the enslaved was a venture into a growing body of literature on transatlantic encounters of historically underrepresented groups and individuals across racial boundaries, including in Barbados (Linebaugh and Rediker 2000; O'Neil and Lloyd 2009; Shaw 2013; Jones 2007).

It was therefore necessary to expand in scope from a specific focus on the Irish to a more inclusive examination of the poor whites for a number of reasons. As mentioned, it was difficult to discern seventeenth-century sites that were particularly "Irish" or could readily be associated with an Irish presence. Additionally, as the seventeenth century drew to a close and the number of laborers arriving from Europe became severely diminished (Beckles 1989), ethnic differentiation among the island's European laboring class became less observable, at least as seen in the historical record. While some semblance of an Irish identity may have persisted into the eighteenth century (see Reilly 2015a), by the 1690s authorities were less likely to use Irish, Scottish, or English as identity markers in official records, instead using poor white as a racial catchall for the underclasses of European descent (Shaw 2013:47). Villages and tenantries were established that were home to poor whites of heterogeneous ethnic backgrounds. The tenantry explored in this volume, Below Cliff, for example, was home to families bearing English, Scottish, and Irish surnames: Fenty, Moore, Goddard, Norris, MacPhearson, Wilkie, King, Croney, Marshall, Gibson, and Downie.[3]

What became increasingly apparent throughout the research process was the intense interaction that had been taking place between these poor white communities, enslaved Africans/Afro-Barbadians (and free Afro-Barbadians, following emancipation in 1834–1838), and the plantation infrastructure, including managers and owners. The realities of such diverse interactions are acknowledged in archaeological and historical literature, but their nuances and effects have seldom been taken as seriously as the power-laden relationship between the enslaved and their enslavers.[4] While not discounting the significance of the plantation power structure planters dominated, this project suggests a prioritization of relationships among racially diverse non-elite individuals as well as the relationship between free plantation residents and processes of capitalist production. In reimagining the plantation and its socioeconomic networks using this framework, do interpretations of the landscape, the archaeological record, social relationships, and racial and class divisions change? If so, how?

Answers to these complex questions were provided in part due to the relatively unique setting in which archaeological excavations were conducted. Tenant homesteads have been commonplace on the island since its first settlement in 1627. Like most systems of tenantry, tenants pay a monthly, quarterly, or yearly rent to an owner for the rights to live and work the land of a particular parcel. Unlike most island tenantries, which were largely established following emancipation and are still inhabited, Below Cliff was settled before emancipation and was later abandoned in the early 1960s. Since its abandonment, several living community members who grew up in the tenantry have remained in the area. I was fortunate enough to collaborate with these local community members who shared fond memories, experiences, and family genealogies. One positive outcome of the recent flurry of media attention garnered by the story of the Redlegs was the genesis of a sociopolitical climate in which the once-taboo subject of Redleg ancestry among the island's middle and upper classes became an openly discussed topic. Therefore, in addition to building relationships with members of the extended Below Cliff community who still live in the region, I also engaged with stakeholders who claimed poor white ancestry but whose forebearers had "made it over the hill," experiencing social mobility and no longer living near the former tenantry.

In addition to the catalyzing effects of methodological challenges and theoretical transformations that affected research, all social scientific endeavors are altered due to local circumstances and political climates. This is particularly true in postcolonial contexts struggling with the "imperial formations" (Stoler 2013) of empire and processes of nation building. Now part of a rich body of literature dedicated to postcolonial archaeologies that espouse strategies for decolonization, Matthew Liebmann summarizes that "this means considering the political climates in which archaeologists generate research questions and interpretations and recognizing that archaeological work is not conducted in a social or cultural vacuum" (2008:8; for foundational texts see also Liebmann and Rizvi 2008; Lydon and Rizvi 2010). Given archaeology's disciplinary ties to histories of colonialism and developing notions of modernity (see Thomas 2004; Díaz-Andreu 2007), researchers need to be wary of how projects affect and are affected by local politics. In Barbados this means maintaining a keen awareness of conflicting and competing ways of remembering histories of slavery and colonialism.

THE POLITICS OF POOR WHITE SCHOLARSHIP IN BARBADOS AND BEYOND

In general, Pan-Africanism is a palpable and present force on the island. Despite the island's nickname of "Little England," many Barbadians identify with their African roots, and this is reflected in local foodways, dance, music, festivals, literature, and education. The English influence is no doubt present, specifically in the structure of government, the continued (though diminishing) strength of the Anglican Church, the official use of the English language, and a relative cultural conservativism. There exists, however, a tension between the influence of the colonial parentage and the embracing and celebration of African and Afro-Barbadian identities (Burrowes 2000; Downes-Alleyne 2017). This tension is particularly noticeable in the debates surrounding the issue of reparations. In recent years, a collaborative CARICOM (a political and economic coalition of 15 Caribbean nations) commission has established a historically grounded, socially engaged, and publicly pronounced movement for reparations for the crimes associated with transatlantic African slavery (see Beckles 2013).

The tensions underlying how Barbadians relate to the nuances of local racial or ethnic identity and colonial/postcolonial legacies are exacerbated by the simultaneous rise of the reparations movement and a growing interest in the story of the Redlegs. While the two related histories are seldom put in direct dialogue, they each nonetheless emerge from the same broader narrative of the development of the plantation agro-industrial system. At the same time, these narratives dramatically depart from one another, competing in a racialized political climate, even if such a climate is not often openly acknowledged. On one political extreme of this debate are those that adamantly proclaim that seventeenth-century European laborers in Barbados were the first "slaves" in the Americas. Such a discourse is more politically motivated than empirically grounded, but it nonetheless represents a reactionary, revisionist response to the growth of the reparations movement and heightened acknowledgment of the horrendous crimes of African chattel slavery (see Handler and Reilly 2017; Hogan et al. 2016). In other words, through their assertions of "white slavery," adherents to this narrative, consciously or unconsciously, suggest mutual suffering by Europeans and Africans alike under the brutal regime of slavery, thus denying validity to central arguments put forth as part of the reparations movement.

These tensions became directly relevant to the development of my archaeological research project, but they also speak to the significance of the research questions being posed. As the initial plans and results of the research began to be disseminated to local audiences through meetings, informal lunches and dinners, and public speaking engagements,[5] I was met with two different types of responses. The first followed the trajectory just described whereby some individuals were excited that someone was taking seriously the story of the "white slaves." One respondent even expressed his gratitude that such a story would finally gain traction, as he was "sick of having slavery shoved down [his] throat" while in school. While the majority of reactions did not approach racially contentious levels, the interest in research on the poor whites was viewed as a welcomed contribution to Barbadian history that could serve to *counter* or *compete with* narratives that focused on the Afro-Barbadian experience.

In contrast, some responded with a keen and detailed interest in what the research could illuminate about the poor white experience on the island in the past and present, without the more unsavory political undertones. Interest extended to the ways in which poor whites were involved in the system of sugar and slavery and how they survived on the margins of the plantation landscape throughout the historical period. Such responses reveal the significance and role of public engagement in archaeological research, as these encounters proved crucial in the development of nuanced research questions. Two events, in particular, were formative and deserve mention. Newlands Greenidge, historian and owner/operator of the Springvale Folk Museum, was actively involved in the project from its first inception. Following the initiation of research in and around the Below Cliff community, Greenidge, who was familiar with the tenantry and neighboring areas, generously shared his knowledge of some of the residents, including the names and contact information of individuals who may have been of some help throughout the research process. He once mentioned an older gentleman who he recalled had grown up in the tenantry. I then asked the man's age and whether he was white or black. At this, Greenidge chuckled and asked, "Why does he have to be one or the other?" The poignant question was humbling, proving critical in recognizing my own assumptions and misconceptions about the Redlegs. Greenidge's dissatisfaction with the reductive nature of these racial categories is part of the broader discussion surrounding race that anchors many of the arguments presented throughout this book.

The other formative event was a lecture I was generously asked to deliver for the Barbados National Trust in March 2013. Throughout the course of the well-attended lecture I presented my initial archaeological findings as well as my preliminary interpretations about life in the Below Cliff tenantry. This included confronting derisive stereotypes leveled against the Redlegs and discussing their place in Barbadian history and society. Following the lecture, questions from the audience sparked a lively, organic conversation about family genealogies and racial identity on the island. One gentleman, likely in his late forties to early fifties, was a crowd favorite. His complexion would likely place him in the social category of brown, indicating a mixed-raced ancestry.[6] He introduced himself as a member of the Fenty family, a common surname found in the Below Cliff tenantry and surrounding community (it is also the surname of the famous Barbadian pop diva, Rihanna, who still has extended family in the surrounding Below Cliff community). Mr. Fenty relayed a childhood story about his grandmother who regularly asked all of her grandchildren to line up for supper. The order of the line was based on the skin complexion of the children, with the darkest children bringing up the rear. Within the same family there was a wide array of skin tones, ranging from pale white to black. The story, reminiscent of Frantz Fanon's notion of "epidermalization" or "lactification" (2008 [1952]), was undeniably laced with racial undertones and bespeaks long, complicated histories of the racial politics of

Figure I.3. Redleg fishermen of Barbados in Bath, St. John, 1908. (Matthew C. Reilly, from the collection of Richard Goddard)

desire and reproduction—a blunt reminder of the racial hierarchies that still haunt the former English colony—but there was a comfortable atmosphere in the hall, and audience members, some possibly sympathizing with his story, laughed along, amused by his entertaining delivery.

Inspired by the comments, a number of families of diverse racial ancestries came to speak with me after the event. During the lecture I used a relatively well-known image of a group of Redleg fishermen taken in 1908 in the small village of Bath along the island's east coast, nearby to the former tenantry of Below Cliff (Figure I.3). To my surprise, many of the Barbadian attendees had copies of the same photograph. The men pictured were the ancestors of those with the photograph. In one instance, two of the individuals present shared surnames but not skin complexion. These genealogically curious Barbadians were able to trace their ancestry to the same person in the photograph. My interactions with these individuals illuminated a slew of familial connections in contemporary and historic Barbados that called into question essentializing racial identities often ascribed to members of the poor white demographic, that is, their definitive categorization of being white. The insights gleaned from the archaeological data and the realizations reached from discussions with Barbadians also challenged notions that precluded poor white interaction with Afro-Barbadians across the island. Far from interpreting this as an indication of an idyllic racial utopia in a poor white community immune to racial tensions, I instead began to consider the unstable intersections of race and class in this marginalized tenantry.

I arrived in Barbados with several preconceived notions of how race and racial identity were historically categorized, partly a result of historical renderings that rely on the myopia of the colonial archive. These notions were symptomatic of what Michael Monahan (2011) refers to as the "politics of purity," whereby racial identities adhere to an all-or-nothing binary of black or white. Additionally, they were partly instilled by historiography and scholarship of Barbados, which seldom deals with the topic of racial intermixture, instead relying on and reifying the black/white binary (for notable exceptions see Handler 1974; Davis 1978; Beckles 1993; Jones 2007; Newton 2008). Despite some cumbersome encounters with Barbadians previously described, specifically those who maintain the legitimacy of "white slavery," I more often encountered individuals who openly discussed the nuances of racial identity on the island and embraced its complexities—a topic that is slowly broaching the public sphere (Stuart 2012). As a friend once told me, "I think you'd be hard pressed to find a truly 'white' Bajan."[7]

The complexities and slippages of racial identity have serious implications for an archaeological project dedicated to the study of the Caribbean plantation landscape. Such spaces were racialized and dependent on rigid divides that defined who was or could be enslaved or in control. Within such a framework, the Redlegs potentially posed a serious threat to racial hierarchies and the functioning of the plantation infrastructure. Therefore, a narrative that directly severs them from any involvement in plantation production conveniently avoids having to consider how poor whites fit into racialized plantation production schemes. Armed with these insights, research sought to identify the ways in which Barbadian poor whites were involved with the plantation landscape from which they were supposedly detached—a product of historiography that is discussed in chapter 2. This entails relationships between poor white tenantry residents and plantation economics as well as between residents and other plantation laborers, namely, free and enslaved Afro-Barbadians. Archaeological and historical data speak directly to such relationships, revealing much about how residents of one Redleg tenantry experienced their plantation home.

COMMUNAL ENCOUNTERS

Despite the formal abandonment of the Below Cliff tenantry in the early 1960s, dozens of local residents remember growing up in "the woods," as they now call the forested area, or had recollections of friends and family members who had lived there. The recent date of abandonment presented the opportunity for an oral history component of the project. Engagement with local and descendant communities has been a mainstay of historical archaeological research for a number of years (for the Caribbean see González-Tennant 2014:28–31; see also Atalay 2012; McDavid and Babson 1997; Marshall 2002; Shackel and Chambers 2004; Merriman 2004; Little and Shackel 2007), and my encounters with local St. John residents offered insights into the poor white experience that differed in form and content from those provided by other Barbadians interested in the research. As local residents and/or people with familial connections to former Below Cliff residents, members of the St. John community offered reflections on their daily lives as well as those of their ancestors. Their own interpretations often stood in marked contrast to vicious stereotypes about poor whites, and even to my own interpretations of archaeological or historical materials. Oral histories were collected to develop family genealogies in addition to the gathering of oral traditions about what life was like in the Below Cliff area in generations past. Such data proved invaluable in interpreting the archaeological record, and the details of these dialogues are discussed in later chapters.

Prolonged residence on the island facilitated the development of meaningful relationships with local community members with whom I shared stories, experiences, fresh produce, work, meals, and drinks. These individuals and families were far more than research informants, and through their hospitality, generosity, and honesty, I encountered the economic hardships that many faced in their daily lives. As can be expected, community members had different perspectives on their economic circumstances, but limited economic means was a reality many St. John residents faced (for discussions of the relativity of impoverishment, see Taylor 2013:14–17). The persistence of economic inequality across the plantation landscape speaks to the historical processes that produce and perpetuate economic hardship. It also allows researchers the opportunity to connect with such individuals as *people* rather than sources of data, despite the scholarly benefit of the insights provided (Richard 2011:167). As a decolonizing practice, such interactions have the potential to inspire self-reflexivity and integrate care into archaeological praxis (Rizvi 2016). The inner workings of the plantation production system had incredibly intimate consequences on plantation residents that were observable through meaningful interactions with St. John residents as they coped with these realities on a daily basis.

Life for those currently living in rural St. John is not neatly characterized by single occupational roles or Monday through Friday, nine-to-five routines. Large-scale sugar production is on the decline in the area, so, in addition to

limited plantation employment, residents participate in small farming operations, raise fowl, fish, commute to Bridgetown for employment, or undertake odd jobs around the community. My regular presence in the area and
my daily excursions into "the woods" to conduct fieldwork fostered relationships with community members that were partly based on mutual labor. I
often exited the woods, excavation tools in hand, to be greeted by workers
in banana fields or commuters walking to and from the bus stop. It was not
uncommon to share some fresh coconut water while enjoying the shade of
a nearby tree. Many of these casual interactions sparked friendships involving a degree of trust. In fact, on several occasions, I was even mistaken for
a community member. This is not to say, of course, that these interactions
took place on an equitable playing field. As an outsider whose presence in
the community was characterized by my role as a researcher, pronounced differences made mutual, candid reciprocity difficult. Mutual labor, however,
does have the potential to develop ties between archaeological researchers
and local communities (McGuire and Reckner 2005). In this case, I was fortunate enough to connect with many who generously spoke openly with me
about their families and daily lives.

In general, and despite stereotypes that marked the Redlegs as destitute, residents were determined not to let poverty define their identities or daily lives.
As one former Below Cliff resident nostalgically commented regarding his
childhood in the now-abandoned tenantry, "You know, we didn't have much,
but we were happy. I'd move back if I could." Given the attitudes and sentiments of St. John residents and former residents of Below Cliff, it is necessary
to negotiate an archaeological analysis that is critical of the historical processes
that engender poverty and inequality while being careful not to allow economic hardship to define the lives of community members, past or present
(see Reilly 2016b). In Barbados, as in most world areas, stigmas against poverty often demoralize individuals who are perceived to be lazy, casting them
as deserving of their destitute lifestyles (Spencer-Wood and Matthews 2011;
Espersen 2018). Those who have benefited from socioeconomic mobility may
acknowledge their humble ancestry, but neoliberal or "bootstrap" ideologies
often generate paternalistic attitudes or blame toward the poor. The discrimination felt by poor white individuals and families is a historical reality that
persists in the present. I am therefore careful to avoid reifying stereotypes or
providing data to quantify or legitimate discriminatory ideologies.

ORGANIZATION OF THE BOOK

I have thus far outlined the politics of conducting research in Barbados and
how these politics come to bear on St. John residents. This book discusses the

general history of the poor whites throughout the long period of colonialism into the present,[8] in part to illuminate the processes that led to their current place in Barbadian society—materially, socially, experientially, and historically. These processes are then discussed at the local level, specifically in the tenantry of Below Cliff. Historical, geographical, oral history, and archaeological data are used in developing interpretations about a former poor white tenantry and the Barbadians who once lived there. While an explicit emphasis on the poor whites will be obvious, the characters in this story include all members of Barbadian society, including planters, managers, enslaved laborers, free people of color, colonial authorities, and visitors to the island. Relationships between poor whites and members of these groups, as well as the fluid boundaries between them, are a pivotal point of analysis in constructing the Redlegs as an indispensable component of Barbadian history and society, rather than being marginal and isolated outcasts.

Chapter 1 provides the theoretical considerations that inform my research questions. Argued by scholars of and from the Caribbean to be one of the world's first modern regions, the Caribbean offers the unique potential to explore modernization and the local consequences of, and responses to, these processes. Furthermore, in presenting the poor white problem, it is evident that modernity and its associated ideologies of race and class have dramatically shaped how the poor whites have been portrayed historically. A review of poor white historical and anthropological scholarship illustrates that such literature tends to treat the poor whites as a historically monolithic group that is, and has been, rigidly bounded by racial and class identity markers. Instead, I turn to historical and theoretical approaches to the Atlantic world, particularly the Caribbean, that challenge the dominant discourses and narratives to present evidence for alternative modernities. These are used to interrogate the production, validity, integrity, and boundaries of class and racial categories in Barbados.

Given the proliferation of historical archaeological research on the plantation, the body of literature associated with these spaces is then briefly reviewed, highlighting contributions as well as gaps. Of particular significance is how the plantation is interpreted as a unit of analysis. Archaeological materials from sites dating to the mid-seventeenth century on the island illustrate stark transformations when compared with later sites, such as Below Cliff, in how the Barbadian plantation landscape was organized from the seventeenth century, through the era of slavery, into the postemancipation era, and to the present. Through an analysis of geographical space, it is possible to question traditional interpretations of landscapes of power and their analogous relationship to ideologies of class and racial hierarchies. Additionally, questions are raised concerning the poor white tenantry as a "marginal" space. These theoretical considerations suggest that these plantation spaces are contested zones in which specific ideologies about labor and class are negotiated. Planters and managers had particular conceptualizations of how space was to be organized and controlled while nonelites, like the poor whites of Below Cliff, demonstrated their abilities to foster their own socioeconomic networks and ideas about efficient and sustainable forms of labor.

Historical context is then provided in chapter 2 to explain the processes through which the poor whites came to occupy tenantries and other marginal spaces across the plantation landscape. For over two decades following the English settlement of the island in 1627, the island's population was primarily European.[9] For the most part, Europeans labored under contracts of indenture on small farms (5 to 30 acres) until the sugar revolution of the mid-1640s drastically altered island society, economics, politics, demographics, and geography (Dunn 2000 [1972]; Higman 2000). European laborers continued to arrive on the island throughout the seventeenth century, but as planters increasingly favored the labor of enslaved Africans, fewer servants came, and those who remained found their services no longer needed. In the decades leading up to the eighteenth century, a sugar and slave society had fully blossomed, and the poor whites, numbering in the range of 10,000 (Sheppard 1977), were cast to the "rab" lands of the island. Through the use of limited historical sources, their existence as militia and small-farming tenants is traced throughout the period of slavery.

The poor whites later enter the historical record more substantially in literature surrounding abolition. Travel writers as well as local historians and radical abolitionists comment on the state of the poor whites. The views these authors espoused would later serve to inform the stigmatypes leveled against the Redlegs in the present, including those deployed by historians and fiction writers. Despite an exodus of sorts following emancipation (Watson 2000b), many poor whites continued to reside along the island's east coast as well as the island's urban center, Bridgetown. Many communities dwindled in the postcolonial period, but the parish of St. John, home to Below Cliff, still holds what is locally known to be the last vestiges of a Redleg community.

Using an island-wide history of the Redlegs as a point of departure, chapter 3 provides a more localized and detailed introduction to the site of Below Cliff and its surrounding community. This chapter explores the research undertaken as well as the interdisciplinary nature of the project using an approach that privileges the community as a unit of analysis. Although primarily archaeological, research also incorporated historical, geographic, and oral history methodologies for a more comprehensive study of the Redlegs.

While the specific research methods employed are discussed, the chapter primarily serves to delineate what, where, and who is the Below Cliff community. Providing the details of the community demonstrates that anthropological and archaeological methods went hand in hand throughout the research process. The collection of oral histories and traditions from former residents of Below Cliff and descendants of former residents proved fruitful in understanding village dynamics, material culture recovered through excavations, local genealogies, and cultural identity. This project also entailed substantial use of primary sources viewed in Barbadian archives, both national and local. Minutes from meetings of parish vestries were consulted, providing detailed information about local residents deemed worthy of poor relief, a requirement of which was being identified as white. Most archival work entailed the use of local vestry minutes as well as registries of baptisms, burials, and marriages—a marked change from previous studies of the Redlegs that relied on traveler accounts, council minutes, and literature surrounding the abolition debate. An important distinction is that the literature surrounding the abolition debate speaks to the poor white experience in general, rather than at the local level.

Chapter 4 presents the class tensions that emerged on Barbadian sugar plantations as planters and other island elites struggled to resolve the "poor white problem," which was broadly conceived of as a question of how to accommodate an impoverished white population in a sugar and slavery society. I begin with a description of a discourse of poor white idleness found in primary and secondary materials that suggests that the Redlegs refused to occupy themselves in "useful" forms of labor. From here, data from Below Cliff are considered to more accurately describe the realities of economic hardship with which residents coped as well as their relationships to broader capitalist processes undertaken on Clifton Hall Plantation on top of the cliff. Those living below the cliff struggled in a harsh environment prone to deadly rockslides while simultaneously grappling with impoverishment. This informs a consideration of artifact use and reuse in interpreting the material culture collected. Additionally, through a critical analysis of baptismal registries, I examine how local authorities perceived and documented poor white occupational identities. Through particular ideologies of acceptable and unacceptable forms of labor, individuals were categorized as either gainfully employed or, in the case of those not given specific occupations, as idle. In opposition to reductive discourses that cast the poor whites as lazy or nonindustrious, I suggest a complex and dialectical relationship between poor whites and processes of capitalism that is not neatly reduced to domination by or resistance to economic forces.

Tied to the notion of poor white idleness is a perception of explicit socio-economic isolation. In direct opposition to such sentiments, the broader economic networks in which Below Cliff residents were involved indicate that poor whites regularly encountered enslaved and free Afro-Barbadians. Chapter 5 addresses the nature of these encounters from the quotidian forms of interaction, such as the exchange of information, goods (specifically locally produced earthenwares), and cultural traits, to the more intimate encounters that weigh heavily on how racial identity was defined and experienced on the plantation landscape. For example, observed similarities in architectural techniques as well as household spatial organization are indicative of cultural exchange between poor whites and Afro-Barbadians. Rather than being concerned with cultural origins of particular ways of life (for critiques of such approaches see Mintz 1974; Mintz and Price 1992 [1976]), I suggest that localized encounters on the plantation landscape facilitated influence in both directions between the seemingly disparate poor whites and Afro-Barbadians. In taking these observations of interaction and exchange a step further, I interrogate the rigidity of the racial categories that sought to separate Afro-Barbadians and poor whites. The categories of white and black were essential to the success of plantation society and a cornerstone of racial modernity, at least as seen through the eyes of those who benefited most from the business of slavery. Spaces like Below Cliff, however, offered a potential to destabilize and fracture these boundaries.

Chapter 6 returns to the notion of Caribbean modernity, suggesting that Below Cliff can more aptly be understood as a plantation space representative of an alternative modernity. Class relations illustrate a dynamic, complex, and, at times, contentious relationship between Below Cliff residents and broader processes of capitalism. Planters, elites, managers, authorities, and others committed to plantation production viewed the habits of Barbadian Redlegs with scorn and perceived them to be detached from productive forms of labor. In contrast, despite the realities of economic hardship, residents were making their own choices as to how they related to broader economic networks and activities. In considering plantation spaces occupied by poor whites, the material signatures of economic inequality are manifest in the archaeological record, representing the quagmire facing Barbadian elites who were committed to the persistence of racial hierarchies that determined one's socioeconomic status. Below Cliff was a tenantry that was largely out of sight and out of mind for planters. Therefore, as laboring classes interacted and even intermixed, it became evident that ideologies of racial separation and purity met with only limited success, even if the consequences of the racialized plantation system led to the harshest forms of human cruelty the enslaved experienced. Tenants were certainly not immune to the effects of living in a highly racialized and industrialized plantation society, but it is evident that ideologies concerning labor and racial identity were being contested and negotiated at the local level. Rather than being indicative of outright or explicit resistance, following Stephen Silliman (2014), I suggest that these behaviors were the ways in which residents lived with and through the realities of plantation modernity to build their own worlds that diverged from the ideals colonial authorities envisioned.

The focus of this volume is the Redlegs, but it is evident that despite historical and contemporary misconceptions of poor white isolation, they played a significant role in the development of broader Barbadian society. The questions presented and addressed are, therefore, significant in understanding the dynamics of plantation spaces, the historical processes that engender and maintain inequality, and how these phenomena affect contemporary notions and entanglements of race and class. Primary sources reveal that planters and island officials had particular ideas concerning the social positioning of the poor whites. Evidence suggests, however, that seemingly marginal spaces like Below Cliff were arenas in which the tropes of modernity and modernization could be contested and had the potential to disintegrate. The material traces of economic inequality and an unforgiving landscape undeniably illustrate the hardships tenancy residents faced. At the same time, on the margins of the plantation, the poor whites coped with harsh living conditions and constructed a space in which dominant notions of race and class were reimagined.

ONE

ARCHAEOLOGIES OF PLANTATION MODERNITY

The history of the West Indies is governed by two factors, the sugar plantation and Negro slavery. . . . Wherever the sugar plantation and slavery existed, they imposed a pattern. It is an original pattern, not European, not African, not a part of the American main, not native in any conceivable sense of that word, but West Indian, sui generis, with no parallel anywhere else. The sugar plantation has been the most civilising as well as the most demoralising influence in West Indian development. When three centuries ago the slaves came to the West Indies, they entered directly into the large-scale agriculture of the sugar plantation, which was a modern system.

—C. L. R. James (1963:391–392).

Plantation agriculture has drastically diminished across the Caribbean over the last century. In fact, on many islands, sugar production, the staple monocrop that long defined the region's economy, has been almost completely abandoned. Sugar production in Barbados, now under the domain of the government, is on its last legs, with only one sugar factory, Portvale, remaining in operation as of 2017.[1] Despite the industry's decline, the plantation infrastructure has left an enduring physical imprint across the landscape in the form of windmills and works in a state of ruin, a mix of dilapidated and restored planter great houses, vast acreage of agricultural fields, and plantation tenantries inhabited by a few remaining agricultural laborers and the descendants of laborers who now look elsewhere to make ends meet. For many Barbadians, their lives, or at least the lives of their ancestors, are inextricably tied to the plantation in one way or another. Individuals relate to the plantation in myriad ways, but its place as a central, if not *the* central, institution in island history and society is undeniable.

This case study marks an attempt, in a long line of such attempts, to illustrate how a particular group lived their daily lives and understood their place in a plantation society. Of the utmost significance, however, is the fact that those being examined here were free plantation residents racially identified as white during a period when the overwhelming majority of plantation residents were enslaved (until 1834) or free people of African descent (following emancipation). Therefore, the poor whites experienced the contours of the plantation in substantively different ways from enslaved laborers or those identified as Afro-Barbadians. Their class and racial positioning were formative, yet not necessarily defining, features of daily life in a racialized and agro-industrial society. This assessment derives from underlying tensions between the socially, economically, and politically encoded tropes of modernity colonial rule imposed and the resulting alternatives that emerged in seemingly marginal plantation locales.

The Caribbean is an ideal world region in which to investigate the early instantiations of the development of modern industrial systems and ideologies associated with labor. That being stated, this chapter suggests a reimagining of plantation spaces to explore the components of Caribbean modernity and how they were imposed, transformed, and experienced along and in between lines of race and class. Central to this endeavor is an underlying question about Caribbean modernity: What did it mean to be marked as poor and white in a society based on white, plantocratic power and race-based slavery? Necessary for undertaking such a project is an explication of modernity as it relates to the Caribbean region and archaeology, the central methodology of this study, more broadly.

Caribbean Modernity

Modernity is a relatively elusive and often haphazardly used term that has been the subject of extensive, diverse, and dense scholarly debate. In her critique of the exceptionalism and cluttered characteristics of modernity, Shannon Dawdy (2010:762) has remarked that "scholars have used modernity as a stand-in for all or part of that inexorable cluster of capitalism, secularism, industrialization, colonialism, the onset of Atlantic slavery, individualism and the divided subject, technological involution, urbanization, global integration, science and rationality, mass literacy, aesthetic modernism, the nation-state, and so-on." The ambiguity of modernity as a theoretical construct has also spawned an onslaught of labels attempting to define and bound the critique, death, acceleration, failure, or nonexistence of modernity; these include postmodernity (Harvey 1990), late capitalism (Jameson 1991), and supermodernity (Augé 1995). In place of an exhaustive review of modernity and its discontents, I instead discuss its direct relationship to historical archaeology in terms of the temporalities and subjects of inquiry as well as its context-specific significance in the Caribbean region.

Still relevant as one of the premier texts in historical archaeology, James Deetz's *In Small Things Forgotten* defined the field as "the archaeology of the spread of European cultures throughout the world since the fifteenth century, and their impact on and interaction with the cultures of indigenous peoples" (Deetz 1996 [1977]:5). Over the years this definition has been expanded, critiqued, altered, and reaffirmed in a number of fashions. Permutations of this definition nonetheless privilege and mark as exceptional the past 500 years or so, creating an often-cumbersome disciplinary schism between those studying the pre- and post-1492 eras. This divide has been critiqued on a number of levels. For instance, some have lamented the ease with which archaeologists have accepted the nature of the discipline to be synonymous with the study of modernity (for archaeology and modernity, see Thomas 2004; Hamilakis 2007; Dawdy 2010; González-Ruibal 2013). The practices of historical archaeology and anthropology more broadly, Dawdy argues, "remain very much embedded in an eschatology of modern rupture" (2010:763), that is, the schism between premodern and modern.

I make no pretense to resolve these grandiose yet important debates. It is incumbent on archaeological research, however, to consider the localized and regional implications for the study and experience of modernity. In short, modernity is perceived differently across space and time. In addition to this truism, rather than being a static entity or a directional progression, it is never complete, and its associated processes alter and function differently based on local contingencies (see Gaonkar, ed. 2001). How modernity is perceived, (re)constructed, and experienced in the past and present is vastly different and often divergent despite historical and contemporary similarities such as colonialism and its associated imperial formations (Stoler 2013). Rather than using overarching and cumbersome definitions or conceptualizations of global modernity, a more regional and localized approach can situate how the clunky manifestations of modernity played out on particular landscapes, within particular psyches, through localized politics, in socioeconomics, and in the shaping of history.

If historical archaeology, by definition, is somewhat wedded to what might arguably be called the modern period, perhaps it is only fitting that it be a useful discipline for exploring what some have deemed the first modern place. It is here, after all, that Columbus first "discovered" the Americas. Since the groundbreaking 1938 publication of C. L. R. James's *The Black Jacobins: Toussaint L'Ouverture and the San Domingo Revolution*, scholars of and from the Caribbean have emphasized the inextricable link between the region and modernity. As Stephan Palmié suggests, due to the early onset of industrializing processes, "the Caribbean might well be regarded as one of the first truly modern localities" (2002:41; see also Benítez-Rojo 1996). David Scott, in explicating James's understanding of Caribbean modernity, argues that the Caribbean was an "inaugural modernity" for two distinct reasons. First, "there were no nonmodern formations in the Caribbean with which the colonial powers had continuously to contend" (2004:125). As Scott notes, James was surely exaggerating this point, and recent historiography has illustrated the depth and severity of European genocide against Caribbean Amerindians (for a review see Beckles 2013). As this case study focuses on Barbados, however, the point is well taken, given that the island is said to have been uninhabited at the time of English settlement in 1627.[2] James's second parameter has been echoed by many scholars who have characterized Caribbean modernity by the onset and rapid expansion and acceleration of agro-industrial production—in most cases, sugar (see Mintz 1974:9–10, 1985; Ortiz 1995).

In this sense, Haitian-born historical anthropologist Michel-Rolph Trouillot's suggestion (2003:36–37) that processes of modernization, or "creation of place," and cultural modernity are not mutually exclusive is paramount to understanding the dramatic transformations enveloping the Caribbean as sugar production spread throughout the region in the mid-seventeenth century. Modernization can be described as the physical, material, and spatial components of settler colonialism and agro-industrial production that expanded throughout the Atlantic world beginning with the Columbian encounter. The implementation and expansion of this system have certainly been important fields of archaeological study (see Woodward 2011; Delle 2014b; Meniketti 2015). Cultural modernity, according to Trouillot, brings the space and place specifics of modernization into a social and temporal framework, thus assisting in defining more abstract cultural attributes associated with a particular time and place. For instance, and of the utmost significance for the purposes of this case study, we might view cultural modernity as the rise of modern notions of race and labor. Modernization and cultural modernity were co-constitutive of each other as local transformations birthed arguably the world's first modern locale, at least in terms of the how modernization is characterized here. The development of Caribbean modernity is therefore tied to the concomitant rise of the plantation complex and the exponential increase in the number of enslaved Africans being sent to the islands. As Scott points out, "Plantation slavery is the fundamental institution through which [the modern] experience is shaped and articulated" (Scott 2004:126; see also Gilroy 1993). Despite ambiguities about the nature of and distinction between bound laborers in seventeenth-century Barbados, given the presence of European and African laborers (see Handler and Reilly 2017; Newman 2013), race-based plantation slavery became indexical of Caribbean modernity. Additionally, industrialized labor found an early home in sweltering sugar factories, capitalism charged into adolescence in the form of joint-stock-company property mortgaging and circum-Atlantic mercantilism (Armstrong and Reilly 2014), and ideologies of racial difference began to crystallize throughout the century (Shaw 2013).

The character of Caribbean modernity described here is a notable departure from other conceptions of modernity that have engaged with the messy ontological and epistemological dimensions of the analytical construct. Temporally, the modernizing processes unfolding in the mid-seventeenth-century Caribbean predate the height of the European Enlightenment by roughly a century. Often associated with the birth of modernity, the Enlightenment marked a turn toward reason, positivism, and secularism (Bauman and Briggs 2003). Such renderings of modernity reveal a Eurocentrism inherent in attributing the advent of enlightened thought to the West, thus divorcing it from any association with colonial encounters (Bogues 2003:2). While colonies may have been seen as "laboratories of modernity" (Cooper and Stoler, eds. 1997:5) where social, economic, and political ideas could be developed and deployed (see Rabinow 1989), the colonial homeland (or at least its representatives) is given primacy for the development of the modern. In short, this suggests that modernity was something that developed in Europe to be transmitted to the colonies. In sharp contrast, it can be argued that in contexts like the Caribbean, modernity was conceived and transformed in unique ways that dramatically affected its character throughout the Atlantic world and beyond. Treating the Caribbean as an inaugural modernity combats such privileging of the metropole, instead demonstrating the heterogeneous nature of colonial/metropole relationships as well as the tensions that transpire in local sites of modernization (Cooper and Stoler 1997; Delle 2014a).

The English visited Barbados in 1625 and officially established it as a colony in 1627. Despite England's relatively late entrée into New World colonial expansion, as compared with Spanish and Portuguese endeavors, the seventeenth century was a formative period in which plantation societies exploded and expanded across the Barbadian and broader-Caribbean landscape. The plantation system, despite significant local variations across space and time, would have an unparalleled impact on Caribbean society, politics, economics, and geography over the next several centuries (for Barbados see Beckles 2007; for the broader Caribbean see Williams 1984; Higman 2011; Thompson 2002). This narrative is, however, a drastic oversimplification of what constitutes the modern period throughout the Caribbean region. There is truth to this macro-history and the tragic realities associated with these overarching processes and events, but at the same time, they can be overdeterminate in how they are remembered, presented, and wielded in the present (Trouillot 1992; Richard 2010:3–4; Hayes 2013; Reilly 2016a).

The broader narrative of Caribbean modernity has largely influenced the way regional history and society are portrayed and perceived in the past and present—the specifics of which will be discussed in more detail. Within the fissures of this historical trajectory, however, exist the alternatives that developed and transformed as a result of the dialectical relationships between individuals and groups thrust into processes of modernization. While such alternatives have been consciously and unconsciously suppressed or ignored (Fischer 2004; Trouillot 1995; Schmidt and Patterson 1995), historical archaeology is well suited to unearth and illuminate localized material manifestations of contexts where and when individuals did not adhere to the prescribed norms of Caribbean modernity. We might therefore look for productive potential in archaeology's fraught relationship with modernity. Whereas Michel-Rolph Trouillot described historicity as "the nightmare of the ethnographer" (1992:33), for those investigating the heterogeneity of the Caribbean, it can also serve as a recurring dream for those willing to embrace the ambiguities, inconsistencies, and dynamic realities of the historical processes that made possible the multiplicity of Caribbean modernity (for archaeological approaches that highlight the intractable nature of colonial and/or modern projects, see Hall 2000; Dawdy 2008).

The "Poor White Problem"

The sugar revolution that erupted in Barbados in the mid-seventeenth century dramatically altered the trajectory of Atlantic-world history, spawning the economic, political, and social structures associated with plantation agro-industry that enveloped much of the Americas. The nuances and permutations of this system have long been the focus of considerable scholarly study. Since the work of Caribbean intellectuals such as C. L. R. James (1963 [1938]) and Eric Williams (1994 [1944]), radical Caribbean scholarship has highlighted the dark legacies and realities of colonialism, capitalism, and slavery (see also Césaire 2000 [1955]; Fanon 2008 [1952], 2004 [1961]; Wynter 2003). While Howard Johnson (1998:ix) has argued that such analyses have had the unintended effect of dismissing the narrative of the white minority's experience, I argue that the experience of wealthy white men loomed large and omnipresent within the very structures and institutions that sought to circumscribe the lives of the enslaved and other exploited colonial subjects (Mills 1997). Although this may be the case for the plantocracy, it presents challenges when considering a poor white minority who coped with economic hardship in a slave society, a largely black postemancipation colony, and, later, an independent nation.

In essence, an investigation of the poor whites of Barbados appears to run against the grain of vindicationist scholarship as espoused by W. E. B. Du Bois. In his formulation, such scholarship sought to "set straight the oft-distorted record of the Black experience and to fill in the lacunae resulting from the conscious or unconscious omission of significant facts about Black people"

(Drake 1987, vol. 1:xviii; cited in Foster 1997:2). As Paul Mullins (2008) has articulated, such an approach appeals to historical archaeologists conducting research in settings where individuals and groups are coping with persistent racism and the legacy of slavery in the present (for a compelling reply concerning the nuances of the African diasporic experience, see Armstrong 2008). In conducting research in a twenty-first-century context still characterized by "white over black" consciousness, ideology, structures, and realities that were developing in the sixteenth and seventeenth centuries, where does that leave an analysis of impoverished whites in a sugar and slave society?

A number of historical studies of poor white or "white trash" populations in the United States, particularly in the Appalachian region, have demonstrated the precarious existence of the white underclass (Hartigan 2005; Bolton 1994; Cecil-Fronsman 1992; Forret 2006; Wray 2006; Isenberg 2016; Merritt 2017). Furthermore, since the 2016 presidential election in the United States, American poor whites have been fetishized and, one could argue, romanticized on a national and even global scale (Maisano 2017). Even though such studies have drawn attention to the significance and heterogeneity of American poor whites, it would be a mistake to assume that the poor white experience in Barbados mirrored that of the United States.[3] Not only were the experiences of these individuals drastically different in terms of their place in society and how race/whiteness operated historically, but also the memory of these pasts has engendered specific narratives and ways of seeing the past that affect how the Redlegs are remembered on the island and abroad. This is not to be dismissive of broader histories of the poor white experience in the Americas, but research questions concerning the poor whites of Barbados must be firmly situated within the context of Caribbean modernity to avoid generalizations or normative readings of whiteness.

Along these lines, a label like "poor white" might seem relatively straightforward, especially in contexts like the United States, but despite historiography and semiethnographic studies of the poor whites, little has actually been said about the label itself and its significance in Caribbean scholarship. As mentioned in the introduction, the existence of thousands of poor whites is seemingly contradictory to the overarching structures and metanarrative of colonial society and economy (for a broader discussion, see Stoler 2002:34–38). In his scathing critique of colonialism, and insistence that Marxist approaches are often insufficient in adequately addressing the realities of imperialist endeavors, Fanon (2004 [1961]:5) argues that "in the colonies the economic infrastructure is also the superstructure. The cause is the effect: You are rich because you are white, you are white because you are rich." In a sociological examination of the poor whites of Barbados, Peter Simmons

(1976:3) employs Fanon's tautology to present the poor whites as evidence
of the shortcomings of Fanon's assessment of colonial society and economy.
In other words, the poor whites are understood to disprove Fanon's assessment. Rather than tearing down Fanon's colonial critique, however, I suggest
that the poor whites reify its astuteness. Their exceptionalism necessitates the
adjective qualifier. The employment of the term alerts users to the out-of-
place-and-time condition of the group.

Historically, Hilary Beckles (1988) has presented the "poor white problem"
as a political question Barbadian authorities faced in the decades surrounding emancipation, a phenomenon discussed in detail in the following chapter. An estimated population of between 8,000 and 12,000 poor whites[4] had
for centuries struggled with poverty, showing little sign of social mobility
despite paternalistic efforts on the part of planters and administrators (see
Lambert 2001, 2005; Sheppard 1977:79–101; Marshall 2003). Barbadian
and colonial elites grappled with the conceptual and practical paradox of a
sizable poor white population in a rigidly bounded racial society (Beckles
1988; Watson 2000b). If we then consider the narrative of white plantocratic
rule and black impoverishment and oppression, the historical "poor white
problem" broaches the boundaries of politics, imposing itself on broader theoretical and conceptual issues in Caribbean scholarship.

We again arrive at the question of where and how to situate an investigation of the poor whites. As discussed, the need for the economic qualifier of
"poor" in the pejorative poor white reaffirms the significance of anticolonial
discourse as well as scholarship that has explicitly illustrated the white over
black realities of Atlantic-world history (see Wolf 1982; Mills 1997; Jordan
1968; Roediger 2007:23–27). A recapitulation of the broader colonial, capitalistic, and exploitative narratives may therefore be unnecessary, but it is
equally futile to argue that the poor whites were and are a unique case that
deserves attention solely for their exceptional character and status. It is an
essential premise of this book that despite their seemingly anomalous and
exceptional status in Caribbean and Barbadian society, the Redlegs were far
more ingrained within local society than has been previously acknowledged.
What is more productive, then, is to interrogate how and why they have been
interpreted as isolated and exceptional, in addition to attempting to uncover
the lived realities of these individuals in plantation society. In other words,
even if it is possible to dismiss stereotypes of poor white isolation, it is necessary to confront the work that such stereotypes do in plantation society. *Why*
were they viewed as insular and exceptional, and what purposes does such a
view serve?

In his explication of the racial contract,[5] philosopher of race Charles Mills has argued that "though there were local variations in the Racial Contract, depending on circumstances and the particular mode of exploitation . . . it remains the case that the white tribe, as the global representative of civiliza-tion and modernity, is generally on top of the social pyramid" (1997:30). In an attempt to cement the status of the racial contract as a political, social, economic, ideological, and philosophical rule, Mills privileges the broader implications of the contract while minimizing the "local variations." It is, however, within these local variations that we are able to observe the suc-cesses and failures of the tenets of the racial contract, or in our case, moder-nity, and begin to unpack how and why they succeeded or failed. To begin this endeavor involves an interrogation of the categories and concepts that were essential to Caribbean modernity—namely, for the purposes of this study, race and class.

Are Caribbean societies made up of primarily class-based or race-based hierarchies? The question is here raised rhetorically, but given that race and class are inextricably linked and mutually constitutive of hierarchies in slave societies, the debate is nonetheless of consequence if poor whites pose a potential problem to the binary power model of white over black. Thomas Keagy (1972:11) raises such issues with his assessment, based on a perceived racial arrogance and a self-imposed socioeconomic isolation, that "the poor whites are believed to occupy the lowest position on the scale of social class on Barbados today." By suggesting that the Redlegs occupy the lowest rung on the Barbadian social ladder, Keagy implicitly gives primacy to a class-based model of island society, relegating racial identity to an important but secondary status marker.

Although not necessarily concerned with the poor whites of the region specifically, Caribbean scholars have long engaged with Marxian analyses of plantation societies to develop ideas surrounding the nature of the relation-ship between race and class (for an archaeological case study, see Delle 2014b). Jamaican social theorist Stuart Hall engaged with this debate throughout his career, shifting perspectives from a cultural Marxist framework, largely stem-ming from his reading of Gramsci, to a postmodern rendering of identity for-mation processes (see Mills 2010:185–212). In his earlier works on race and class (1977, 1980, 1986), Hall foregrounds class, suggesting that the colo-nial Caribbean is best understood as a "social class stratification system in which the race-colour elements in the stratification matrix constitute the vis-ible index of a more complex structure" (Hall 1977:171). While Hall would later turn toward a more representational and identity-centered approach to race (Hall 1991, 1997), his work is in keeping with Caribbean scholarship that sought to make racial interventions into Marxist frameworks. Jamaican scholar Rex Nettleford similarly voiced the insufficiencies of vulgar Marxism to account for the realities of race and racism in the Caribbean. In drawing on the failure of scholars to adequately address race as an essential component of the "substructure" (in keeping with the Marxian lexicon), he insists that "race (and ethnicity) must be worked into the Marxian dialectic to meet the realities of Caribbean existence" (Nettleford 2003:8).

In highly racialized spaces like the plantation, the shortcomings of class-centric analyses become increasingly apparent. In his study of the white working class in the postrevolutionary United States, Marxist historian David Roediger bemoans that "the point that race is created wholly ideologically and historically, while class is not wholly so created, has often been boiled down to the notion that class (or 'the economic') is more real, more fundamental, more basic or more *important* than race, both in political terms and in terms of historical analysis" (2007:7, emphasis in original, see also Roediger 2017). Such an assessment compels scholars of the modern period in the Caribbean to critically engage with the dialectical entanglement of race and class to avoid one-dimensional approaches in which "race disappears into the 'reality' of class" (Roediger 2007:8; for Barbados see Mack 1965). Both phenomena are equally "real," even if biological race has been proven to be a myth (Sussman 2014), and necessitate analyses that are attentive to the ways in which they operate across space and time. How stratification was imposed and implemented across Caribbean landscapes and the intimacies of the race/class dynamic were far more than discursive abstractions; rather, they were grounded in particular and power-laden locales—none more ostentatious than the plantation.

ARCHAEOLOGIES OF THE PLANTATION LANDSCAPE

The plantation is an emblematic space of early Atlantic-world capitalism representing transatlantic flows in the form of goods and bodies. In this arena in the seventeenth century, new labor regimes were developed that were a marked transformation from labor systems practiced in western Europe and West Africa (Blackburn 1997; Newman 2013). Additionally, as the "cultural hearth" of the plantation system that would come to dominate England's American colonies for centuries to come, Barbados is an ideal setting to observe the transformations that occurred at local levels before, during, and after the shift to sugar production. While the specifics of the sugar revolution and its aftermath, particularly how it affected the white underclass, are discussed in detail in the following chapter, I first turn to how plantation archaeology has informed my approach to analyzing these transformations.

Plantation studies have been a mainstay of historical archaeology since the 1960s, thus remaining an integral part of what can be termed African American or African diaspora archaeology (see, for example, Fairbanks 1984; Orser 1990; Singleton, ed. 1999, and 2009). The contributions of archaeologists conducting such research have been invaluable in unearthing and interpreting the material signatures of the lifeways of enslaved Africans and their descendants. This scholarship has produced an enormous body of literature, too much to list here, illuminating the nuances, complexities, and harsh realities of everyday life for those forcefully tethered to the plantation. Additionally, the landscape of the plantation has been a focal point of analysis, with archaeologists investigating how space was imagined, produced, experienced, and laden with power dynamics. For the purposes of this study, the work of James Delle (1998, 2014b) is particularly useful, specifically his Marxist analyses that view plantation landscapes as material spaces that were purposely designed and produced to maximize profit and control labor. Using this framework, plantations can be viewed as spaces in which negotiations took place, albeit in unequal capacities, between management and the enslaved, as these groups struggled to surveil and claim space as their own, respectively.

Despite common features and basic tenets in production strategies, the plantation as a unit of analysis varied across space and time, as should the archaeological study of the space. In such analyses, however, plantation space is often divided into specific and familiar bounded units that include the village, great house, fields, works, and provision grounds. By subscribing to this framework, archaeologists adhere to plantation divisions that were designed, constructed, and often mapped by planters or plantation managers. Despite planter attempts to circumscribe movements of the enslaved and plantation tenants on and away from the plantation,[6] such landscape subdivisions are not necessarily useful modules of analysis for investigating how plantation laborers or residents experienced the world around them. While understanding the power structures inherent in plantation organization is crucial for unpacking the harsh realities of these emblematic spaces of human brutality and enslaved responses to them, such analyses privilege the relationship between laborers and authority figures and/or power structures, oftentimes obfuscating significant and formative relationships between nonelites. What is often lacking is a careful mediation to avoid an essentializing adherence to binary models of plantation analyses: control or resistance, "the world the slaves made," or "the world that was created and controlled by planters" (Singleton 1999:12).

The idea that plantations were purposely constructed to control labor and maximize profits in an overtly capitalist system has been the subject of considerable study, including by archaeologists (for the Caribbean, see Delle

1998, 2014b; Lenik 2011; Hicks 2007; Bergman and Smith 2014; Hauser 2015; Meniketti 2015; Ryzewski and Cherry 2015; Singleton 2015). Additionally, as Lynsey Bates (2015) has demonstrated, due to landscape constraints, planters frequently made choices about whether the control of labor or production efficiency was more important. Plantation design and planter/managerial strategies for laborer surveillance and subjection were certainly significant in affecting how laborers (enslaved and indentured, in the case of Barbados) experienced life on the plantation, and the power structures inherent in the institution of bound labor. As a distinctive institution, slavery has been described by Orlando Patterson as "approaching the limits of total power from the viewpoint of the master, and of total powerlessness from the viewpoint of the slave" (1982:1). Patterson's astute observations have long inspired scholars of slavery, but a shift in focus away from the master/slave dynamic or dialectic can be revelatory of the ambiguous in-between spaces and conditions of slavery and freedom on the plantation (Bates et al. 2016). Such a reorientation is proposed here, focusing analysis on networks among laborers at plantation peripheries. The intended goal is not an obfuscation of power relations or class economics (Orser 1988), but a privileging of the ways in which residents negotiated their roles in plantation production processes and navigated communal relationships.

In considering the inability of planters/managers/overseers to control every aspect of the lives of plantation laborers, specifically the enslaved, archaeologists have largely focused on two arenas of responses or cultural behaviors in the face of plantocratic domination: resistance and the persistence/transformation of African or Afro-Caribbean cultural traits. The two most overt forms of resistance were absconding from the plantation, sometimes followed by the establishment of maroon communities, and open rebellion. While the former has received a fair amount of archaeological attention (Agorsah 1994, 1999, and 2007; Goucher and Agorsah 2011; Weik 2012; Sayers 2014; White 2010; Fellows and Delle 2015), the latter is more difficult to trace archaeologically (see Orser and Funari 2001; Norton 2013).[7] While not necessarily focusing on acts of resistance, other archaeological approaches have similarly presented the enslaved as agentive actors within the plantation infrastructure. This heterogeneous body of literature, in addition to discussing colonial, creole Caribbean life more broadly, has taken a variety of forms, including the study of African symbolism (in its infinite permutations) and production techniques in the making of ceramics, religious beliefs and burial practices, the function and significance of local (il)licit pottery markets and other economic activities, subtle acts of resistance, provision ground production and economies, and consumer choice and personal preferences in consumption patterns and identity formation (for book-length treatments on the Caribbean see Handler and Lange 1978; Armstrong 1990; Delle 1998, 2014b; Haviser 1999; Farnsworth 2001; Wilkie and Farnsworth 2005; Hauser 2008; Hauser and Kelly 2009; Kelly and Hardy 2009; Kelly and Bérard 2014; Arcangeli 2015; Meniketti 2015; Singleton 2015; Bates et al. 2016; Chenoweth 2017).

Although a gross oversimplification of the high quality and quantity of work done under the banner of African American or African diaspora archaeology, the conceptualization of the plantation and its integral components needs to be expanded to incorporate the nuances of landscapes home to laborers that may not have been of African descent or were of mixed ancestry. Therefore, while I am sympathetic to calls to broaden archaeological horizons beyond the plantation (González-Tennant 2014:43; Potter 1991), there are important reorientations to be made on these emblematic landscapes of colonial modernity. In the Caribbean, historical archaeological research on the plantation rarely extends beyond planters and the enslaved, thereby avoiding the heterogeneity of the white population and nonenslaved laborers (but see Armstrong and Hauser 2004; Ryzewski and McAtackney 2015; Chenoweth 2017). Given that African chattel slavery was the dominant form of labor on plantations throughout the historical period, such a scholarly focus is understandable. In contexts where other forms of labor were used, and nonenslaved people were in residence, however, the place of these nonelites in plantation production, and the nature of their social relationships, need to be considered to generate a more comprehensive interpretation of plantation life. Additionally, such considerations reveal how nonelites understood their relationship with the plantocracy as well as with their plantation neighbors. To pose this challenge as a question, how did indentured servants and their descendants fit into the plantation scheme as laborers and tenants? How did such tenants relate to enslaved and, following emancipation, free Afro-Barbadians with whom they shared a similar economic status but not necessarily an inscribed racial identity?

It should also be emphasized that plantation studies need not be constrained by temporal boundaries determined by the commencement of slavery and emancipation. While emancipation or the collapse of the plantation economy may serve as a convenient bookend for individual case studies, plantation spaces maintained active lives even when the fields went fallow and the windmills began to crumble. Even in the case of Below Cliff, which was entirely abandoned in the 1960s, the plantation landscape is today traversed by local community members. Additionally, it holds particular memories that can sometimes only be sparked by engaging with its physicality. As anthropologist Maurice Bloch notes, despite the passage of time, "topography infused with history is particularly significant in that it facilitates this re-experiencing as though one was there" (Bloch 1998:120). What transpired on plantations even after they fell out of agricultural use is nonetheless significant in revealing the memories and stories that these spaces hold. As active spaces, community members engage with these landscapes, and archaeologists need to take seriously the living biographies of these contexts without allowing temporal restrictions to limit ongoing interactions between people and the materiality of the plantation.

LIFE AT THE MARGINS

In assessing the subtleties of plantation dynamics, spaces deemed marginal emerge as being of extreme consequence. From a political-ecological perspective, marginality is associated with those areas deemed unsuitable for profitable agricultural production—what Barbadians call "rab" lands. Poor whites have traditionally been portrayed as being marginal in socioeconomic capacities, including in their minor role in the island's sugar industry, their perceived isolation, and their tendency to reside in tenantries on the peripheries of plantations (Sheppard 1977; Keagy 1972). Contrary to such interpretations, poor white communities in Barbados provide evidence that spaces designated as marginal or peripheral were actually centers of heightened social interaction, production, and activity among laborers, both enslaved and free.

Marginality also comes to bear on how power is experienced across the landscape. In some cases, margins offer the potential for circumstantial autonomy for those experiencing various forms of oppression. These opportunities exist through geographical distance, physical barriers, limited viewscapes, or apathy from those in positions of power. In their analysis of marginal spaces in select Caribbean locales, Hauser and Armstrong (2012) suggest that the marginal character of such realms may facilitate lifestyles of "not being governed" for those technically under colonial rule. Using James Scott (2009) as their point of departure, they carefully demonstrate that archaeological research amply allows for the "exploration of individual action in the face of seemingly overpowering external constraints" (311) through individual or group adoption of "strategies of settlement and subsistence [that] evade the apparatus of the state" (313). Critically, as they acknowledge, evasion does not entail immunity from the material and discursive forces of colonialism. Following this line of thought, while the tenantry of Below Cliff was physically separated and out of sight from the central features of Clifton Hall Plantation (the great house, works, sugar fields, and slave village), warranting residents certain degrees of autonomy, they were nonetheless affected by the functioning of the plantation economy and the realities of living in a society infused with racial and class hierarchies.

These interstitial zones present opportunities for alternative ways of life to the cumbersome demands of dominant economic systems and modes of production on the plantation. They need not be, however, spaces that can be discretely associated with conscious or explicit resistance. Resistance, in principle, privileges the relationship between laborers and elites, as the former directly combat or are insubordinate toward the latter. Resistance can take the form of banal, everyday acts or outright rebellion to challenge and change circumstances of oppression. Alternatively, resistance can be mounted to slow or halt processes of change being imposed on individuals and groups (see González-Ruibal 2014:6–12). Each form of resistance entails an inherent intentionality on the part of actors, which places the burden of proof on archaeologists seeking to demonstrate explicit resistance in the past. The historical record can often provide direct evidence of resistance or revolt, as can archaeological evidence. There are, however, risks associated with using flimsy archaeological evidence to suggest intentionality on the part of actors in the past. Matthew Liebmann expounds on such interpretive pitfalls by cautioning against "contemporary researchers throwing their own voices and opinions into the mouths of people in the past" (2012:8). To avoid such acts of ventriloquism, in the chapters that follow, I use historical and archaeological evidence not as proof of direct resistance to forces of colonialism and capitalism but, rather, as evidence of practices of *residence* that "involve individuals staking out claims for themselves" (Silliman 2014:61) that did not neatly comport with elite understandings of the place of poor whites in island society.

Given that the marginalized inhabitants of Below Cliff were not immune to the imposition of ideologies concerning race and class, social relationships and interactions taking place between nonelites in the tenantry were affected by various markers of difference (for Barbados see Shaw 2013). In tenantries inhabited by poor whites and villages occupied by enslaved Afro-Barbadians, legal distinctions between free laborers and the enslaved were certainly taken seriously, no doubt having a tremendous influence on how such individuals perceived themselves and others, even after emancipation. Despite marked legal and social differences between the enslaved (and later, free Afro-Barbadians) and poor whites, Karl Watson suggests that "their [the poor whites] history is far more akin to the history of the blacks [than the white elite], with whom they share centuries of marginalization, discrimination, oppression and poverty" (2000b:131). The detailed implications of this assessment in terms of lived experience and cultural attributes will be discussed in later chapters. At this juncture, however, I draw attention to

Watson's claim of shared degrees of poverty. Archaeologies of the plantation
have tended to sidestep discussions of class and class formation in favor of
the imposition of and response to racial, ethnic, and gender stratification
(Spencer-Wood and Matthews 2011:4; for exceptions, see Orser 1988; Epperson 1990; Delle 2014b). Analyses along lines of gender, racial, and class difference afford opportunities to explore multiple dimensions of social inequality
that can emphasize "the struggles among members of society over the exercise of social power" (McGuire and Paynter 1991:1; Delle et al. 2000). Taken
a step further, exploring the intersections of these analytics exposes how they
can be operationalized and experienced in different ways among nonelite
populations. Karl Watson's assertion about the socioeconomic position of the
poor whites in Barbadian society makes clear that issues of class and race
must be addressed together rather than in isolation.

Class, Racialization, and Whiteness

Archaeologists regularly encounter the material manifestations of economic
inequality. Unequal access to goods and amenities are visible in everyday
items as well as in developing and dilapidated landscapes. Careful attention
to the processes that led to the establishment of poor white tenantries on
the same landscape as villages for the enslaved certainly entails an engagement with the forces and relations that engender inequality, specifically those
between planters/overseers/elites and nonelite laborers (enslaved and free) in
an agrarian capitalist system. These dialectical class relations are no doubt
important and crucial in understanding social relations in plantation societies (see Delle 2014b; Sayers 2014). However, approaches to class that focus
on the relationship between planters and laborers potentially obfuscate differences and schisms *within* classes, including among those marked as subordinates. The construction, reconstruction, and negotiation of difference among
nonelites make apparent the need for an engagement with how such individuals simultaneously coped with economic inequity and interacted with one
another, their material possessions, and the environment. In short, promoted
here is an approach that addresses the entanglements of race and class as they
affected nonelites plantation residents.

The poor white experience of economic hardship was shared by enslaved
and free Afro-Barbadians, albeit under very different circumstances. While
these rigid racial boundaries were by no means impermeable (see Jones 2007;
Stoler 2002; Reilly 2016a), such differences come to the fore in the historical
record as elites debated how to govern, manage, assist, or condemn diverse
underclass populations. Additionally, members of the poor white community in the past and present experience class antagonisms and their own

economic circumstances in a multitude of ways, thus drawing an important distinction between "individual descendants of historical communities [and] a descendant community" (McGuire 2008:212). Multiple, and sometimes conflicting, narratives arise between individuals within these communities, engendering schisms in how economic inequality is interpreted and remembered (Jones and Russell 2012:280, McDavid 2011). Conflicts and competition may arise due to social stigmas associated with poverty. Members of the present-day poor white community offer conflicting opinions on their own economic circumstances; it is with such sentiments in mind that scholars must carefully consider the use of the terms *poverty* and *impoverishment* (Reilly 2016b).

The castigation of the poor is inherently tied to class antagonisms, informing approaches to archaeological studies of impoverishment and homelessness (Mayne and Murray 2001; Spencer-Wood and Matthews, eds. 2011; Rimmer et al. 2011; Zimmerman and Welch 2011; Kiddey 2017). A long-standing engagement with analyses of class and economic inequality has engendered an explicit archaeological approach to poverty. As Spencer-Wood and Matthews argue, "Poverty is a way of positioning some at a disadvantage that simultaneously enriches the few, impoverishes others, and marks the poor with symbols of marginality, failure, and Otherness. Poverty, therefore, is a struggle for resources *and* reputation" (Spencer-Wood and Matthews 2011:1, emphasis in original). Like Wurst and Fitts (1999), Spencer-Wood and Matthews acknowledge that an engagement with poverty entails a relational definition of class (see also Mrozowski 2006:12–13). For the purposes of this case study, poor white economic realities may have been similar to the circumstances of free and enslaved Afro-Barbadians, but they experienced the plantation landscape in markedly different ways given their racial identity. As free and white plantation residents, the Redlegs were marked in the historical record and in historiography by their impoverishment and were socially condemned due to their perceived idleness.

As a discipline that works with things, archaeologists might understandably be uncomfortable with absences. Absence and nothingness have been considered from the perspective of materiality and the experiential (see Fowles 2010; Owen 2015), but poverty, from a materialist perspective, can be constituted by a relative quantitative absence of things. Despite limited archaeological materials, those materials that are present have observable attributes—like those connoting artifact reuse—that demonstrate the ways in which those who suffered from economic hardship combated their circumstances. Artifact paucity may limit certain modes of quantitative archaeological analysis while simultaneously offering other qualitative forms.

Poor whites and Afro-Barbadians were similarly afflicted by class realities in plantocratic Barbados. The assignation of racial identity, however, assured that each group experienced class relations in markedly different ways. It is therefore impossible to disarticulate class from race in highly racialized spaces like the plantation. Race continues to be a central analytic and political underpinning in archaeological literature (Franklin 1997, 2001; Dawdy 2006b; Mullins 2008; Matthews and McGovern 2015; Agbe-Davies 2015; Battle-Baptiste 2011; Hayes 2013; Voss 2008; Orser 2001, 2004, 2007; Shackel 2011; Babson 1990; Epperson 1990; for a prehistoric/historic dialogue about race and archaeology, see Gosden 2006). Whether viewed as being practiced, essential in the construction of identity and space, an embodied social construction, a politically salient illustration of contemporary inequality, a fluid emic and etic identity across space and time, or an "ideological assertion of otherness, inferiority, and fragmentation" (Epperson 1990:29), *racism* rather than *race* has more often been the critical object of study.

Race, as an analytic, is not easily separable from racism, nor should it be. Indeed, historical processes of racialization that unfolded during and after European colonization of the Americas have demonstrated that race and racism are inextricably linked. This entanglement was arguably most palpable on the plantation. The emergence of slave societies has even sparked a lively chicken-or-egg debate, asking whether race or slavery was the foundational piece of the equation (see Smedley and Smedley 2012:93–120). The creation of a white racial category is equally crucial in understanding how processes of racialization unfolded. Whiteness has transitioned from being a taken for granted, unmarked social category to a central object of study within a growing body of anthropological literature (Brander Rasmussen et al. 2001; Hartigan 1999, 2005; Tyler 2012; for pertinent sociological and philosophical literature see Wray 2006; Wray and Newitz 2013; Jacobson 1998; Monahan 2011; Dyer 1997; Frankenberg 1993 and 1997). Despite divergences and disciplinary threads that characterize this literature, most scholars agree that there were and are particular boundaries or limits to a white identity (see, for instance, Maghbouleh 2017). These boundaries were engendered, policed, contested, and altered, including in Barbados (Jones 2007). Finally, class and gender are viewed as significant and co-constituting identities that drastically affect the way in which race is defined, perceived, embodied, and experienced.

The making of race was of the utmost significance for the success of the plantation system in places like Barbados. It follows that I wholeheartedly agree with Charles Orser Jr.'s assertion that "the use of racialization in history constitutes a significant vector of social inequality" (2007:10), making historical processes of racialization a valuable arena of analysis for social archaeology. Examining these processes as they affected Barbadian poor whites, however, becomes particularly challenging. As Cecily Jones highlights in her historical analysis of poor white Barbadian women, white elites regularly expressed their "uncertainty as to the precise quality of 'whiteness' of this underclass" (Jones 2007:19). Additionally, as described in more detail in chapter 5 herein, poor whites implemented their own strategies to resist the limitations racial taxonomic systems posed. What this suggests is that paying critical attention to fissures in racializing discourses, and the ability of racial identities to be manipulated, can be just as fruitful as a strict focus on historical processes of racialization. In short, racialization had dire consequences, especially for those victimized by plantation slavery, but race could at the same time be made and unmade.

In the ensuing chapters, it will become evident that discourses and practices of racialization came to be crucial in defining, reproducing, and attempting to maintain modern constructs of racial difference and boundaries in Barbados. These broader discourses and ideologies constitute a significant component of what encapsulates modern Caribbean history. Given my interest in exploring alternative modernities, however, it will be crucial to interrogate the salience (or lack thereof) of its hegemonic parlance (Stoler 2002). In other words, in presenting evidence that destabilizes racial discourse, we can recognize the inability of their essentialist character to explain how racial identities are locally produced, reproduced, experienced, and embodied.

It is this very essentialism and reification of categories and concepts that inspired Michael Monahan's philosophical theorization of race in *The Creolizing Subject: Race, Reason, and the Politics of Purity* (2011). Monahan argues that traditional approaches to racial analysis suffer from an adherence to a "politics of purity" whereby one's racial identity is ascribed to concrete and bounded "all-or-nothing" racial categories. This inherent danger in analyses of race has been particularly problematic in studies of poor white populations. Rather than being an a priori identity, colonial whiteness had to be created and maintained through constant effort. Poor whites regularly posed a challenge to those boundaries, suggesting that white purity may be better described as an elite ideal rather than a reality (for a summary of skin color and social class, see Jablonski 2012:142–156).

With this in mind, Monahan suggests an interrogation of the epistemological roots of these racial categories to better understand the biological, social, and political dimensions of racial ontology and identity, and how such categories are always in a state of becoming, that is, never complete. If class formation processes are infused within this discussion, which Monahan explicitly omits (2011:122), the approach is useful for examining Barbadian poor white

racial and class identity and positionality. What are the boundaries that separate the Redlegs from free people of color? Furthermore, while the legal designation between the poor whites and the enslaved may appear straightforward,
how are these boundaries maintained, for example, if an enslaved man has a
child with a poor white woman? In interrogating these embodied and multiple
personal identities (Harris and Robb 2012), the very whiteness of Barbadian
Redlegs becomes a critical avenue of analysis.

In this study, I propose an approach to race that borrows from critical whiteness studies but is more anthropologically informed. While recognizing the
significance of broader ideologies of racial distinctiveness, as well as hierarchies
and power dynamics, localized analysis of cultural interaction and relations
will attempt to interrogate the stability of racial identities as they were developed, imposed, and embodied in the past (Stoler 2002). In essence, to avoid
the theoretical "poor white problem," it is necessary to critically engage with
physical and conceptual boundary maintenance between poor whites and the
larger Barbadian society in the past and present, and to draw out the fragility and porousness of those boundaries (Forde-Jones 1998; Jones 2007; Wray
2006). Sociologist Rogers Brubaker has highlighted the danger of group-based
analysis along lines of ethnicity that is equally applicable to investigations of
race. He warns that undisciplined grouping practices homogenize individual
variation, problematizing the very nature of groups as a useful analytical construct. He further claims that such practices essentialize and reduce groups to
a few underlying characteristics, ultimately missing other significant aspects of
individuality and identity (Brubaker 2004:9–10). Ultimately, if racial identities
(imposed and/or self-perceived) can be contested, they can be reimagined to
generate a more accurate depiction of village and tenantry life on a Barbadian
plantation. Throughout this book, I present evidence suggesting that localized
and nonelite understandings of race and class did not always adhere to dominant (plantocractic) notions of how individuals were to be defined.

As mentioned, the development of dominant ideologies about race, in addition to alternatives to them, was and is intimately tied to similar processes
affecting socioeconomic class. Despite arguments claiming that Barbados is,
and has historically been, an entirely class-based society, often using the poor
whites as justification for this ascertain (Keagy 1972), race-based hierarchies
played an integral role in the development of social classes on the plantation
landscape. Archaeological research is well suited to analyze class and race
formation processes as they unfolded and continuously became reimagined
in emerging capitalist/colonial spaces. The processes that took place in Barbados beginning in 1627 would significantly alter the trajectory of Atlantic-
world history. The sugar revolution, beginning in the 1640s, would establish

a high-functioning and remarkably profitable agrarian capitalist network that not only transformed global trade but also substantially altered how race, class, and labor were conceptualized, managed, and (re)defined in localized plantation settings.

CROSS-CURRENTS OF GENDER

Race and class are the themes most explicitly discussed throughout this book. This does not, however, preclude the fact that issues of gender are implicit within the overarching discussions of race and class. In her analysis of empire and imperialism, Anne McClintock suggests that "no social category exists in privileged isolation; each comes into being in social relation to other categories, if in uneven and contradictory ways. But power is seldom adjudicated evenly—different social situations are overdetermined for race, for gender, for class, or for each in turn. I believe, however, that it can be safely said that no social category should remain invisible with respect to an analysis of empire" (McClintock 1995:9). In essence, while discussions may be framed through a particular lens such as race, class, or gender, it is not necessarily the case that the other categories are irrelevant or indeterminate. Rather, the categories and concepts are stitched together, especially in the Caribbean where, as Stuart Hall argues (2017:64), they are "interpenetrating, mutually reinforcing as well as mutually destabilizing." This point, of course, has not been lost on archaeologists, and the entanglements of these concepts are inherent in disciplinary literature, especially as archaeologists find inspiration in intersectional thought popularized by Kimberlé Crenshaw (see Hancock 2016). As Mrozowski and colleagues have pointed out, "As a field concerned with understanding the material dimensions of capitalism, historical archaeology must examine how material culture relates to the social categories constructed within the capitalist system, particularly race, class, and gender" (2000:xiv). While reluctant to use the now oft-used notion of intersectionality, largely to avoid having multiple analytics exist on a symmetrical plane, I nonetheless recognize how race, class, and gender can intersect, if not fluidly, at least haphazardly and often violently.

I have chosen to center this project on race and class as the data presented in the following chapters most directly speak to these concepts; this is most explicitly illustrated in the moniker *poor white*. Despite this focus, however, gender is subtly and consciously tethered to these discussions. In considering relations between Below Cliff residents and processes of capitalism in a colonial context, it is inevitable to confront gender divisions and sexuality in labor patterns on the plantation landscape (see Voss and Casella 2012; Delle 2000; Gilchrist 1999; Baugher and Spencer-Wood 2010). Gender is featured alongside discussions of labor in elite discourses about acceptable and proper forms of industriousness. These are manifest in parish baptismal registries, which serve as powerful tools that demonstrate labor patterns; it is important to note, however, that in these records a column is reserved for only the child's *father's* occupation. This suggests that women were perceived to be irrelevant within island labor patterns. When, in rare instances, women's occupations are given in such records, they usually adhere to gendered stereotypes whereby women occupy traditional "women's work," such as seamstresses or domestics. Conversely, data presented speaks to the diverse roles played by both men and women at the household and community level (for the Caribbean see also Armstrong 2003:280).

Issues of race are intricately tied to reproduction practices, policies, and perceptions; racial boundaries and their rigidity or porousness are therefore dependent on gender relations (Jones 2007). The Barbadian plantation landscape was an incredibly intimate realm of colonial encounters in which enslaved Africans and Afro-Barbadians, planters, managers, and poor whites interacted with one another. Such encounters are rife with sexual liaisons, exploitation, masculinity and femininity, intimacy, sexual policies, and politics (for archaeologies of colonial encounters and sexuality see Voss and Casella 2012). As will become evident in later chapters, particular practices and policies sought to police racial boundaries through punishments against poor white women who developed sexual relationships with Afro-Barbadians. In general, island authorities were determined to maintain a perceived "racial purity" among island residents. In response, evidence suggests that poor white women exhibited sexual autonomy, actively choosing to reproduce with Afro-Barbadians, thus blurring the color line.

Just as there were prescribed ideologies concerning racial and class identities, Barbadian men and women were expected to adhere to particular roles that circumscribed their economic activities, reproductive habits, and places in society (Reilly 2014). As demonstrated by Marisa Fuentes (2016; see also Beckles 1999) in her analysis of Barbados's urban center, Bridgetown, however, dismantling the violence of the colonial archive makes clear that Barbadian women had their own notions of their places in plantation society, which often conflicted with, contradicted, and transformed elite discourses. In spaces like Below Cliff, an environment was fostered that allowed for the development of vastly different understandings of race, class, and gender relations than those prescribed by modern Caribbean systems and lifeways.

An Archaeology of Alternative Modernities

The plantation system came to be dependent on essential, definitive, and reductive racial categories in addition to specific conceptualizations of labor practices. There were, of course, exceptions to this generalization, but it nonetheless connotes the underlying principles and practices that defined the system of sugar and slavery. In Barbados, as was the case throughout the Caribbean, there were certainly ambiguities that complicated colonial ideals and designs. For instance, manumissions were uncommon but possible, resulting in a population of free people of color (see Handler 1974). Additionally, mixed-race individuals, often referred to as mulattos, born to free women of color or white women were nominally free. If, however, we turn to island census data, it appears that mixed-race individuals and free people of color were relatively uncommon in island society, at least according to official records. While acknowledging the unreliable nature of these population figures, Jerome Handler's compilation of statistical data on Barbadian freedmen in the late eighteenth to early nineteenth century illustrates how few individuals on the island were considered free people of mixed ancestry or "coloured." In the freedmen population of St. Michael (the parish home to the island's urban center, Bridgetown) in 1773, 136 were registered as "coloured" and 78 were listed as "black," thus composing 0.73% and 0.42% of the total St. Michael population, respectively. Although these percentages would rise to 2.65% and 2.25% shortly before emancipation, it is still evident that free individuals of mixed ancestry composed a small minority of the St. Michael and island population (Handler 1974:17–21). Therefore, on a densely populated island, census records indicate that only a small minority of individuals fell outside of the comfortable white and black categories (and, by extension, free and enslaved).

There are two possible readings of these statistics. If accurate, they reflect an overwhelming success of colonial designs of racial segregation and the institution of slavery on all levels of island society. This entails an almost complete refusal on the part of all Barbadians, regardless of class, to procreate with individuals outside of their own racial group. If taken at face value, assuming the veracity of racial categories, it would appear that ideas of racial purity and hierarchies were well maintained in Barbados. Alternatively, and more plausibly, such statistics reflect the power wielded by the producers of the historical record. A substantial body of literature grapples with the strategies employed by such authorities and archival producers that suggest alternative ways of reading official documents (Cohn and Dirks 1988; Stoler 2009; Comaroff and Comaroff 1991; for Barbados see Shaw 2013; Fuentes 2016). Reading archival absences, critically engaging with documents to uncover particular slants and biases, and understanding the motivations of those producing such documents implies that what is taking place on the ground is not necessarily what is represented in the historical record. This point is paramount to the historical archaeological endeavor, which has long prided itself on recovering evidence that can illuminate the lives of those lost to history or narratives that counter such histories (see Shackel and Roller 2013; Schmidt and Patterson 1995). While this disciplinary foundation is no doubt significant, historical archaeology is in an advantageous position to illuminate not only resistance on the part of historical actors against power structures and oppressive forces like colonialism, capitalism, racism, and sexism (to name a few), but also the sheer failures of modernity and its associated ideologies. Through his work in East Africa, Alfredo González-Ruibal (2006:196; see also González-Ruibal 2014) argues that in addition to exposing and critiquing the numerous tentacles of the modernist narrative, archaeological techniques and sensibilities "seem particularly suitable for unveiling the darkest side of the modern project" seen in "territories devastated by war, famine, disease and forced re-settlement, all fostered by a dream of reason gone berserk." If these sites exemplify the destructive forces and failings of modernity in the most physical modes possible, ideological failings are more difficult to discern and less visible, but no less significant.

Proposed here is an archaeology of alternative modernities. Even in one of the most efficiently managed and profitable colonial territories, alternatives to the dominant tropes of modernity existed. Evidence of these alternatives can be found in the materials produced, consumed, used, and discarded by community members, the spatial orientation of the areas they inhabited, how they made their livings, the domestic structures in which they resided, and the choices individuals made in spouses, places to worship, and places to be buried. These seemingly mundane items, practices, and choices encompass what constitutes everyday ways of living that were distinct from the prescribed and desired behaviors and attitudes associated with localized modernity. To be clear, as mentioned, there is an explicit difference between this approach and modes of resistance. Resistance, even when conceived in Certeauian terms of everyday practices (1984), still implies a conscious effort on the part of actors to counter domination or oppression through various means. Everyday practices enacted in spaces home to alternative modernities rely less on a particular, knowable psyche or intention. Rather, I argue that modern ideologies, manifest in the actions taken by authorities and officials to circumscribe the lives of nonelites, were sometimes only partially successful in affecting those that they sought to control. Before expanding, however, it is useful to engage with more blatant forms of resistance to substantively unpack how such transgressive behavior that deviated from the established order and ideologies of modernity offered the potential for alternatives.

Despite my supposition that alternative modernities need not be associated with discreet acts of resistance, the concept owes much to a growing body of literature, including that of the Black Radical Tradition (Robinson 1983; Johnson and Lubin 2017), that has shed light on suppressed historical instances of actors directly contesting the major tenets of modernity, including colonialism, capitalism, racism, sexism, and imposed change (see González-Ruibal 2014). Peter Linebaugh and Marcus Rediker's *The Many-Headed Hydra* (2000) presents a circum-Atlantic historical account of rebellion and resistance on the part of the "hewers of wood and drawers of water," or the laboring masses of the modern world. Their work, though critiqued for being romanticized at times, masterfully illustrates the refusal of individuals and groups to adhere to burgeoning ideologies about modernity, particularly class exploitation and racial hierarchies. The work highlights transatlantic examples of rebellion and resistance by heterogeneous racial and ethnic groups who found common ground in their experiences of discrimination, exploitation, and marginalization; the rebellion plot planned in Barbados was one such example that involved European indentured servants and enslaved Africans (123–127; see also Ligon 2013:74–75). Ultimately, despite the efforts of those in positions of power to paralyze the "many-headed hydra," the authors argue that such ideologies and discourses only ever meet with partial success and that explicit rebellion and resistance are evidence of solidarity on the part of the masses.

Susan Buck-Morss (2009) and Sibylle Fischer (2004) engage with similar themes, centering on the Haitian Revolution to discuss radical antislavery and universal human liberty in the wake of the only successful slave rebellion in the Atlantic world. Buck-Morss rhetorically asks, "What if that every time that the consciousness of individuals surpassed the confines of present constellations of power in perceiving the concrete meaning of freedom, *this* were valued as a moment, however transitory, of the realization of absolute spirit? What other silences would need to be broken? What *un*disciplined stories would be told?" (2009:75, emphasis in original). Through these questions, Buck-Morss illustrates a philosophical and practical exclusion of Haiti from discourse surrounding Enlightenment ideals of liberty, despite the rebellion's demonstration of them. Fischer (2004) extends the Haitian conversation to the Dominican Republic and Cuba to illustrate the extensive knowledge of the Haitian Revolution among Caribbean inhabitants (of all classes and backgrounds), and what its success potentially meant throughout the region. Fischer reveals that discourses of universal human liberation and radical antislavery were purposely suppressed via cultural, political, economic, and social maneuvering to deny the blossoming alternative modernity that a free Haiti exemplified.

Ultimately, these works illustrate stark silences or purposeful suppressions in the historical record that limit interpretation and memory. Michel-Rolph Trouillot's separation of "history as told" and "history as happened" takes these silences to task to account for how Haiti is remembered, how and why silences are produced, and what they deny. In presenting the Haitian Revolution as an impossibility or nonevent, Trouillot suggests that "built into any system of domination is the tendency to proclaim its own normalcy. To acknowledge resistance as a mass phenomenon is to acknowledge the possibility that something is wrong with the system" (Trouillot 1995:85). This passage is significant for a number of reasons. First, the practice of proclaiming a system's normalcy is an ongoing process that continuously unfolds through the actions of those who have a hand in dominating, but also those who unconsciously reaffirm the nature of the system and its associated characteristics. Within this latter category we need to include the reproduction of history by actors from all levels of society who uncritically adhere to the narratives and discourses of modernity. Second, as stated, evidence that something is wrong with the system need not be seen *only* in outright resistance; structural cracks can also be manifest in the everyday actions of those who never recognized the "normalcy" of the system to begin with. With this in mind, I turn to the poor whites to sketch a preliminary picture of what modern spaces were *supposed* to be and the alternatives that fomented at the margins.

The historical interpretation of the poor whites has traditionally been one of racial purity, isolation, idleness, and destitution. Historical and contemporary accounts of the poor whites comfortably claim that the entirety of the population suffers from a racial arrogance that makes the prospects of miscegenation in the past and present nearly impossible (although some accounts have claimed that racial intermixing is a mid-twentieth-century phenomenon; see Keagy 1972, 1975; Price 1957). Additionally, seemingly innocuous stereotypes such as idleness and social isolation are essential to the narratives of Caribbean modernity. In profit-producing spaces such as the Caribbean plantation, those deemed idle and lazy are severed from the socioeconomic landscape. By being nonentities in the sugar production process, poor whites' poverty is expressly portrayed as being a self-inflicted result of their own idleness and isolation. This portrayal of the Redlegs resolves the precariousness of an impoverished population with white skin. In other words, the logic implies that the only reason these people are poor is because of their own laziness and refusal to participate in the sugar industry. Such interpretations imply the success of dominant ideologies of racial superiority and inferiority that permeated Caribbean socioeconomic life. While impoverished, a rather counterintuitive phenomenon in Caribbean plantation society for white residents, the perceived racial purity of the Redlegs coupled with their self-inflicted poverty assuaged planter fears of unadulterated mixing of races that shared an economic status (Beckles 1993; Jones 2007).

The evidence presented throughout this book goes beyond the deconstruction of these stereotypes. I argue that such stereotypes were constructed for the purpose of maintaining the illusion that modernity and its associated ideologies were successfully imbedded in island society. These ideologies and their material manifestations changed as ideas about race transformed during the seventeenth century and continually warped to compensate for the palimpsest of modernity. Two essential tropes of Caribbean modernity are interrogated, deconstructed, and analyzed at the local level to view their successes and failures. The first involves the relationship between these racial groups and capitalist production processes. The second is the strict boundary between races that paralleled and informed the island's socioeconomic hierarchy. As the story goes, island (and absentee) whites held positions of power, reflected the civility and bourgeois character of "Little England," and ensured that plantations were functioning efficiently. Enslaved Africans and Afro-Barbadians provided the necessary dehumanized labor to ensure productivity in the fields, in the works, and in the great house. The degenerate poor whites lived a backward lifestyle on the margins of the plantation landscape and experienced squalor and destitution due to their own idleness. Their refusal to labor in the same capacity as the enslaved and free people of color was due to pride in their white identity. If this is the narrative of Barbadian modernity, what were and are the plausible and very real alternatives?

Through a reorientation of analysis of plantation space, I suggest that seemingly marginal spaces like Below Cliff were home to alternative modernities. In this space, the boundaries between white and black racial identities were contested (even if unconsciously) and blurred, in a figurative as well as a biological sense. While some labored on the plantation, there was not a wholesale commitment to the sugar economy. Rather, residents of Below Cliff were small farmers and fishermen who subsisted on their own production, traded with neighbors (including the enslaved and free people of color), consumed locally produced goods in addition to imported material, and interacted and intermixed with individuals of diverse racial ancestries. The existence of such spaces that facilitated these particular lifestyles threatens the dominant narratives of Caribbean modernity and destabilizes the very concepts and ideologies that were (and still are) essential for its perceived success and reality. Archaeologies of colonialism can therefore highlight the inherent messiness of modern projects that were never fully what those with the most power may have wanted them to be (see Hall 2000; Dawdy 2008; Cipolla and Hayes

2015). The historical and archaeological evidence presented throughout this book illustrates that residents of Below Cliff, while coping with a harsh environment and hardship, were maintaining a lifestyle that did not neatly comport with colonial logics surrounding the functioning of plantation society.

TWO

REDLEGS ON THE PLANTATION LANDSCAPE

> One segment of the white community was represented by the poor whites who had survived the consequences of the sugar revolution and formed a group that was separate and distinct from the other classes in the social order of Barbados. Although their lot was little better than that of the slaves and inferior to the more prosperous of the free coloured people, they kept very much to themselves, remaining distant and aloof from other underprivileged groups in the community.
>
> —F. A. Hoyos (1978:96)

How did Barbados come to be the tropical home for thousands of impoverished inhabitants of European extract? How did their precarious existence on the landscape lead to a reputation like the harrowing depiction quoted above? In a general sense, these are questions of history. They demand an understanding of the English settlement of Barbados and the development of the plantation infrastructure. This chapter explores the historical trajectory that explains the poor white presence on the Barbadian landscape. Broader narratives of Caribbean historiography that address the forces of colonialism, capitalism, plantation production, and slavery are also constitutive of the poor white experience in Barbados and are therefore fundamental to situating this localized narrative in a colonial Caribbean framework. At the same time, however, and due to the archaeological nature of this case study, historically contextualizing the Redlegs is equally about the present. Archaeology is "a discipline that is able to make the past present through its remains" (González-Ruibal 2013:10). More specifically, archaeology "deals only indirectly with the past. The object of its study is the present, or, more precisely put, time as it is inscribed in the present" (Olivier 2013:124).

The historical and material pieces of evidence that speak to the Redleg experience in places like Below Cliff constitute a dynamic relationship between Redlegs in the past, the poor white community of the twenty-first century, and all residents of and visitors to Barbados. The Redlegs have been and are the victims of derisive stereotypes including idleness, drunkenness, incestuousness, uncleanliness, arrogance, and ignorance. While the origins and nature of these stereotypes will be addressed in turn, more pressing questions will explore the function that these stereotypes serve(d) in broader Barbadian society. This chapter is organized chronologically, not to adhere to a linear or progressive sense of time, but to make lucid the role that memory plays in situating the past in the present (Olivier 2011). The sequence of events that transpired on the island from settlement in 1627 speaks to the implementation of a sugar and slavery system that attempted to circumscribe the roles of laborers and rigidly divide society into bounded racial groups. Unraveling the specifics of this narrative speaks to how the history of the Redlegs is understood in the present.

From the earliest English settlement of the island to the twenty-first century, a so-called white underclass has persisted in Barbados despite economic hardship and socioeconomic marginalization. Despite marginalization in the past and present, the earliest European laborers were crucial in the development of early colonial society. Furthermore, following the establishment of a plantation slave society, planters lamented the decline of the white population and made efforts to bolster the number of white inhabitants able to serve in the militia. Despite limited socioeconomic power, the poor whites were also inculcated in the debates surrounding emancipation. Their anomalous existence in plantation society was described by authors who frequently used their condition to make political arguments for or against slavery. In short, rather than being marginal within or isolated from the inner workings of Barbadian history and society, evidence proclaims the critical role of the poor whites in these historical processes.

On a broader scale, the narrative of Barbadian poor whites is enmeshed with social, economic, and political phenomena that moved people, things, and ideas throughout the Atlantic world. An Atlantic-world approach takes seriously the multitude and magnitude of continental connections that began in the late fifteenth century. In contrast to previous approaches that privileged European empires and their links with Old and New World outposts and colonies, an Atlantic-world approach acknowledges that "the links and exchanges were as often between people of many different origins as they were within strictly imperial lines" (Kupperman 2012:1). Viewed from this perspective, we can explore more fluidly the nuances and complexities of Caribbean and Atlantic interactions, exchanges, and connections (Curet and Hauser 2011; Greene and Morgan 2009; Palmié and Scarano 2011). While this analysis will be locally situated in Barbados, the island's history involves tremendously diverse ethnic groups, each of which contributed to the development of Barbadian society. It is therefore important to note that the narrative of the poor whites is not one characterized by isolation or exceptionalism, despite analyses of this group that have fallen victim to such tropes. Rather, an inclusive approach acknowledges the European, Amerindian, African, and Barbadian influences on the emergence of a poor white demographic and the specific realities of their daily lives. This fairly extensive historical background will be somewhat familiar to those well versed in the historiography of the Caribbean region, but the shift in perspective is important. The broader narratives of sugar and slavery are well known, but when told from the vantage point of the experiences of the white underclass, they demand careful attention to explicate how and why poor whites lived at the margins of plantation society.

GEOGRAPHY AND SETTLEMENT

Barbados is the southeasternmost island in the Caribbean region, though it technically falls outside of the Lesser Antilles chain (see Figure I.1). Unlike most of its Windward and Leeward island neighbors, which are volcanic in origin, Barbados is a limestone island. Geologists refer to it as an accretionary prism or wedge, "created when part of the North Atlantic Plate buckled and crumpled as it slid under the Caribbean Plate over millions of years" (Barker 2011:29). Although formed by tectonic activity, the island is relatively flat compared with neighboring islands, making it an ideal landscape for intensive agricultural production. Most of the island is covered by a thick coral limestone cap except in the northeastern Scotland District, where erosion has exposed the shale and sandstone sediments (MacPherson 1963:73–74). The island experiences a hot and humid rainy season from June to November and a milder dry season from December to May. Its easterly location also places it outside of the hurricane belt, making destructive storms less frequent but nonetheless dangerous occurrences for residents.

Due to the rough waters of the eastern coastline, the four main towns are situated along ports of the western and southern coastline: from south to north Oistins, Bridgetown (the capital), Holetown, and Speightstown. Holetown was the first settlement English settlers established in 1625, and densely populated settlements have hugged the western and southern coastline since that time. The area's calm waters and gentle topography made a suitable place to establish permanent settlements and develop urban and rural landscapes. The Scotland District, however, covers nearly one-seventh of the island and is home to some of the most rugged terrain, which led early settlers to name the region after its resemblance to the highlands of Scotland. Hackleton's Cliff extends south from the center of the Scotland District into the southeastern parish of St. Philip. The plateau above the cliff boasts some of the most fertile land on the island and has been home to some of the largest and most successful sugar plantations. The region below the cliff, home to the tenantry of Below Cliff, the focus of this case study, is prone to frequent rockslides and land slippages due to the instability of the escarpment and the dramatic slope that leads from the cliff down to the coast.

The early colonial history of the island is unique for the Caribbean due to the fact that "there is ample evidence that Barbados was uninhabited when it

Figure 2.1. Hapcott map of 1646 depicting a presugar landscape of what would soon become Trents Estate. (Courtesy of the John Carter Brown Library at Brown University)

was settled by the English in the 1620s, and it is quite possible, and would be consistent with archaeological evidence, that it had no human inhabitants a century earlier" (Campbell 1993:11). Amerindians were brought to the island from Guiana as part of the first settlement expedition (Handler 1969, 1977), but the uninhabited nature of the island provided terra nullius for early English arrivals to establish settlements without considering relations with local indigenous populations. The 1620s and 1630s were watershed decades in terms of Caribbean ventures for the English, which witnessed the settlement of Barbados (officially in 1627), St. Christopher (1623), and Montserrat (1632), among others. Although many of these island holdings would be contested by Spanish, French, and Dutch forces due to their geographic position "beyond the line" (Bridenbaugh and Bridenbaugh 1972), Barbados would enjoy relative immunity from outside threats.[1] The early years of settlement, however, were marked by tumultuous internal conflict over which discovery party held proper claim to the island.

Despite persistent tensions among competing factions of settlers (see Harlow 1926:9), the arduous task of clearing land and establishing the earliest farmsteads on the island began almost immediately. To settle outstanding debts, the Earl of Carlisle rented land to tenants or gave parcels as payment of debt to interested investors. Initial plots were small, few individual parcels exceeding 100 acres in size, and most plots dotted the western coast of the island. As Dunn notes, "The great majority of patents issued by Governor Hawley from 1637 to 1639 fell into the range of thirty to fifty acres. To an English peasant farmer thirty acres would not seem paltry, for it was a larger tract than most husbandmen enjoyed at home" (Dunn 2000 [1972]:51). Although most of the plots were small by comparison to later Barbadian sugar plantations, larger plots owned by individual landlords did appear on the landscape in the early years of the settlement. As Menard (2006:17–18) points out, however, most landowners were unable to provide enough capital to develop large plantation systems. Therefore, many of the larger plots—those in excess of 50 acres—were divided and leased to tenants to generate an income on land that landowners could not afford to put into production themselves.

This phenomenon is well illustrated by the 1646 Hapcott map (Figure 2.1). The land being depicted is that of Fort Plantation, which would later become Trents Plantation, a site of ongoing archaeological excavations examining how the transformations associated with the sugar revolution affected laborers (Armstrong and Reilly 2014). The map was drawn for the purposes of a mortgage as several small plots were being consolidated into a larger estate that would eventually produce sugar. The landscape depicted is undergoing a shift from small tenant farms to processes of capitalization and large-scale agro-industrial production (Armstrong et al. 2012). The map is significant in that it projects a visual representation of presugar Barbados, an era that is often given limited scholarly attention in comparison to the sugar revolution of later years. Additionally, it represents the landscape that early arrivants of all laboring status and background would have experienced. The map also bears significance for early histories of the Redlegs, as many small farmers would have likely rented small plots like those depicted until they were rendered landless by processes of land consolidation as a result of the growth of the sugar industry.

In the early years of settlement, the arrival of ships with provisions was infrequent and unreliable, forcing many settlers to provide their own means of subsistence on plots while experimenting with various cash crops to develop a successful agricultural economy. As for provisions, early Barbadians relied on a wide produce base as indicated by Oldmixon's 1708 history of the island: "Having clear'd some Part of the Ground, the English planted Potatoes, Plantines, and Indian Corn, and some other Fruits" (B3). This mixed-agricultural and subsistence economy is partially reflected in the Hapcott map, in which a parcel of land is specified to be a "potato piece."

In addition to subsistence agriculture, throughout the course of the first two decades of the English occupation there were significant attempts to build a cash-crop economy based on tobacco, cotton, and indigo. Small plantations functioned primarily under the labor of indentured servants from England, Ireland, Scotland, and Wales.[2] Hilary Beckles notes that the European population in Barbados grew at a faster rate than in Virginia and Maryland, with the numbers in Barbados exceeding each colony by the mid-1640s (Beckles 1989:18). In 1667/1668 an anonymous author estimated that by 1643 the total number of "effective men" on the island stood at 18,600, a number that consisted of land proprietors and European militia members (Handler and Shelby 1973:118). Therefore, the total white[3] population, inclusive of women and children, was likely higher. While the preferred form of labor during this period was certainly European indentured servants, enslaved Africans were present in smaller numbers from the first years of settlement, reaching a population of roughly 6,400 by 1643, according to the same anonymous author.

During the first decades of settlement, the majority of servants coming from what would become the British Isles (the United Kingdom and Ireland) voluntarily signed contracts whereby the laborers agreed to a certain number of years of servitude (usually between three and seven years) in exchange for passage across the Atlantic and food, clothing, and shelter during their time of service. Following the termination of their period of indenture, contracts often awarded servants a small plot of land or a small sum of money or its equivalent in cash crops. As the demand for labor grew, however, especially with the advent of the sugar revolution in the 1640s, coerced servitude impressed on vagrants, criminals, children, and military/political prisoners became far more common. In reference to the servant trade from Bristol, England, Vincent Harlow describes that "a minor offender would, on conviction, be persuaded by an officer of the court to beg for transportation in order to avoid hanging. These transportees were assigned to the mayor and aldermen in town, who sold them to the planters, and grew rich" (Harlow 1926:298). Additionally, prisoners from Cromwell's invasion of Ireland in 1649 and the Battle of Worcester in England in 1651 contributed to the servant population of the island. The growth in the number of servants arriving to Barbados under such circumstances inspired Henry Whistler to comment during his early 1655 visit to the island as part of Cromwell's West Indian expedition that "this Illand is the Dunghill wharone England doth cast forth its rubidg" (cited in Handler 1971a:136). This comment reflects Whistler's class positioning and bias but nonetheless speaks to the perceived character of many indentured servants. In terms of sheer numbers, while population figures are unreliable, Jill Sheppard has surmised that "by 1655 a total of twelve thousand prisoners of war was alleged by the planters of Barbados to be employed by them, which would have represented nearly half the total white population" (Sheppard 1977:18). This approximation could have been an exaggeration, but it demonstrates planter reliance on indentured laborers, whether voluntary or coerced.

Early scholarly attempts to historically contextualize the institution of indentured servitude have argued that the exact origins are unknown but that its underlying principles can be found in the apprenticeship system of sixteenth-century England (see Galenson 1981; Smith 1947; Tomlins 2010). When such principles are extended to colonial territories, however, the rationale behind the terms of indentureship becomes clearer. For instance, Nicholas Canny has illustrated that early English settlers who made up part of the Munster Plantation in late sixteenth- to early seventeenth-century Ireland had trouble binding their English laborers/apprentices to their land. In essence, contract or apprentice laborers were arriving to work on Irish plantations and simply moving to more desirable plots (Canny 2001:152). Within the context of new colonial landscapes, new labor practices were necessary to control and manage laborers. Despite the new forms of bound labor that emerged in the Atlantic world that have been recently highlighted by Simon Newman (2013:62), it is evident that Old World precedents of labor management influenced how laborers would be bound to masters and property on the Barbadian landscape. Along with the use of enslaved natives from the Americas and Africa, this practice was employed from the earliest years of English settlement of the island.

The principles underlying the institution of servitude and the legal structures governing it mark explicit disparities between indentured servitude and slavery. Contracts tended to be one-sided, constructed to benefit the servant's master, and the period of indentureship could be readily extended as punishment for minor infractions committed. Despite the exploitative nature of the contracts, as opposed to the conditions of enslavement, the period of servitude usually lasted no longer than ten years (if the servant survived that long), at which time the former servants were supposed to be awarded their freedom along with a small plot of land.[4] Additionally, a child born of an indentured servant was free as opposed to a child born of an enslaved woman, who was born into slavery. In some instances, political or military prisoners were sentenced to life terms as servants, but their legal status was still distinct from that of the enslaved. These distinctions were codified into early Barbadian law beginning in the 1640s and survive in full textual form in the 1661 *Act for the good governing of Servants and ordaining the Rights between Masters and Servants* (Hall 1764:35–42) and the *Act for the better ordering and governing of Negroes* (for selections, see Engerman et al. 2001:105–113). Despite divisions in labor forms that make it erroneous to equate servitude with slavery, during the earliest decades of island settlement and into the second half of the seventeenth century, European indentured servants and enslaved Africans worked alongside one another. Their interactions in the fields, on the plantations, in the towns, and at the markets were formative experiences that greatly affected the development of island society and culture as sugar production came to engulf the island (Shaw 2013).

The Rise of Sugar and Slavery

A tremendous body of literature surrounds the sugar revolution and the social, economic, political, and geographical transformations that occurred in its midst and wake (for classic examples see Dunn 2000 [1972]; Mintz 1985; Williams 1994 [1944]). For Barbados in particular, the literature is equally bountiful (Beckles 1989; Menard 2006; Newman 2013; Gragg 2003; Parker 2011; Puckrein 1984). Russell Menard (2006:4), following arguments laid out by Bridenbaugh and Bridenbaugh (1972), has argued that the processes associated with the sugar revolution were underway years before the proposed late 1640s start of the "revolution" and instead suggests that these processes would be more adequately described as a "sugar boom." While his claim has merit, the argument ultimately runs the risk of undermining the sheer enormity of the changes that the sugar agro-industrial complex brought on the Atlantic world. While the full scope of these changes is beyond the realm of this work, they are discussed in reference to how they affected labor schemes and how the body of European indentured servants and former servants fared during and after the transition to sugar and slavery.

Prior to the growth of the sugar economy on the island, the early settlers experimented with a number of other cash crops that met with varying degrees of success. Most of these ventures involved plots of smaller than 50 acres and were worked by modest numbers of indentured servants and less frequently by enslaved Africans or Amerindians. The familiar plantation landscape associated with the sugar industry had not yet been established, and laborers were likely living in close proximity to the planter houses (Armstrong and Reilly 2014). In the late 1620s, trying to match the success of the crop in Virginia, farmers turned to tobacco. While some farmers met with moderate success, the price of tobacco would drop during the 1630s and Barbadian tobacco would come to have the reputation of being "illconditioned, fowle, full of talks, and evillcolured" (Menard 2006:20–21). Whether a fair assessment or a form of propaganda to boost the tobacco industry in Virginia, by the mid-1630s cotton had become the crop of choice and would frequently be used as the most popular exchange commodity on the island. Like tobacco, however, cotton often failed to turn substantial profits, and those farmers who were able to acquire sufficient capital looked elsewhere to invest and make their fortunes. Sugar had been grown in small quantities since the 1630s, but the name often associated with the sugar revolution is James Drax. Drax began planting the crop extensively in 1643 after receiving investment and technology from Dutch growers in Pernambuco, Brazil (see Parker 2011).

Although capital and labor intensive, sugar cultivation grew exponentially throughout the 1640s and 1650s. Smaller plots of 10 to 50 acres that once grew tobacco, cotton, other cash crops, or provisions were quickly consolidated to establish larger sugar estates, some exceeding 200 or 300 acres. Small tenant farmers growing crops on land with loosely defined property boundaries would be bought out, allowing boundaries to be rigidly and legally defined. Land became capitalized to make way for burgeoning sugar estates backed by joint stock companies in England as well as through Dutch and Jewish investments. Richard Ligon's *A True and Exact History of the Island of Barbados* (2013), originally published in 1657, was based on his experiences on the island from 1647 to 1650; the volume still stands as one of the richest primary sources of the seventeenth-century Caribbean in terms of ethnographic detail. Ligon also provides a firsthand account of the rise in property values associated with the sugar revolution. Using the plantation of Major Hilliard as an example, Ligon notes, "For, before the work began [sugar cultivation], this Plantation of Major Hilliards, of five hundred acres, could have been purchased for four hundred pound sterling; and now the halfe this Plantation, with the Stock upon it, was sold for seven thousand pound sterling" (Ligon 2013:136).

The rise of the sugar industry drastically altered labor practices and ideas about acceptable forms of labor on the island. As sugar began to engulf the landscape in the mid-1640s, an insatiable demand for more land and labor provided the impetus for a heightened English involvement in the African slave trade. This, however, did not signal a halt in the importation of indentured servants from Europe. On the contrary, as Hilary Beckles (1989:18) has illustrated, the European population on the island continued to increase throughout the 1650s, though not at the same rate as it had in previous years or as fast as that of enslaved Africans. The exponential growth of the white population from 1,400 in 1628 to an estimated 30,000 in 1668 illustrates the socioeconomic allure of the colony for planters or investors but also demonstrates the influx of the laboring population.

As planters sought to maximize profits and efficiently manage a growing labor force, the labor of enslaved Africans began to be favored over that of European indentured servants. This shift has been analyzed on a number of economic and social levels (see Beckles 1985; Beckles and Downes 1987; Newman 2013), but despite observable labor shifts, the servant trade persisted along with the white underclass on the island. In fact, despite Richard Dunn's assessment that the shift from servants to slaves was remarkably fast (2000 [1972]), Hilary Beckles's (1989) analysis of this transition illustrates that it was a gradual process that took place over the course of several decades from the 1640s to the 1670s. While seventeenth-century demographics are unreliable, the slave population grew from 5,680 in 1645 to 38,746 by the time of the 1680s census (Dunn 1969), a number that is surely underestimated given that planters regularly underreported the numbers of enslaved peoples they owned (Handler 1974:14). Eventually, as the sugar and slave system engrossed the island, the white population reached a plateau and even began to decline. By 1715, there were nearly 16,888 white inhabitants as compared to 41,970 enslaved individuals in 1712 (Molen 1971:289; for sources on population estimates throughout the period of slavery see Handler 1971a).

The transformations associated with the sugar revolution also affected the role of laborers on early farms and, later, large sugar plantations. While the earliest laborers were likely used for brute strength to clear the island and work the fields, early sugar estates also needed the assistance of skilled laborers. As Beckles notes, "The grinding, boiling, curing, refining and distilling processes of sugar manufacture demanded industrial machinery which had to be assembled, maintained, and at times modified." He continues that "this meant that a labour force with basic literacy and a familiarity with advanced industrial technology was necessary" (Beckles 1985:34). In the early years of sugar production, these tasks were seldom allocated to enslaved laborers who were believed to be incapable of handling such responsibilities.

Therefore, while European servants were certainly used as field hands along with enslaved Africans, they also benefited from positions of prominence and responsibility on the plantation in the form of skilled labor.

Ligon's account illustrates the hardships indentured servants endured from their arrival to their experiences laboring and living on the island. In addition to noting their meager clothing allotments, humble housing, poor diets, a "seasoning" period, and long hours working in the fields from sunup to sundown (Ligon 2013:50), his comments on the often-brutal treatment they received has attracted scholarly attention. One of the most frequently cited passages on the subject of servants' treatment at the hands of their masters claims that "I have seen such cruelty there done to Servants, as I did not think one Christian could have done to another" (2013:73). While he goes on to note that the conditions for servants would improve greatly in the very next sentence, it is evident that planters had few qualms about using European servants in field gangs and treating them with excessive force.

The harsh treatment of servants and the frequent involuntary nature of their servitude quickly raised eyebrows in England, and a lively debate was sparked in Parliament. The catalyst was the publication of Marcellus Rivers and Oxenbridge Foyle's *England's Slavery* (1659) in which these Royalists describe their ordeal of being sold into slavery in Barbados following their capture during the English Civil War. As a result of the account's vivid description of capture, imprisonment, and harsh treatment, planter and merchant Martin Noell was called before Parliament to defend his exploitative treatment of white laborers or "slaves." Despite Noell's claims that he had not been mistreating his laborers, in addition to his noting of the great profit that their labor was bringing back to the motherland, Parliament expressed its unease in using Englishmen in such a fashion (Beckles 1982). This petition, in addition to the few other firsthand accounts of European labor in Barbados (for examples, see Handler and Reilly 2017), suggests that Europeans of a particular status, including those who suffered mistreatment in colonies like Barbados, were appalled by the laboring conditions of servants and lamented their slave-*like* status (Amussen 2007:19). It is crucial to point out that such accounts, despite their ability to shed light on the plight of European laborers, should not be viewed as providing fuel for those interested in advancing the narrative of "white slavery." Rather, they point to the development of conceptualizations of labor that determined permissible treatment and status based on racial differences. Social and economic forces ensured that as the seventeenth century wore on, a distinct racial hierarchy would be rigidly ingrained within Barbadian law and society as the use of white bound labor began to wane.

Despite legislation during the 1670s mandating planters to keep one white servant for every ten enslaved Africans for the purposes of keeping a sizable island militia,[5] planters made their commitment to slavery clear, as illustrated by one of the most prominent planters, Colonel Henry Drax, son of James Drax. Drax is responsible for a 1679 document in which he provides potential planters with a set of instructions for profitable operation of a sugar estate. Drax states that "I shall Not leave you many white Servants[,] the ffewer the better" (Thompson 2009:575). The census of the following year indicates that Drax was true to his word; Drax enslaved 327 people and employed only 7 white workers despite the militia requirement (576). Drax offers no explanation as to why having fewer white servants is for "the better," but given the purpose of the document, it is likely that he found the use of enslaved labor far more profitable. The influence of this document became widespread and was the basis for the infamous plantation instructions penned by Belgrove in 1755. In short, the instructions Drax put together explicitly illustrate the shift to the use of enslaved labor as a more efficient model of profit extraction from the plantation.

The processes of land consolidation described here also had a direct impact on servants who had completed their period of indenture. Many servants signed contracts that promised 10 acres of land following their release. Expanding sugar plantations, however, left little space available for the practice of small farming. Records indicate that servants were hesitant to sail for Barbados due to the lack of available land and the island's reputation for the harsh treatment of servants. In 1679 Governor Atkins commented that "few white servants come, from the scarcity of land available for them when they have served their time; they prefer Virginia, New York, and Jamaica where they can hope for land" (see Shilstone 1933). Small plots that remained were usually located on "rab" land, or land unsuitable for agricultural production. Those who were fortunate enough to acquire small plots of land often found it nearly impossible to generate a profit within a society based on large-scale sugar production, often failing to compete with larger planters.

The sugar and slavery society that emerged in Barbados drastically altered the trajectory of Atlantic-world history. Simon Newman has recently called for a shift in geographical focus for the advent of plantation slavery, arguing, "In numerical terms the Chesapeake was a sideshow, and during the seventeenth century a great more white bound laborers and enslaved Africans went to Barbados: for every enslaved African who stepped ashore in the Chesapeake before 1701, nearly fifteen had disembarked in Barbados" (Newman 2013:25–51). While the profits that planters had enjoyed in the late 1640s and 1650s began to level off as the seventeenth century wore on, the system that they had engendered would be transposed onto the Jamaican and South Carolina landscape; the former quickly overtaking Barbados as the richest of England's American colonies (Dunn 2000 [1972]).[6] The effects that these changes brought on systems of labor and the laborers themselves were equally astronomical as the use of enslaved labor overtook that of indentured servitude. Planters would rely on enslaved Africans and Afro-Barbadians for roughly two centuries, until emancipation in 1834, at which time labor exploitation continued under a different guise (Carter 2012). As sugar and slavery became ingrained within West Indian society, the white underclass slipped into the backdrop of Barbadian political and economic life while still remaining part of its social fabric.

THE REDLEGS AND THE RISE OF TENANTRIES

Prior to and during the sugar revolution, the ethnic origins of the white servant population were significant in determining one's place in Barbadian socioeconomic hierarchies. While servants arrived by the thousands from England, Scotland, Wales, and Ireland, it was the Irish that "constituted the largest block of servants on the island, and they were cordially loathed by their English masters" (Dunn 2000 [1972]:69).[7] Evidence suggests that, based on colonial antecedents and conditions in Barbados, planters and authorities held particular disdain for Irish indentured servants who were typically cast as rebellious and culturally inferior to other servants (Beckles 1990; Block and Shaw 2011; Handler and Reilly 2015; Newman 2013:81–83; Reilly 2015a; Welch 2012). As Block and Shaw have argued, "In the English colonies, servants of all nationalities were subject to harsh working conditions, but Irish Catholic subjugation was magnified by English Protestants' sense of cultural and religious superiority" (Block and Shaw 2011:35). Whereas the early years of colonial settlement had experienced an influx of impoverished but voluntary servants from an English countryside that was experiencing overpopulation and landscape transformation (Newman 2013:17–35), the late 1640s witnessed an influx in prisoners of military conflicts, vagrants, and criminals, particularly from Ireland.

As the seventeenth century drew to a close and the trade in indentured servants drastically diminished, significant social transformations affected the white underclass on the island. While evidence suggests that an Irish, English, or Scottish identity may have been marginally important to individuals and communities based on surnames and settlement clusters across the island (see Reilly 2015a), by the turn of the century, racial identity far outweighed ethnic origin as a marker of socioeconomic status. As a result, groups or individuals who may have previously been diligently identified as

Irish, English, or Scottish began to be grouped together as poor whites (Sheppard 1977:41). The rise of an unemployed white underclass on the island is concomitant with a dwindling in their appearance in the historical record. While there is substantial literature concerning European indentured servitude on the island in the seventeenth century, as well as the social positioning of the poor whites in the decades surrounding emancipation in the nineteenth century, there is a paucity of material that concerns the poor whites during the majority of the eighteenth century—a century that was entirely dominated by the sugar and slavery system.

As African chattel slavery became the preferred mode of labor exploitation for planters, the closing decades of the seventeenth century witnessed a departure of the majority of poor whites from their roles as laborers on sugar plantations. Many swarmed to the urban center of Bridgetown (for the nuances of the urban population in Bridgetown, see Welch 2003) while others would come to occupy newly established tenantries on the margins of plantations, whether as militia tenants, small farmers, or plantation employees. Despite the decline in use of white labor on the plantations, Jill Sheppard argues, "it would be a mistake . . . to regard the plantations as having been totally denuded of white servants" (1977:43). In this capacity, however, Sheppard is only referring to servants in their roles as laborers on the plantations. She illustrates that throughout the eighteenth century, whites served as managers, drivers, bookkeepers, housekeepers, groomsmen, and herdsmen. Heather Cateau presents similar data, presenting the various positions open to waged white workers on the plantation: "The standard occupations available on plantations were attorneys, overseers and bookkeepers, but many estates had additional white personnel. This group included: carpenters, plumbers, coopers, masons, ploughmen, coppersmiths, millwrights, wheelwrights and blacksmiths" (Cateau 2006:8). Plantation records provide evidence of whites fulfilling such roles, but they provide few details as to where and how these individuals lived. Many of these plantation employees were not allotted housing near the works complex and would have likely resided on tenantries on the marginal lands of the plantation. Not all tenantry residents, however, were employed by the plantation, and a more detailed analysis, as seen in chapter 4, of such tenantries illustrates the diversity and nuances of tenantry life during the period of slavery.

While the phenomenon of plantation tenantries would become far more prevalent after emancipation, at which time formerly enslaved Afro-Barbadians established villages on the boundaries of the plantations, evidence suggests that poor white tenantries appeared on the Barbadian landscape as early as the 1650s.[8] Plots allocated for tenantries typically lay at the very margins of the plantation at a substantial distance from the great house and, in some cases, villages for the enslaved. Few of these tenants would have occupied positions of prestige on the plantations since overseers and, occasionally, bookkeepers were provided with housing in close proximity of the great house.[9] With the exception of when tenants would pay rent or work on the plantations, inhabitants of poor white tenantries were, for the most part, out of sight and out of mind.

Burial and baptism records from the parish of St. John during the period of slavery confirm that poor white tenants fulfilled a number of functions on plantations, working as gardeners, distillers, laborers, shoemakers, masons, blacksmiths, carpenters, schoolmasters, domestics, hucksters, and seamstresses (BDA RL1/26). While their pale complexion warranted them a number of legal and social privileges, such occupations provided tenants with few opportunities for social mobility. Ethnographic analogies are no doubt tenuous, but Harry Rosenberg (1962:55) has described the limited options for social mobility available to the St. John poor white community of the 1960s. Migration to Bridgetown became a viable option as positions for clerks became more readily available, and the plantation infrastructure also offered social mobility for select individuals, but many Redleg families found it difficult to "make it over the hill." It is therefore unsurprising to see similar surnames as tenantry residents for several generations. Heather Cateau has argued that positions such as bookkeeper or overseer on a plantation were used as "stepping stones" for social mobility (Cateau 2006:7), but Gary Lewis has amply illustrated that despite the social prestige of being a bookkeeper rather than a laborer, such positions offered marginal economic benefits, allowing many plantation employees to fall into the category of the working poor (1999:3–4).

Throughout the eighteenth century, poor white militia tenants were seldom called on to fulfill their military duties. There were no substantial slave rebellion threats between 1692 and 1816, and imperial conflicts failed to reach the shores of the island. Although Barbadian law decreed that planters supply one militiaman for each 20 acres owned (Hall 1764:138–155), it is unknown how strictly this act was enforced or if tenants' roles in the militia had any bearing on their daily lives. More likely, militia tenants operated as small farmers, growing provisions as well as crops to sell in local markets, a practice William Dickson observed during a late eighteenth-century visit to the island. Dickson notes that "in Barbados many whites *of both sexes*, till the ground, without any assistance from negroes, and poor white-women often walk many miles loaded with the produce of their little spots, which they exchange in the towns for such European goods as they can afford to purchase" (Dickson 1789:41, emphasis in original). Dickson's observations speak to gendered divisions of labor in addition to highlighting the subsistence patterns of poor whites who occupied small plots of land.

Given the close proximity of many poor white tenantries to the coast, fishing was a common occupation among community members and constituted a substantial component of the local diet. The significance of fishing in such tenantry communities has received relatively little attention, as such activities are overshadowed by the socioeconomic dominance of sugar plantations. Pedro Welch (2005:20) has argued that "in several small island communities in the Caribbean, farming the marine environment, not sugar, represented the main economic activity." While Welch provides evidence for a viable poor white fishing industry in postemancipation contexts, island residents were using their proximity to the coasts from the earliest days of settlement. Henry Colt commented that Barbados was home to "more fish and better fishing" than neighboring Caribbean islands (Harlow 1926:92; cf. Welch 2005:21). Evidence also suggests that poor white tenants displaced by the transformations of the sugar revolution relied heavily on fishing in the seventeenth century (and for centuries to come). During a meeting of the St. John parish vestry on April 10, 1676, vestrymen voiced their concerns about an individual who desired to claim ownership to fishing rights in the parish. The minutes from the vestry meeting describe the individual as "greedy" and "avaricious," arguing that a private claim to the industry would be a devastating blow to the local economy (BDA D273, 1649–1682:35): "Which will not only be prejudiciall to ye Inhabitants in General by depriveing of the benefit of ffresh ffish for there Tables, but also to the poorer Inhabitants who draw there principle livelihood and subsistence by there Trade and occupation of ffishing, By sole or parte where of they supply there necessities, and with ye remainder ffeed there ffamilyes, off which should they be deprived it would inevitably bring them to see great poverty that they must either have releiffe from ye parish to support there ffamilyes or be inforced to departe ye island." The passage can be read in a number of ways. It can be seen to reflect compassion on the part of parish vestrymen who sought to prohibit fishing rights falling into the hands of a single individual. A more sinister interpretation of the passage, however, may indicate that the vestrymen feared that severing access to the sea would force impoverished villagers to rely on parish relief, which would inevitably come out of the pockets of planters in the form of poor relief taxes—poor relief being another privilege afforded to free whites on the island. The relationship between the vestry and poor white inhabitants of St. John is discussed in more detail in later chapters, but it is evident that poor whites relied heavily on access to fresh fish for inexpensive protein since at least the mid-seventeenth century.

In addition to fishing, many poor whites were small farmers, growing their own provisions as well as crops for sale through internal markets. When Rev. Nicholls, who was born in Barbados, was asked by Parliament in the late eighteenth century if white people work to any degree in Barbados, he responded, "Those who are called tenants . . . do commonly work in their grounds with their negroes, if they have any, or else cultivate the whole with their own labour; that ground is commonly in provisions, not in canes" (HCPP 1790:334). A generation later, William Dickson would similarly comment, "The white militia tenants, and even some small proprietors and their families, certainly do work *like* Negroes, in the comparatively easy employment of raising provisions, cotton, &c. Probably they think themselves degraded by working in that manner; but they must do it, or starve, - or plunder the Negroes, as they often do" (Dickson 1814:429). Both passages are indicative of a tenuous relationship between the poor whites and their neighbors of African descent, with whom they shared a similar economic status. The specifics of this relationship (including the ownership of the enslaved among the poor white community) are discussed in later chapters, but the passages are illustrative of the common practice of subsistence farming among poor white tenants.

The temporal jumps made throughout this section provide a necessary overview of the broader history of Barbadian Redlegs. As mentioned, in the long period between the sugar revolution and emancipation, it is difficult to trace the poor whites in the historical record in any qualitatively or quantitatively significant degree. Poor white plantation tenants were not reliable sources of income for planters, so they seldom appear in wills and deeds (the enslaved are far more often enumerated and occasionally given a first name in such documents). Poor whites more regularly appear in vestry minutes where they are listed as the beneficiaries of parish poor relief (Marshall 2003). Such sources, however, reveal little about the daily lives of these individuals. What is made clear in this discussion is that, despite social, political, and economic changes that affected the island, there was a relative degree of consistency concerning the daily lives and habits of the poor whites. Employment opportunities waxed and waned with broader trends on the island and beyond, but fishing, subsistence farming, plantation labor, and limited forms of skilled labor and professional occupations were the common means through which poor whites made a living. Limited opportunity for social mobility ensured the persistence of these ways of life, but their categorization as white was nonetheless crucial in attempting to circumscribe their roles in Barbadian society.

THE MILITIA

Despite the decline in the white population as the seventeenth century drew

to a close, white Barbadians consistently composed the overwhelming majority of the island's militia. The enslaved could occasionally be called to muster
and even be armed (Handler 1984), but such instances were rare. Given that
the most common position associated with poor whites in social memory on
the island is that of militia members, it is worth discussing the extent of their
service and the impact it had on the poor whites more generally. The militia was originally established to prevent foreign imperial invasion. Forts and
other defensive structures were quickly constructed following the English
settlement of the island. The settlers, however, would ultimately never have to
face any substantial conflict with imperial forces, and as the sugar revolution
swept across the island, a new fear would develop among island elites. As the
white population declined and that of the enslaved rose exponentially from
the 1640s to the 1660s, a fear brewed among the plantocracy of internal conflict in the form of slave revolts. Despite conspiracies of a servant rebellion in
1634 and joint servant and slave conspiracies in 1649, 1686, and 1692 (see
Handler 1982), planters were increasingly wary of slave rebellions as they witnessed a depletion in the number of able-bodied white militiamen.[10]

Their concern over the depleted state of the militia was augmented by their
distrust of those who were serving. As mentioned, the Irish were perceived
to be a particularly rebellious group, and their numbers in the militia caused
officials to comment on the deplorable state of the militia. In 1667 Governor
Willoughby made such ethnic preferences clear, stating that "we have more
than a good many Irish amongst us, therefore I am for the downright Scot,
who I am certaine, will fight without a crucifix about his neck" (see Sheppard 1977:35). As discussed, as the seventeenth century closed, the ethnic
identities of the island's white underclass became less significant, and records
indicate that there was a general want of any white servant who could serve in
the militia, regardless of ethnic origins.

Concern about the state of the militia was again raised in the 1690s as
officials complained that harsh treatment and the lack of available land were
driving whites from the island and preventing others from arriving. This,
in turn, depleted the numbers available to serve in the militia. A report to
the Lords of Trade and Plantations in 1695 laments the condition of the
island's defensive force as well as the treatment of white servants (Fortescue
1903:446): "I dare say that there are hundreds of white servants in the Island
who have been out of their time for many years, and who have never a bit of
fresh meat bestowed on them nor a dram of rum. They are domineered over
and used like dogs, and this in time will undoubtedly drive away all the com-
monalty of the white people and leave the Island in a deplorable condition, to
be murdered by negroes or vanquished by an enemy, unless some means be

taken to prevent it. Nor can we depend upon these people to fight for defence of the Island when, let who will be master, they cannot be more miserable than their countrymen and fellow-subjects make them here." This passage reveals not only the weakened state of the militia but also the harsh treatment servants experienced and the poverty former servants suffered.

Those who served in the militia did so under a status of militia tenants, a practice implemented in the 1671 "Act to prevent depopulation." The act "provided for the rating of two tenants, with leases of at least three years on plots of two acres of land, as the equivalent for Militia purposes of three freemen or servants" (Sheppard 1977:38). A later act in 1697 required that one white militia tenant be supplied for militia service by planters for every 20 acres owned (Hall 1764:138–155). While it is unclear how rigidly planters adhered to such requirements, it is evident that they were partially responsible for the establishment of white tenantries within the boundaries of sugar plantations. For the plantocracy, the militia was another arena in which to affirm their status since wealthy planters held positions as officers. However, indentured servants and plantation tenants served as the rank and file of the defense force. As for the enslaved, a mid-seventeenth-century ordinance allowed for their arming (with edged weapons, not firearms) only in the case of emergencies, and they were never fully enlisted (Sheppard 1977:58; Handler 1984). Given that there were no imperial conflicts or internal slave rebellions from 1692 to 1816, however, militia tenancy was likely not a defining feature of the lives of poor white militiamen. Without much consideration paid to the island's militia, those who served made for a rather unimpressive sight. Left to their own devices as subsistence farmers and fishermen, poverty came to be a defining attribute of the militia as the period of slavery closed. Special Magistrate John Colthurst would lament the state of the militia in a journal entry from February 1836 (Marshall 1977:72): "The militia of Barbados (the private men) is chiefly composed of the very lowest order of whites, the greater number of whom were born in the colony, and are a most idle and good for nothing set—proud, lazy, and consequently miserably poor. They usually live round the coast as fishermen. The estates being taxed for the militia, it is the practice to give many of these persons a few acres of rough lands belonging to those estates, provided they serve as militia men. These men are universally called Redshanks. They seldom wear shoes or stockings, therefore their legs are tinted highly from constant exposure to the sun and all weathers." Colthurst even included an illustration of "Sergeant Redshanks" (Figure 2.2) that shows the emaciated, impoverished state of a poor white militia member.

It is also important to note the presence of an Afro-Barbadian militia member trailing Sergeant Redshanks. Colthurst would comment that "a few

Figure 2.2. *West Indies Barbados Militia Sergeant Redshanks Moving to Muster.* Original watercolor illustration from John Bowen Colthurst's *Journal as a Special Magistrate in the Islands of Barbados and St. Vincent, 1835–38.* The watercolor is likely by Colthurst himself (Marshall 1977:32, 72). (Courtesy of the Boston Public Library)

of [the Redlegs], during slavery, possessed a slave or two" (Marshall 1977:72). It was quite possible that select poor whites owned enslaved peoples in tenantries across the island, as will be discussed, but I have found no evidence to suggest that this was the case for any member of the Below Cliff tenantry. Many poor whites lacked the economic means necessary for such a purchase, but limited means in no way demonstrates any contempt for the institution of slavery. We have no accounts describing how poor whites actually felt about slavery, but the fact that some poor whites owned enslaved peoples suggests that the relationship between poor whites and Afro-Barbadians was complicated and often contentious. The nature of these relationships is the focus of later discussions, but for the moment, the status of many poor white male tenants as militiamen reinforced a particular boundary between them and their enslaved neighbors. Serving as a buffer between planters and the enslaved, the racial and economic status of the poor whites would become contested, challenged, essentialized, and overtly political in the decades leading to and following emancipation.

The "Poor White Problem" in the Age of Emancipation

The legal and social demarcations separating Redlegs and Afro-Barbadians became accentuated in the decades leading to and following emancipation. As antislavery activism and thought swelled in Europe and rebellions erupted throughout the Caribbean region (including Barbados in 1816), the poor whites, as well as free people of color, became "liminal" groups of interest as planters and colonial authorities debated the issue of slavery.[11] David Lambert, following Homi Bhabha, defines liminal groups as "those which were neither obviously dominant nor subjugated, occupying a position of 'in-betweenness' in the colonial order" (Lambert 2005:81). Specifically referring to early nineteenth-century Barbados, Lambert summarizes, "Neither white and dominant, nor black and subjugated, the poor whites and free people of colour were unsettling figures in slaveholding culture" (2005:81). This statement neatly encapsulates the role these groups played in island and Atlantic debates surrounding slavery. In the decades preceding emancipation, a number of visitors and local writers would comment on the state of the poor whites to support their arguments for or against the institution of slavery. These arguments are significant in that racial and class diversity was being acknowledged and attempts were being made to justify the existence and socioeconomic positioning of these demographics. Furthermore, as writers continued to use these populations to justify their political, economic, or humanitarian positions, poor white and free people of color became essentialized identities where certain characteristics defined individuals who were perceived to be of these particular categories.

In 1789, William Dickson would publish his *Letters on Slavery* based on his observations made on the island while serving as secretary to Barbados's governor, Edward Hay. The work is a radical antislavery treatise that depicted the horrors of the slave system and the current state of the English colony. The poor whites frequently appear in the narrative, being described as "totally ignorant and regardless of all laws human and divine" (Dickson 1789:37). Due to their racial arrogance, according to Dickson, he goes on to claim that "many of the poor whites are disposed to take, and too many of them do take, every advantage over the negroes which the laws leave in their power" (41). In general, Dickson was attempting to illustrate that "the poor whites in Barbados have no idea that the blacks are, any way, intitled [*sic*] to the same treatment as white men" (57), arguing that racial identity was no correlate for one's intellectual capacity or degenerative status. In effect, negative comments toward the whole of the poor white population sought to support his argument for emancipation and equal rights for the enslaved.

Dickson's progressive attitudes toward slavery were not shared by most members of the plantocracy, but many planters did acknowledge that social reform was necessary for certain segments of the population. Joshua Steele was one such planter who arrived in Barbados in 1780 to take command of two large plantations (Guinea and Kendal) that had been left to him following the death of his wife and stepdaughter. Steele promoted the implementation of ameliorative measures to improve conditions for the enslaved as well as promote more "rational" or "enlightened" plantation management techniques. Although it is unlikely that he ever implemented these plans, Steele sought to provide each member of his enslaved population with two acres of land to become self-sustaining. Eventually, he planned to manumit his enslaved who would, by that time, have the necessary skills to survive as small farmers. Additionally, Steele established a Barbadian branch of the Society for the Encouragement of Arts, Manufactures, and Commerce, which, along with other goals, sought to provide the necessary materials and structures to enable poor whites to emerge as a middling industrious class on the island (see Lambert 2005:41–72). Contrary to Dickson's depiction, Steele argues that with the proper support, the poor whites were capable of functioning within a Barbadian class-based society.

Sir John Gay Alleyne, a noted Barbadian planter and prominent politician of the second half of the eighteenth century, was also a member of Steele's Society for the Encouragement of the Arts. Alleyne harbored far less sympathetic attitudes toward the enslaved but supported reform efforts within white creole society. Despite serving as the attorney for Codrington Plantation, an estate owned by the Society for the Propagation of the Gospel, Alleyne believed that religious conversion and education in general should be restricted to the white population. Putting these beliefs into action, Alleyne ensured that education at the Codrington School was only provided for white boys (Bergman and Smith 2014:424–425). Similar educational and training initiatives were implemented for the sole benefit of the white population, many of them being poor whites. Given the dominance of slave labor, many opportunities that would have been available to white women, such as being employed as a midwife, seamstress, domestic servant, or cook, were reserved for the enslaved. The lack of opportunity for poor white women leads Melanie Newton (2008:29) to argue that "plantation slavery made white female poverty an endemic feature of the Barbadian social landscape." As a result, social reform efforts like industrial training schools were put in place to improve the conditions of poor white women (Forde-Jones 1998; Jones 2007; Reilly 2014).

Poyer's 1808 *History of Barbados* similarly provided support and encouragement for the poor whites, but unlike many of his contemporaries, Poyer explicitly voiced his racially motivated rationale. Poyer, a Barbadian-born middle-class white man, was a staunch apologist of the institution of slavery, and his *History* defended the institution against abolitionists. Poyer feared that a growing body of middle-class free people of color threatened the racial hierarchy that for so long had defined Barbadian socioeconomic life. In a letter to Lord Seaforth (the incoming governor of Barbados) in 1801, Poyer argued that the maintenance of a "well constituted society" depended on the preservation of "distinctions which naturally exist. . . . First between White inhabitants and free people of Colour, and Secondly between Masters and Slaves" (1941:162). As such, he argued that the poor whites were hard-working, industrious individuals who struggled to make a living due to the rise of free people of color (see Lambert 2005:73–104).

Several traveler accounts also depict encounters with the poor whites in pre-emancipation Barbados. Two authors, in particular, offer explicitly malicious portrayals of the poor whites: George Pinckard (1806) and Henry Nelson Coleridge (1826). Although not overtly political like the works of Dickson, Steele, or Poyer, these accounts provide details about fleeting interactions with poor white individuals, which then inform their generalizations about the population as a whole. For instance, Coleridge offers this lengthy yet qualitatively significant description of the Redlegs following his encounter with a poor white woman in the Scotland District (Coleridge 1826:272–274):

> In consequence of the large white population in Barbados there exists a class of people which I did not meet with in any other, of the islands. . . . These men are called the Tenantry, and have an indefeasible interest for their lives in a house and garden upon the respective plantations. . . . The greatest part of them live in a state of complete idleness, and are usually ignorant and debauched to the last degree. They will often walk half over the island to demand alms, and if you question them about their mode of life and habits of daily labor, they stare in your face as if they were actually unable to comprehend the meaning of your discourse. The women who will work at all, find employment in washing and mending the clothes of the negroes; and it is notorious, that in many cases whole families of these free whites depend for their subsistence on the charity of the slaves. Yet they are proud of Lucifer himself, and in virtue of their freckled ditchwater faces consider themselves on a level with every gentleman in the island.

Expressing similar sentiments, Pinckard claims that the poor whites are "descended from European settlers, but from misfortune, or misconduct, in some of the race, are reduced to a state far from independence; often, indeed, but little superior to the condition of free negroes" (Pinckard 1806:132). Pinckard would go on to comment on the possibility of racial degeneration, expressing fears associated with racial intermixing. Despite several accounts that reify the "white" identity of Barbadian Redlegs, there were underlying trepidations among colonial elites that racial intermixture would disrupt the rigidity of racial categories.

In the late 1820s, shortly before emancipation, Frederick William Naylor Bayley, the son of a military officer, visited Barbados and commented on the poor whites he came across in Bridgetown (1833:62): "Of all the classes of people who inhabit Bridgetown, the poor whites are the lowest, and the most degraded: residing in the meanest hovels, they pay no attention either to neatness in their dwellings or cleanliness in their persons; and they subsist too often, to their shame be it spoken, on the kindness and charity of slaves. I have never seen a more sallow, dirty, ill looking, and unhappy race; the men lazy, the women disgusting, and the children neglected: all without any notion of principle, morality, or religion; forming a melancholy picture of living misery, and a strong contract with the general appearance of happiness depicted on the countenances of the free black, and colored people, of the same class." These accounts illustrate the harsh depictions of the poor whites that came to define them within a plantation society that was typically dependent on white superiority, power, and control. While being careful not to conflate the poor white experience with that of similar populations elsewhere, this phenomenon bears striking similarities to the discourses produced about "white trash" during a similar time period in the American South (see Hartigan 2005:59–108; Wray 2006). By this time, the direct relationship between impoverishment and physical health, appearance, degeneration, etiquette, nourishment, and hygiene was being observed and acknowledged on both sides of the Atlantic. On visiting Ireland, for instance, this led noted abolitionist Frederick Douglass, with regard to the relationship between physical appearance and well-being, to famously comment that an individual "may carve out his circumstances, but his circumstances will carve him out as well" (Douglass 2008 [1854]:38). Despite the similarities in this developing discourse, the poor white situation was unique in the Caribbean given poor whites' proportionally high population percentage on a densely populated island.

Eighteenth- and nineteenth-century observers harshly and strategically incorporated the poor whites into their accounts of Barbadian society. These accounts served to bound and marginalize the poor whites as both exceptional and isolated in a plantation society that was coming to grips with the inevitability of emancipation. In 1832, two years prior to emancipation (or the start of the apprenticeship period, which lasted from 1834 to 1838), Edward Eliot, who delivered a series of sermons at the Bridgetown Cathedral, would comment on the state of the poor whites. Arguing that most of the carpenters, masons, tailors, smiths, and shoemakers were free people of color, he noted that this was "at a time when a large white population are in the lowest state of poverty and wretchedness" (Eliot 1833:225–226). The problem of poor white poverty was exacerbated by full emancipation in 1838 with a flood of free Afro-Barbadian laborers on the market. With historical roots in the period of slavery, Hilary Beckles has argued that "by the end of slavery in 1838 a heterogeneous white working class had fully developed, and society was characterized by an element of 'black over white' at its lowest levels" (1988:1). Additionally, without the threat of a slave rebellion, the island's militia was soon disbanded. As Watson notes, "This in effect meant that those whites who occupied rent-free land on the plantations in return for services rendered in the militia, suddenly became squatters, with no legal claim to the land they occupied" (Watson 2000b:134).

The "poor white problem" quickly emerged as a question of what to do with a largely underemployed population that was sinking further into the depths of poverty. Throughout the mid to late nineteenth century, Barbadian officials viewed emigration for the poor whites as a viable solution. Beginning in the 1850s, Governor Francis Hincks orchestrated efforts to send hundreds of Redlegs to neighboring Caribbean islands. Arguing that immigration to distant regions such as England, Canada, or New Zealand would be a drastic change in climate, Hincks, and later his replacement Governor James Walker, would propose that the Redlegs would find suitable homes in St. Vincent, the Grenadines, the Bahamas, or Jamaica. Many of these proposals were rejected for a number of political and economic reasons, but eventually it was determined that St. Vincent, Grenada, and several islands in the Grenadines would be suitable island homes where they would receive 5 to 10 acres of land (Watson 2000b:138–148). Citing a report that "confirms that as many as 400 poor white Barbadians had settled in St. Vincent and that another 100 had been sent to Bequia [the Grenadines]," Karl Watson has estimated that "between 1860 and 1870 some 600 and 700 poor whites left Barbados to settle in the Windwards" (147). Poor white communities can still be found on St. Vincent, Grenada, and Bequia today. Inhabitants of these communities are often locally known as Barbadians. Despite the emigration of hundreds of poor whites, however, thousands remained on the island and continued to be viewed as a problem for local administrators and planters.

By the start of the twentieth century, the condition of the majority of the poor whites had improved little despite efforts for reform through poor relief and education (see Sheppard 1977:79–101). These conditions, however, were not unique to the poor whites. Widespread poverty and growing unemployment swept across the island as global sugar prices declined and England looked to other Caribbean territories (such as Cuba) and to the beet-sugar-producing regions of eastern Europe to purchase sugar (for labor conflicts during this period, see Carter 2012). This led to a tremendous outflow of Barbadians to Panama to work as laborers building the canal (estimates reach as high as 45,000 laborers) (for more on Barbadians in Panama and the effects of return migration and money, see Richardson 1985). Additionally, health issues such as malnutrition and hookworm plagued the poor white population. A 1917 Rockefeller Foundation study revealed that 65% of the poor whites suffered from hookworm compared with 36% of the black population (Watson 2000b:134).[12] Official efforts to promote emigration in the mid to late nineteenth century and migration to Panama in the late nineteenth to early twentieth century were factors in the decline of the total white population, which dropped from 16,207 in 1861 to 12,063 in 1911. It is estimated that the poor whites consistently made up the majority of the white population throughout the island's history (Sheppard 1977:70).

Throughout the twentieth century, the poor white population continued to decline in number. As agricultural production diminished, emigration continued to be a factor in population decrease. Additionally, many rural poor whites made their way to Bridgetown with hopes of social mobility. Despite social unrest due to large numbers of unemployed, which climaxed in riots in 1937 (see Browne 2012), many poor whites were able to take advantage of employer preference for light-skinned employees and were able to procure jobs as clerks, bank and office workers, cashiers, dock workers, and skilled laborers in the city (Sheppard 1977:109–110). By the 1960s and 1970s it was observed that the poor whites could only be found in two discrete areas: the urban context of Bridgetown and in the rural community of Newcastle or Church View in the parish of St. John (Keagy 1975:20). These communities are adjacent to the abandoned tenantry of Below Cliff and received an influx of residents when Below Cliff was formally abandoned in the early 1960s. Historical and semiethnographic works of the 1950s to the 1970s attribute the dwindling of the poor white population to social mobility and outward migration but are torn on the issue of miscegenation (Price 1957; Keagy 1972, 1975). The implications of such arguments surrounding racial identity and intermixture are discussed in detail in chapter 5, but it was evident that those traditionally defined as Redlegs were dwindling in number by the time of independence in 1966.

THE REDLEGS IN HISTORICAL PERSPECTIVE

The history of Barbados can be grossly oversimplified into a chronological framework similar to the trajectory followed in this chapter: English settlement, the sugar revolution, sugar and slavery, emancipation, postemancipation labor unrest, and independence. This periodization might be convenient, providing temporal markers for major socioeconomic shifts and transformations, but it presents a set of challenges for microlevel analyses like the one in this book. The seismic shifts associated with the sugar revolution and emancipation, for instance, certainly had a tremendous effect on the daily lives of Barbadian Redlegs, but one of the major limitations of the historical record is that it provides a top-down perspective that is foregrounded in the construction of historical narratives.

Sugar monoculture and the associated exploitative systems of slavery and colonial rule have appropriately received the lion's share of historical attention. The story of the Redlegs is certainly not divorced from these violent historical realities. Additionally, these realities do not always tell the whole story. For instance, not all Barbadians lived on sugar plantations and not all enslaved peoples were the property of wealthy sugar planters. As Melanie Newton (2008:30) highlights, "An 1824 Barbados government report concluded that, out of 5,206 slave owners on the island, 3,671 had no land, and most of that number possessed a handful of slaves." This figure can be partly attributed to the high number of slave owners living in the urban center of Bridgetown, but it also means that a number of the propertyless, poorer whites also owned enslaved peoples. As mentioned, there is no evidence to suggest that residents of Below Cliff owned enslaved peoples, but it is certainly clear that the legal bonds between poor whites and Afro-Barbadians could be contentious, exploitative, and even inhumane. For poor whites who did or did not own enslaved individuals, how are we to qualitatively investigate their socioeconomic relationships with people with whom they would have shared a similar economic status but contrasted greatly in terms of racial identity and/or legal status? Whiteness afforded immense privileges, even for the most impoverished of those legally considered white, in the form of social reform, educational initiatives, and poor relief (described in more detail in the following chapter), but how was that privilege socially or materially manifest in the everyday lives of Barbadian Redlegs? Answers to these complicated questions can only insufficiently be addressed by the words of planters, colonial officials, or island visitors. From a localized context like a poor white plantation tenantry, however, it is possible to glean insights into communal life that complicate broader narratives about Barbadian sugar society.

THREE

BELOW CLIFF

Excavating and Engaging with a Plantation Community

The several deep chasms below, over which they project, are imbrowned with the
thick foliage of lofty trees. The adjacent steep declivity is crowded with irregular
precipices, and broken rocks; the whole view terminating in the tempestuous sea,
over whole craggy shore the foaming waves incessantly break. All solemnly awful,
if not horrifying scenes! Except when the eye is relieved by a glimpse, or sometimes a full sight, of the neighbouring plantations.

—Griffith Hughes (1750:23–24)

When first investigated as an archaeological site beginning in the fall
of 2012, the tenantry of Below Cliff bore little resemblance to its
former self. In fact, it likely resembled the view from atop Hackleton's Cliff
described by St. Lucy's Parish rector, Griffith Hughes, in his mid-eighteenth-
century natural history of the island. This description, in the epigraph,
details a vibrant, tropical scene devoid of human activity, until one gazes on
the relieving sight of the plantation. Similarly, when viewed from above in
the present, the lush tropical forest that now dominates the landscape elicits
a tranquil, unkempt, and picturesque aesthetic (Figure 3.1). The encroach-
ment of vegetation since the tenantry's abandonment in the early 1960s
has provided twenty-first-century passengers aboard the Island Safari tour
mentioned in the introduction with a bucolic photo op to capture the rural
beauty of the Barbadian countryside and the undulations of the Atlantic.
Unbeknown to visitors gazing from above, however, the vestiges of a dynamic
community of generations past rest quietly beneath the canopy. As a visitor
to the parish of St. John, my role as an archaeologist tasked me with the
challenge of reimagining a built and cultural landscape that had largely been
erased due to the passage of time, the movement of people, and the rapid
expansion of the tropical environment.

The material culture the former inhabitants of the tenantry community
produced, consumed, used, reused, and discarded littered the ground surface
and resided in the depths of the soil below the canopy of the thick forest. Perhaps Hughes gazed on but ignored this same tenantry community during his
survey of the island. In a volume concerned with climate, geography, diseases,
and biodiversity of the island, Hughes, as can be gathered from the epigraph,
draws a sharp distinction between the disorderly ruggedness of Hackleton's
Cliff and the neighboring, manicured plantations. As discussed in this chapter, ambiguity remains as to whether or not the tenantry below the cliff was

occupied in 1750, the year Hughes's volume was published, but given the marginality of its inhabitants, it would not be surprising if the tenantry was rendered invisible in his otherwise vivid description. If that is indeed the case, it fits a broader pattern in which Caribbean islands are reduced to the binary of untamed "nature" and the productive plantation landscape. A poor white tenantry does not fit this model, but the material record, along with archival and oral sources, tells a different story. Fragments of everyday items provide clues as to what life had been like for those residing on the boundaries of sugar plantations. Archaeologists depend on these pieces of material culture, along with other lines of evidence, to access images of the past that speak to our present and future.

In recognizing that archaeology is not solely about the past, it also needs to be acknowledged that the landscapes that archaeologists attempt to reimagine are active spaces, even if uninhabited at the time of investigation. The physical transformations undertaken in Below Cliff since its abandonment hinder attempts to lucidly reconstruct what community life may have been like, but the twenty-first-century landscape holds meaning for those who interact with it, alter it, are affected by it, and hold memories about its past and present. With that in mind, this chapter has multiple dimensions: it concerns the nature of undertaking a study of a community, the people who make up that community in the past and present, and the ways in which archaeological, anthropological, and historical methods were employed to better understand a marginal space on the plantation landscape inhabited by those known as the poor whites or Redlegs. In other words, if the previous chapter provided the necessary context to explicate how poor whites fit or did not fit into Barbadian society in the *longue durée*, this chapter uses an in-depth analysis of an intimate community to deconstruct broader narratives and present an alternative that privileges what can be discerned from localized investigations.

Taken from roughly the same vantage point as in Figure 3.1, Figure 3.2 provides the only known surviving photograph of the Below Cliff community. The photograph, purported to be part of the same 1908 series that includes the photo of the Redleg fishermen found in the introduction (see Figure I.3), depicts a vibrant community devoid of the tree cover that dominates the twenty-first-century landscape. Boarded homes are in close proximity to one another, and many uneasily rest on limestone blocks nestled into the steep topography. Community members are vaguely visible as they congregate in cleared spaces between households. In the background, neat rows of cane stalks follow the landscape as it extends to the rocky Atlantic coastline. The contrast between the photographs demonstrates the power of

Figure 3.1. Landscape view of Below Cliff taken from the ridge of Hackleton's Cliff in 2013. (Matthew C. Reilly)

the tropical environment and the fragility of a colonial landscape so heavily invested in sugar production. Archaeological and historical methods can therefore allow viewers of these photographs to pivot from one to the other. These methods provide a window into community life on a landscape that has undergone tremendous transformation in the last century. If the landscape captured in the 1908 photograph has been rendered largely invisible, the material vestiges of community life and the associated recollections of community members provide unique perspectives that make great strides in attempting to bring that landscape back to life.

AN ARCHAEOLOGY OF A POOR WHITE COMMUNITY

This book is more aptly described as an archaeology of a community than community archaeology (for archaeologies of communities see Canuto and Yaeger 2000). The distinction between the two reflects not only conceptual approaches to the study of a community but also methodological implications for how research is undertaken. For the better part of two decades, archaeological research has made tremendous strides in engaging with the public at large and the immediate communities that are associated with archaeological projects. Branded as community or public archaeology, this collaborative approach between researchers and community members seeks

Figure 3.2. Below Cliff from Hackleton's Cliff, 1908, believed to be part of the same series as the photograph in Figure I.3. (Matthew C. Reilly, from the collection of Richard Goddard)

to develop community-relevant research questions, address the interests of stakeholders, incorporate willing community members in the archaeological process, and facilitate a dialogue for interpreting the archaeological materials collected in the course of excavations (for collaborative archaeology in the Caribbean see González-Tennant 2014; Haviser 2015a, 2015b; see also Marshall 2002; Little and Shackel 2007; Silliman 2008; Okamura and Matsuda 2011; Atalay 2012).

Despite commendable attempts at inclusivity on the part of researchers committed to community archaeology and my own engagement in, and support for, community involvement, I make no pretense of placing this project under the banner of community archaeology. Community members were certainly involved in the development of a research strategy, in the archaeological research process, and in the interpretation of acquired data. In general, however, I share Terrence Epperson's (2004) concerns about the practice of community collaboration. As he notes, well-intentioned archaeologists attempting to engage and collaborate with community members often fall short of equal exchanges in the research process. Rather than an exchange in which all participants stand on equal footing, community archaeology can often suffer from, in the words of Epperson, "superficial inclusion" (2004:103), in which archaeologists shoulder the majority of methodological and interpretive responsibility. More recently, Sonya Atalay has made similar observations, noting that while the theoretical basis for community collaboration is present in archaeological thought, "what remains to be established are effective methods for putting collaborative theories and concepts into practice" (Atalay 2012:3). While sympathetic to the desire for a more praxis-oriented community archaeology, in presenting data gathered from and about Below Cliff, it is not my intention to speak for or with the extended Below Cliff community (but coauthored publications are in preparation). Rather, my identity as an outsider (to the community and to the country) was an important factor in how research was designed and undertaken. At times, my own perspectives differed from those of Below Cliff community members, and my interpretations should not be viewed as an extension of their thoughts, beliefs, or understandings despite my best attempts to incorporate their perspectives into my analyses.

While engagement with the broader Below Cliff community was an essential component of the research process, the approach taken here is more aptly described as an archaeology of a community. By this I mean an archaeological study that takes the community as its principal focus of analysis. Here the community largely refers to the socioeconomic and kinship networks of individuals who operated in and around the physical space of the tenantry known as Below Cliff (see Handler and Lange 1978:30). Community boundaries, however, can be fuzzy—geographically, temporally, and conceptually. In the case of Below Cliff, the physical space was abandoned in the 1960s, meaning that the living Below Cliff community is geographically and temporally distant from the space and time under direct investigation. Today the community is made up of individuals who spent their childhoods in the tenantry and now reside in neighboring villages. Other former residents have scattered to more distant regions of the island or abroad. Some grew up in neighboring villages but had familial, social, or economic relationships with Below Cliff residents. Others, from all parts of the island, had ancestors who once lived below the cliff. Given these parameters, members of the local and extended community need not know one another to be connected to Below Cliff. Additionally, these categories of community members are not mutually exclusive; individuals can have multiple and diverse connections to Below Cliff in the past and present.

When the tenantry was still inhabited, the community consisted of those who had their homes constructed on land belonging to Clifton Hall Plantation. Extended community members also included those who lived in neighboring tenantries or villages who were related to residents of Below Cliff or maintained social, economic, and even familial relationships with them. Finally, enslaved and free Afro-Barbadians who lived in Below Cliff, above the cliff at Clifton Hall Plantation, and in the neighboring villages and tenantries were also integral members of the Below Cliff community. Given the emphasis on everyday social, familial, and economic interaction, I have chosen to consider planters as only tangential members of the broader Below Cliff community. Owners of Clifton Hall and other members of the plantocracy are not absent from the story of Below Cliff. They appear in the historical record and in the oral sources provided by community members. While economic and social transactions certainly took place between planters and community members, members of each group operated, in most cases, in vastly different circles. From daily social interactions, to seating arrangements at the parish church, Below Cliff community members and the plantocracy inhabited different, if intersecting, worlds.

The parameters established here for community membership are in no way contingent on racial identity. Despite the tenantry being locally known as being inhabited by poor whites, and parish registries listing free tenants as residents throughout the period of slavery, the racial identities of those living below the cliff are not necessarily an invitation for or prohibition from community membership. As Mieka Brand Polanco (2014:4) notes in her study of a "historically black community" in rural Virginia, imposing a single racial identity onto a diverse community "not only casts an image of a monochromatic, monohistoric landscape, it also masks the fact that in this settlement neither racial identity nor historicity—nor even the physical boundaries of the community—are fixed." This is not to say, however, that racial identity, history, or physical boundaries were meaningless—quite the contrary. Living in a highly racialized and class-biased society, Below Cliff community members have been acutely aware of the significance of racial dynamics as well as their socioeconomic status. What makes the dynamics of community life interesting, however, is how members navigate social, economic, racial, and physical divisions in their daily lives.

Observing the dynamics of community life is not a practice that is solely relegated to interpretations of the past. Below Cliff is an active community, even if its last inhabitants left the tenantry over 50 years ago. While the physical space of Below Cliff is now densely forested, select members of the extended community are still familiar with the narrow pathways that meander through "the woods," as well as the foundations of former houses that still dot the landscape. Additionally, former residents and the descendants of residents surround the tenantry in neighboring communities and beyond;

these community members were able to provide invaluable insights into the nuances of daily life in Below Cliff, an active place in their memories and recollections. The intricate relationship between the past, present, people, places, and material things of the Below Cliff community compelled an interdisciplinary framework that included archaeological, anthropological, and historical methodologies. The implementation of these methodologies brought to light a vibrant community in the past that persists, albeit in different forms, in the present. One of the first tasks, however, was to understand if and why Below Cliff was a poor white community.

BELOW CLIFF AS A POOR WHITE TENANTRY

Prior to Below Cliff's abandonment in the early 1960s, its long occupational history is directly tied to broader processes affecting island society. The earliest historical reference pertaining to the area below the cliff is found in a 1653 deed for what would become Rous's and, later, Clifton Hall Plantation (BDA RB3/3:11). This particular deed is of interest because few such documents survive from this early period when sugar production had not yet completely enveloped the eastern regions of the island. The document details the transfer of a 259-acre property from George Martin to Thomas Cooper for over 50,000 pounds of muscovado sugar. During this early period, such transactions used a variety of exchange goods including cotton, tobacco, and sugar before sugar became the overwhelmingly dominant means of payment. Despite a mixed-commodity economy in the earlier years of the sugar revolution, the goods and chattels described as part of this sale demonstrate that sugar production was in full swing on this property prior to 1653. The inventory provided indicates that the property consisted of a mill, a boiling house, a curing house, copper bins for boiling, ladles, skimmers, 1,000 sugar pots, and 60 enslaved individuals (25 men, 25 women, and 10 children). Additionally, indentured servants and their time remaining to serve are noticeably absent on the inventory. At a time when land was being cleared in the more remote areas of the island to make room for sugar production, the sugar and slavery system was firmly in place on these acres.

It is evident that what would become Rous's and Clifton Hall Plantation was a property that quickly adopted the sugar and slavery model in a fashion that became typical, in terms of the materials and infrastructure needed, over the course of the following decades. Somewhat atypical, however, is the description of the actual land being transferred along with the goods and chattels. As described in the deed, the property comprised "by estimacion the land above ye Cliffe two hundred and nine acres and fifty acres below the Cliffe joyneinge to the said land above ye Cliffe" (BDA RB3/3:11). When experiencing the landscape firsthand, this division makes practical sense. The escarpment of Hackleton's Cliff runs through the eastern portion of the property separating the land on top of the cliff, at an elevation of roughly 230 meters above sea level, from the land below the cliff, beginning at roughly 175 meters above sea level. From most vantage points on top of the cliff, the drop of nearly 50 meters is almost completely vertical. According to the deed, the land below the cliff is further divided into ten acres of "free land" and 40 acres of "leased land." The distinction made between these two zones indicates that the property was, at the time, not a cohesive unit of sugar production. Rather, it shows that while sugar production was the industry par excellence atop the cliff, the acreage below the cliff was leased or rented, for purposes unclear. The ambiguity about the acres situated under the cliff makes it difficult to assess whether this reflects a single renter who was using the space for crop production or the land was being leased out to a number of tenants. Given that 10 acres are listed as "free land," it might be the case that the owner had begun the process of leasing parcels but had yet to find a renter for the remaining 10 acres. It is clear, however, that from the earliest years of colonial habitation and cultivation in the area the lands below and on top of the cliff were viewed and used differently from each other.

The challenge of tracing the history of a place like Below Cliff is that, from an early date, there was little to no economic interest, from the perspective of those in power, in what was taking place in that area. In fact, in an extensive 1744 will for Samuel Rous (BDA RB6/33:139–145), the owner of Rous's Plantation, his entire property is described in detail with reference to how his holdings should be divided among his heirs, yet the land below the cliff is not mentioned at all. After 1653, while much can be gleaned about Clifton Hall as a functioning plantation, no known will or deed makes mention of Below Cliff with the exception of its inclusion in the total acreage of the plantation's property. Despite silence on the part of the individuals who actually owned the parcels of land, hints concerning the existence of Below Cliff as an active place of residence are found in official parish registries for baptisms, marriages, and burials, as well as in records associated with poor relief. By the mid-seventeenth century Barbados was divided into 11 parishes that functioned as administrative units. Given that the Anglican Church held significant power on the island, there was little separation between church and state (see Campbell 1982). Parish churches were often tasked with administrative duties such as collecting taxes, maintaining highways, recording official registries, and allotting poor relief (Marshall 2003). The last two undertakings are of particular interest given that poor whites regularly appear in the records associated with these tasks.

Unlike the historiography of the poor whites that examines the population in broad swaths, the approach taken here operates at the community level, making it exceedingly difficult to find traces of a small tenantry in official documentation. When traces are uncovered, however, they shed light on the character of the community below the cliff in terms of the officially sanctioned racial identity of its residents as well as their economic circumstances. Again, the depth of these official records is limited, particularly as they were recorded and maintained by members of the plantocracy and other colonial officials. Members of the vestry who met on matters related to the parish were often the largest plantation owners, making these white men some of the most socially and economically powerful people on the island. They harbored particular sentiments about the individuals and groups over whom they governed, and details are often lacking when it comes to the specifics of the poor whites. Despite these shortcomings, parish records provide some of the necessary evidence that confirms Below Cliff's existence as a poor white tenantry during and after the period of slavery.

Beginning in 1825, place of residence was regularly recorded for parish registry entries for baptisms, marriages, and burials. For the parish of St. John, during the period of 1825 to 1849 (the years encompassed in a single volume of baptisms), 232 individuals were baptized with a given place of residence of Below Cliff, Below the Cliff, Living on Clifton Land, or Tenant on Clifton Hall (BDA RL1/26, RL1/27). For the same years, 135 individuals listed in the registry of burials were provided with similar places of residence during the same period of time (BDA RL1/29). The variety of place names given for the acreage below the cliff indicates that the space wavered in terms of official recognition. It was known to residents of the parish, even to the point of being described in these records, but it falls short of the consistency noted of official plantation names. Despite irregularity in the listing of the community name, these registries confirm that people were living below the cliff on Clifton Hall property during the era of slavery. Tenantry living became a dominant feature on the Barbadian landscape in the postemancipation era as a result of what became known as the Contract Law when many formerly enslaved laborers found themselves contractually obligated to work on the same plantations and reside as tenants in newly established villages on the peripheries of the plantation (Beckles 2007:147–151; Bergman and Smith 2014). This transition signaled the explosion in the number of Afro-Barbadians living in plantation tenantries, a phenomenon that had previously been primarily associated with poor whites, select free people of color, and militia members (Handler 1974:114).

The high number of baptized individuals residing in Below Cliff may suggest that the community's residents were predominantly white, given that baptism for the enslaved and free people of color was relatively uncommon throughout the period of slavery. As Jerome Handler (1974:161–165) notes, however, slave baptisms were becoming increasingly popular in the nineteenth century, and many free people of color were choosing to be baptized into the Anglican Church in the years leading up to emancipation. In fact, in 1822, of the 1,382 individuals receiving an Anglican baptism, 753 were enslaved and 261 were free people of color (164). In the immediate postemancipation period, baptisms for the formerly enslaved reached new heights. In the baptismal records for the parish of St. John, multiple baptisms taking place on the same day regularly provide only a first name for the individual and note "adult" as their age, likely indicating their identity as a formerly enslaved Afro-Barbadian (BDA RB1/27).

If the baptismal registries are only able to confirm that Below Cliff was inhabited during the period of slavery, a comparison of burial records and the parish vestry minutes detailing poor relief reveals that many of these residents were identified as poor whites. Inspired by poor relief systems in place in England, parish vestries in Barbados attempted to assuage the economic hardships suffered by those deemed to be the "deserving" poor from the earliest years of settlement. This relief, however, was only extended to those identified as white, and "non-whites, whether slave or free, were deliberately excluded from participation" (Marshall 2003:167). During meetings of the parish vestry, poor relief was regularly discussed. Minutes from these meetings include detailed lists documenting the names of relief recipients and the amounts that they were provided on a quarterly basis. These minutes reveal insights into the attitudes island elites harbored toward poor whites, but they sometimes provide the necessary details to piece together the makeup of local communities.

For instance, at a meeting of the St. John vestry on March 25, 1802, the minutes record 58 entries of poor relief to be allotted to specific adults (mostly women) and children (BDA D273). Several of those listed as receiving poor relief are also found in the registry of burials beginning in 1825, with a place of residence given as Below Cliff or one of its permutations. Mary Charge (75), Sarah Downey (68), Henrietta Gibson (64), Mary Ann King (77), Elizabeth Norris (36), Margaret Howard (64), Jane Brooks (90), and Henry Mayers (45) each passed away at an age when they could have been receiving poor relief in 1802. While no other matches of full names appear, several additional matching surnames are found on the lists—names that can still be found in neighboring communities today—including Goddard, Fenty, and Moore. Having sufficiently met the standards of being "deserving" of poor

relief, including being identified as white, records of these individuals confirm that several members of the Below Cliff community would have been
readily categorized as poor whites or Redlegs, thus providing historical con-
firmation for the oral sources provided in the neighboring communities.

FROM RESIDENCE TO RUIN AND RECOVERY

In the early 1860s a small Anglican church, St. Margaret's, was built in
nearby Glenburnie to cater to the growing population living in the broader
Below Cliff region. The registries for St. Margaret's were kept in a similar
fashion to those for the official parish church. Given the closer proximity to
the Below Cliff community, St. Margaret's boasts an expansive set of baptismal, marriage, and burial records that provides details about the dynamics of daily life in Below Cliff as well as long-term kinship and genealogical
patterns during the latter years of the tenantry's occupation (St. Margaret's
Registries [SMR]). In the first years of the church's existence, a large number of baptisms for infants from Below Cliff demonstrates that the tenantry
was already a thriving community and likely had been in preceding decades
(potentially centuries). It is difficult to estimate an official population given
that the geographical boundaries of the tenantry were and are ambiguous.
Three plantations—Clifton Hall, Newcastle, and Colleton—each owned
land below the cliff, and it is difficult to determine where one property ends
and the next begins. The area chosen for archaeological investigations, however, was centered in the acreage of Clifton Hall Plantation. Following the
names of those listed as residing in Below Cliff or on Clifton Hall land, however, it can be approximated that at any given time the community was home
to several dozen households and upwards of 200 people.

Almost exactly a century after the establishment of St. Margaret's Church,
however, Below Cliff would be officially abandoned and nearly erased from
the island landscape. The historical record is silent as to how or why the tenantry was abandoned. Following a single baptism for a child said to reside in
Below Cliff in 1965, the tenantry disappears from parish registries entirely.
Ethnographic data collected in the area in the 1960s (Rosenberg 1962) and
1970s (Davis 1978) provide some clues surrounding the decline of the tenantry, while more details were provided by the extended Below Cliff community of the twenty-first century. Unlike emancipation, which caused the
large-scale restructuring of the plantation landscape in a relatively short
amount of time, the abandonment of Below Cliff was a slower process that
involved multiple contributing factors. The broadest process affecting the
space was the decline of the sugar industry. As sugar production decreased
in profitability due to more competitive markets, including beet sugar, some

plantation laborers shifted to small-farming techniques while others sought opportunities in Bridgetown and abroad. For those who decided to move elsewhere, social mobility, or "making it over the hill," was relatively rare (Rosenberg 1962:55), but select success stories are well known across the island. Pressing health concerns were also a cause for moving. In the 1940s, the parish medical officer, a Dr. Carter, lamented that in his old age he could no longer make the difficult climb to Below Cliff, encouraging residents to move if they expected to receive parish-sponsored medical attention. Hurricane Janet struck the island in 1955, causing extensive devastation, providing yet another catalyst for Below Cliff residents to move to affordable lands made newly available in the surrounding area rather than rebuilding in the tenantry.

The processes contributing to the abandonment of the area below the cliff aided the transition from it being referred to as Below Cliff to "the woods" by those who knew the space best. Like many similar tenantries around the island, a once-vibrant community quickly became engulfed in forest, as it once had been in the early seventeenth century. Labeling the phenomenon "vanishing villages," Barbadian historian Woodville Marshall (1988:4) notes that this process was relatively common in the rural districts from the mid-nineteenth century to the mid-twentieth. Having previously inhabited unstable areas prone to rockslides or land slippages, many residents sought more desirable acreages and better access to amenities. In most cases, the boarded homes that once dotted these landscapes were removed and reassembled in new locales. Over time, vegetation reconquered the former tenantries, nearly erasing evidence of prior occupation.

The challenges posed by the reality of reforestation vary greatly from those noted by archaeologists searching for former villages of the enslaved. Following emancipation, many former villages were plowed and planted in cane, forcing plantation laborers to take up residence at newly established tenantries on the peripheries of the plantation. As Handler and Lange note, "A great deal of Barbados's arable land has been cultivated for many years and the mechanical deep plowing of fields in recent times, as well as architectural and other alterations in plantation yards and adjacent fields, have undoubtedly assisted in disturbing and even erasing many cultural features associated with slave life" (1978:56; see also Handler 2002:124–127; in some cases, undisturbed village contexts have been discovered on the island, see Armstrong and Reilly 2014). However, the disturbances deep plowing causes allow for walking surveys of recently cut cane fields, exposing ground surfaces where clusters of artifacts can be observed that are likely associated with domestic sites in disturbed contexts (Finch et al. 2013).

In the case of Below Cliff, however, the methodological challenges were slightly different. Below Cliff never hosted large-scale or deep-plowing sugar cultivation, but in the forested environment, visibility is minimal due to a foliage-covered ground surface, large trees, and thick brush. Select trails maintained by local residents and island hikers offer limited and narrow means through which to navigate the wooded area but only offer a very confined representation of the space as a whole. Steep topography also contributed to field challenges, making it difficult to even walk in certain areas. Throughout the duration of archaeological work undertaken in the woods, boulders were sporadically encountered that had come loose from the escarpment, tumbling down the cliffside and into the former tenantry. The instability of the physical environment would have been even more problematic for those living under the cliff. Without the appropriate conditions to conduct walking surveys along regimented transects, reconnaissance in the woods was undertaken using informal walking surveys. A small survey team used pathways as general guides to explore the tenantry, taking regular excursions off the beaten path to investigate heavily wooded areas that might contain clues about previous places of occupation. These informal surveys proved successful in confirming the location of several features associated with domestic life. At multiple locations along pathways and deep in the woods, stone features were encountered that hinted at a variety of activities. The specifics of the types of activity undertaken, however, left only ephemeral and faint traces on the landscape. In the short amount of time since Below Cliff had been abandoned, many housing platforms had tumbled down, retaining walls had eroded from their places, and animal pen walls had become disarticulated. Nonetheless, these stone ruins were the most visible remaining vestiges of daily life in the Below Cliff community.

Below Cliff as a Living Community

With the exception of the occasional rockslide, the woods are now a very peaceful and quiet place. The sounds of everyday life are absent and the footpaths that meander through the area no longer receive the traffic they once did. The stone ruins found below the cliff hint at the prior human occupation, warranting the designation of Below Cliff as an archaeological site. My encounters with community members and laborers husking coconuts in the woods or cultivating bananas in neighboring fields, however, served as a reminder that Below Cliff is not a place solely relegated to the past. My encounters and interactions with such individuals serve to blur the boundaries between past and present, recognizing the depth and complexity of the relationship among people, places, and time.

Beginning in November 2012, I slowly developed relationships with members of the broader Below Cliff community. Through chance meetings in the woods, introductions from mutual friends, or time spent in the immediate area, I soon met members of families whose surnames are found in the historical record and who have been fixtures of the region below the cliff for several generations. Members of the Watson, Gibson, Goddard, Fenty, Farnum, Norris, King, Mayers, and Downey clans all contributed to my understanding of the broader Below Cliff community. Many, if not most, of these individuals have very light complexions and would likely be imposed with the label poor white or Redleg. Community members are fully aware of these terms and cognizant of their implications. While the terms are seldom self-applied or used in conversation, many openly recognized and discussed various degrees of European ancestry. Others, however, were also keen to point out their African ancestry. In effect, the racial identity of community members was most often referred to on a sliding and informal phenotypic spectrum, with people being referred to as light, dark, brown, colored, or red more often than white or black. The significance of the complex racial character of this community is taken up in more detail in later chapters, but, for now, it serves to demonstrate that the community continues to maintain and acknowledge a degree of European or white ancestry.

During the course of research, I regularly shared drinks, meals, small talk, produce, rides, and my day's findings with those living and working in the area of the woods. On certain occasions, I joined community members in their daily work routines (Kusenbach 2003), noting how they conducted their tasks and the nature of their engagement with the environment and other community members. My relationship with local residents also included informal conversations about their own family histories, kinship networks, and their recollections of the surrounding area, specifically Below Cliff, in the past. These encounters and interactions illustrate that Below Cliff is still an active space; activity here relates to the physical undertakings unfolding in the geographical setting of Below Cliff as well as the active process of memory and recollection on the part of those who once lived there, or those who had kin or ancestors who had lived there.

In my use of oral sources and engagements with local residents I made a conscious choice to avoid formal interviews and the use of recording devices. Formal interviews in the presence of recording devices have been noted to have a stifling effect on interviewees who may feel pressured to provide what they perceive to be "complete" or "accurate" information that is desired by interviewers (Polanco 2014:73–113). This is not to say that interviewees would otherwise provide untrue information but suggests that a more formal atmosphere can connote a "just the facts" mentality. Informal conversations, especially those that include multiple community members simultaneously, breed a more comfortable atmosphere that allows participants to freely recollect stories, people, and places in a setting that allows them to feed off of the memories of other individuals. As Polanco notes, in these casual contexts, "residents produce narratives that are reflective of a complex experiential relationship to the past" (2014:113). Residents were aware that I was taking notes for the purposes of this study, but most felt more at ease without the watchful eye of a camera or the formality of an audio recorder; this comfort allowed them to speak about the past as it related to their present.

Aside from conversations at local rum shops, in the homes of community members, and in the course of daily work regimens, I took several trips through the woods with former residents for the explicit purpose of providing an "opportunity to re-experience their connections with landscape and to reminisce" (Harrison and Schofield 2010:76; see also Anderson 2004). These excursions revealed invaluable insights into the history of Below Cliff as well as the nuances of everyday life for community members. The stone ruins of a former house were often given life histories or biographies, assigned names that stood for the individuals who had once lived there. These stones and otherwise lifeless features could be intimately tied to the occupations of male heads of household, a mother's famous recipe, or kinship networks that sprawled across households. In general, the now-quiet community came to life.

The walks through the woods also revealed much about the inner workings of recollection and memory. For instance, for one member of the Norris family, who continues to use Below Cliff to collect coconuts, Below Cliff has never been a place of the past. Rather, it is an active space associated with labor. This former resident was thus concerned with local agricultural practices and the occupations of community members. In contrast, one of his younger cousins had spent very little time in the woods since his childhood departure. For this former resident, the space is one imbued with childhood memories of playing with his siblings, socializing with schoolmates, monitoring the comings and goings of plantation workers and fishermen, and watching his mother cook in the family's detached kitchen. Those who were physically able and willing to participate were only male former residents, restricting the nature of recollections along lines of gender. Despite these constraints, the method of bringing former residents into the physical environment to spark their recollections proved fruitful (Bloch 1998). The gathering of oral sources in this setting again reveals the active nature of Below Cliff, as it sparked particular recollections based on individuals' relationship to the space.

Barbadian historian Ronald Hughes noted many years ago the importance of oral sources in his ethnohistorical research on a small tenantry due
north of Below Cliff known as St. Elizabeth's Village. Documenting the
complicated nature of racial identity, land ownership practices, and daily
life in the village, Hughes notes that oral sources collected often represent
a "sadly neglected field of historical research" (1979:70–71). Oral, archival,
and archaeological sources provide intersecting data sets that allow for interpretations that the historical record alone is ill-equipped to provide. Despite
calls for an "informed imagination" (Shaw 2013:9) in the reading of historical archives that have acknowledged and significant silences (Trouillot 1995),
archaeological and oral data have the potential to circumvent archival shortcomings (see Schmidt and Patterson 1995; Jones and Russell, eds. 2012).
Despite disciplinary gulfs between history and archaeology (see DeCorse and
Chouin 2003), the use of diverse historical archaeological methodologies,
including using the wealth of knowledge provided by a living community
(for Caribbean case studies see Armstrong 2003; Wilkie and Farnsworth
2005), allows for a more comprehensive study of the Below Cliff community.

ARCHAEOLOGY BELOW THE CLIFF

The memories and recollections community members shared were indispensable in providing unique perspectives on the former tenantry. At the same
time, archaeologists need to be attuned to "the memory things hold" (Olivier 2011:28). The things encountered during the course of excavations below
the cliff provide time-depth inaccessible from oral sources in this community
in addition to intimate details about daily life not reflected in the historical
record. While these three data sets inform and complement one another, it
is the archaeological assemblage that provides an entirely new source of data
through which to comment on the history and lives of Barbadian Redlegs.
Archaeological strategies were devised in the hopes of addressing a broad set
of questions. Given that the historical record is rather ambiguous, dateable
material culture was sought to confirm the earliest occupation of the tenantry. More open-ended questions concerned the daily lives of Below Cliff
residents and their place in Barbadian society.

The excavations undertaken in the tenantry were household oriented,
using domestic settings to explore the intimate domains of the household,
the public realms beyond the immediate house features and yards, and the
entangled relationship between the two (Robin 2002; Robin and Rothschild
2002; Fogle et al. 2015). Similar to methods employed for the study of sites
associated with slavery in the Caribbean (see Armstrong 1990; Haviser 1999;
Armstrong and Kelly 2000; Wilkie and Farnsworth 2005; Armstrong and

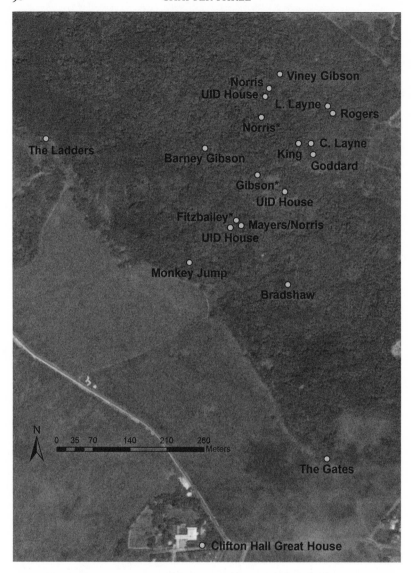

Figure 3.3. Satellite image of Below Cliff with households plotted and named through the collection of oral histories. Select houses were located but were unable to be associated with a specific family by former residents. These house sites are depicted as UID. Households marked with an asterisk were the sites of excavation. (Matthew C. Reilly)

Reilly 2014; Bergman and Smith 2014; Handler and Wallman 2014; Kelly and Bérard 2014), material culture recovered from households and their surrounding features, particularly yard areas, can speak to internal practices and preferences as well as a household's relationship to broader socioeconomic networks and processes. While certainly living under radically different legal codes, discriminatory practices, and labor regimes than the enslaved, those living below the cliff can be studied archaeologically using similar methodologies. In short, the archaeological methods employed sought to capture the essence of everyday life for those living below the cliff in the midst of a highly racialized plantation society.

Three households were chosen for excavation following shovel test pits (STPs) and select surface collections conducted at seven house sites found during preliminary reconnaissance and surveying. Shovel test pits, when possible, were placed inside and outside known housing platforms that were identified by the presence and articulation of limestone foundations or "groundsels," as they are locally known. Steep inclines presented challenges in terms of excavation and also caused erosion in certain areas. That being the case, test pits varied greatly in depth and artifact density. In some cases, bedrock was reached in just 5 cm while others reached depths of over 60 cm. The degree of foundation articulation, stratigraphic control, and artifact abundance for each STP were considered to determine which house sites were the ideal location for unit excavation.

Archaeological potential was then coupled with insights provided by community members. In the case of three households, visible features and materials recovered from STPs were complemented by knowledge of the families who had last lived in the structure. In some cases, the occupations of select family members was known, along with the names of children and those in the extended family that lived nearby. Some of the most crucial insights came from members of the Norris family, who were able to provide detailed information about the orientation of households and associated features like garden plots, trash pits, detached kitchens, and animal pens. The information provided also allowed for the creation of a rough map of the community as former community members remembered it. Although many families had already left Below Cliff by the time some former residents were born, they did their best to remember family households, stories, and the landscape. Using a GPS device, points were plotted at each individual house site and assigned a family or individual name according to the information provided. In some cases, when housing platforms had long been abandoned, they were given a brief description. The result is the map seen in Figure 3.3. Due to dense vegetation and unavailability of LiDAR data (for use of LiDAR in the Caribbean, see Opitz et al. 2015), the creation of a detailed plan view or topographic map was not possible. Therefore, this map serves as the best visualization of one zone of the former community. Foundation stones were found beyond the limits of platforms plotted on this map, but former residents confirm that the area pictured was the heart of the Below Cliff community.

Sampling strategies and oral sources determined three specific households for excavation, each pictured on the map. Rather than assign each house site with a number or context code, the standard methodological approach for archaeology, the names provided by community members were used to provide a more familial persona to the abandoned domestic site. The three residences are those of the Fitzbailey, Gibson, and Norris families—the Norris residence being the most extensively excavated. For each house site, a platform for a boarded house was discernable (at least partially), artifacts were observed on the ground surface and in STPs, and information about the former residents was provided through oral sources.

The Fitzbailey Household

The Fitzbailey house site is the closest to the cliff side of the three houses excavated, but it received the least attention archaeologically. Located in what is now a sizeable coconut grove frequented by a former community member, the housing platform consists of a single limestone wall set into the hillside. Oral sources confirmed that the Fitzbailey family had last lived at this spot. It was also noted that Mr. Fitzbailey operated a small shop up the hill and that the family was "dark." This latter comment was a point of interest for conducting excavations at this household. The ambiguous designation of "dark" raises significant questions about the racial identity of the family as well as those who lived at the site previously. Oral and historical sources point to this former tenantry being a predominantly poor white or Redleg community, but there were also mixed-race and African-descendant families. With this in mind, excavations at this household were designed to provide a comparative assemblage to determine whether any qualitative or quantitative differences were found between households of different racial identities/ancestries.

Excavations failed to collect an assemblage that could serve comparative purposes. In general, extremely claylike soils (found in select regions of St. John) made excavations difficult, and material culture was relatively scarce. For instance, in a one-meter-square unit placed along the outer edge of the northeastern wall of the foundation, excavations went to a depth of roughly 60 cm, with the lowest 10 cm made up of sterile clay. In total, 68 artifacts, including coarse earthenwares, imported ceramics, glass, tobacco pipe stems, charcoal, metal, nails, and brick, were collected from the unit, with most recovered from the surface. The relative paucity of artifacts is not necessarily a problem for archaeological interpretation and can speak to issues related to access to goods, economic status, and artifact reuse patterns. Given the poor soil quality and lack of stratigraphy, however, it was determined that excavation efforts would be made elsewhere.

The Gibson Household

The Gibson household is located northeast and downhill from the Fitzbailey house site. Adjacent to a small plot of tall grass that had once been used for small-scale cane production, the housing platform had once held the residence of Gorringe Gibson (née Norris), the aunt of two former residents who provided insights about the household. Born in 1901 to Lambert and Louisa Norris, Gorringe married Robert Hampden Gibson in December 1921, a month after the birth of their first son, Byron. In total, Hampden, as he was regularly called, and Gorringe baptized nine children at St. Margaret's Church (SMR). It is possible, however, that the registry is incomplete, as one community member noted that the couple had as many as a dozen children. The uncommonly large size of the Gibson family led to challenges in understanding the archaeological signature left by their presence. It is possible that the family moved to that house site to accommodate their growing family. Before their occupation of the space, it is unknown who lived at the site.

In addition to being able to easily assemble and disassemble the walls of these boarded homes known as chattel houses, this architectural style also allowed for household expansion with relative ease. In the case of a growing family, like the Gibsons, new groundsel stones could be placed accordingly to support new walls for the addition of rooms. For the Gibson house site, this resulted in a complex array of piecemeal walls that, when abandoned, were left in no discernable order. In fact, when strategizing excavations in consultation with community members, walls that were thought to be part of the house foundation were instead noted to be the walls of animal pens. These walls, taller and better-preserved than those of the house foundation, were constructed with great care to securely contain what would have been a valuable economic asset. Their close proximity to the house, however, made it difficult to discern the spatial organization of the larger domestic space. STPs and one-meter-square units were placed inside the foundation and outside its walls in the immediate yard area. Of immediate interest was discerning the occupational history of the structure. Had Hampden and Gorringe been the first to build a structure at this spot when they arrived in the 1930s? If not, how long had the space been inhabited? The excavation process answered these questions in short order, while the material culture recovered contributed to the ongoing investigation of the lives of poor white Barbadians on the plantation landscape.

More agreeable soils allowed for more extensive excavations; six conjoining one-meter-square units were placed along the exterior of the northern foundation wall, forming a three-by-two-meter trench that spanned a portion of the home's front yard. Similar to the Fitzbailey household, however, relatively few artifacts were recovered from the units. From the three STPs and six units (reaching depths of up to 75 cm), a total of 67 artifacts were recovered, including coarse earthenware, imported ceramics, glass, brick, a utensil handle, nails, seeds, plastic, charcoal, and metal. The scarcity of material culture prohibits quantitative interpretations based on evidence from this household alone, but the contexts within which particular artifacts were found are instrumental in speaking to occupation periods and habitation practices of Below Cliff residents.

Two discernible stratigraphic layers were observed in excavation units based on soil color and texture. The first layer, reaching a depth of about 40 cm, contained all of the sherds of recovered whitewares from these units, dating from about 1820 into the present. The inclusion of small quantities of plastic indicates that this layer of occupation is likely associated with the Gibson family. Following the soil change, however, the only ceramics recovered in the lower stratigraphic level were barley molded white salt-glazed stonewares, introduced around 1740. The material record is limited, but it is possible that the levels represent two discrete periods of occupation. If this is the case, it indicates that residency patterns below the cliff are defined by a complex relationship between simultaneous long-term inhabitation and ephemerality. In other words, while the broader Below Cliff community was inhabited for a long period of time, individual homesteads could be abandoned and reinhabited at a later date. The archaeological evidence indicates that Below Cliff was inhabited at least as early as the mid-eighteenth century and that housing platforms were used and reused throughout its period of occupation.

The Norris Household

The Norris household was the site of the most extensive excavations, the largest assemblage of recovered material culture, and the richest oral history. The house, which had once been the childhood home of one of the community members providing oral histories, is highly visible on the landscape due to a raised foundation that sits along a steep hill to the northeast of the former Gibson residence. The oral histories provided reveal the tight kinship network represented in the immediate area. Through marriage or consanguinity, many neighboring households were related, and members of the Norris family were apt to point out the webs of interconnectedness. As many families began to vacate the tenantry in the 1940s, this homestead became a central

Figure 3.4. Northeast wall of the housing platform of the Norris homestead. (Matthew C. Reilly)

fixture for a number of reasons. Its geographical location placed it roughly in the center of surrounding households. In terms of kinship, the inhabitants had extended relations throughout the area. Finally, for a number of years, one family member ran a small shop out of the household. Despite the small dimensions of the foundation, a 6.6-by-3.9-meter rectangle, the structure had once been two stories, housing the shop on the ground floor and the family's residence above.

The foundation of the Norris household was the most complete and articulated of all the foundations observed in the woods. Given the steep topography running downslope from southwest to northeast, a platform roughly one meter in height was built along the north and southeast sides of the foundation. This provided a level platform on which to construct the groundsel (Figure 3.4).

Adjacent to the northeastern and northwestern walls, a large pile of limestone rubble cluttered the area. Former residents noted that it had been there during their childhoods, and it likely represents the ruins of a foundation or platform from a previous occupation. Therefore, before excavations commenced, surface evidence indicated that multiple occupation episodes were likely. Limestone walls in the immediate area delineated other features

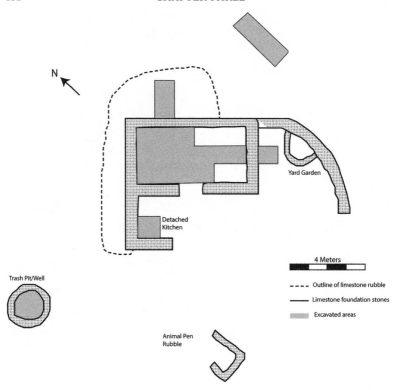

Figure 3.5. Plan view map of the Norris homestead. (Matthew C. Reilly)

associated with the home, including a small garden plan, a detached kitchen, small animal pens, and a trash pit (possibly a former well). Some of these features were easily discernible based on the limestone ruins, while the function of some features was described by community members (Figure 3.5).

Excavations were designed to assess the material record of many of these discrete activity areas, including the interior and exterior of the house, the detached kitchen, the trash pit, and the path that ran along the northeast platform wall. The Norris household was chosen for the most extensive excavations because of the diversity of household and community activities taking place within a relatively condensed space. Daily household activities, ranging from cooking, eating, socializing, and chores, were taking place in an area that was also home to a shop that sold household goods, making it a location that many community members would frequent. In breaking down analyses of a house site that treats such spaces as "fixed and unproblematic containers for certain kinds of social actions and interactions that were seen as private and enclosed or public and exposed in relation to the type of spatial container where they occurred" (Robin 2002:246), the boundaries between interior and exterior space become more fluid. As such, this archaeological approach to the household recognizes the importance of including spaces beyond the structure's walls (see also Armstrong and Kelly 2000; Fogle et al. 2015). However, units within the walls of the foundation were equally important. Unlike most slave quarters, which frequently had compact dirt floors that were swept regularly, chattel houses boasted wooden floors, allowing many artifacts to collect under the planks.

At the Norris house site, 20 one-meter-square units were excavated, along with the excavation of the adjacent trash pit feature. Three conjoining one-meter-square units were placed in the path below the northeast wall of the platform, in addition to three units placed abutting the exterior walls of the foundation and a single unit against the back wall of the detached kitchen. Inside the structure's foundation, 13 units were excavated; here, in addition to the recovery of material culture, excavations sought to examine the architectural signatures of the occupational history of the structure. Finally, the trash pit adjacent to the house was excavated as a feature. The pit, circular in shape, has a diameter of 125 cm and is lined with limestone blocks. The feature was bisected and, due to safety concerns and waterlogged soil, was excavated to a depth of roughly 120 cm, despite not reaching bedrock.

The assemblage recovered represents goods produced from the late eighteenth century to the late twentieth century, ranging from sherds of pearlware to the plastic packaging for an athletic shirt. Mid to late twentieth-century rubbish, including empty beer bottles, plastic, and metal tools, were found on the surface around the house site, likely being associated with the use of the woods for agricultural purposes after the tenantry's abandonment. Excavated material from below the surface primarily consists of domestic materials that include coarse earthenwares, buttons, tobacco pipes, drinking vessels (glass and tin), animal bone, and imported ceramics. Materials were collected from all levels of excavation within a complex matrix of stratigraphy. Units from the structure's interior reached depths of roughly two meters, exposing lenses of soil associated with at least two periods of occupation and two episodes of (re)construction. The surface and first level of excavations represented the most recent period of occupation, that of the Norris family. This was followed by a 30-cm level of loose limestone fill, another lens of organic soil, a thicker layer of limestone fill with larger blocks (roughly 50 cm), and finally, a mix of limestone boulders and soil before bedrock was reached (Figure 3.6). Aside from imposing challenges for safe and efficient excavations, the loose levels of limestone likely represented episodes of household (re)construction.

Figure 3.6. Northeast profile of house-interior excavation unit. (Matthew C. Reilly)

Stratigraphy observed indicates that limestone fill was used to construct a flat housing platform for the original structure. At some point, possibly following a destructive event like a hurricane (massive storms hit the island in 1780 and 1831) or a rockslide, a new housing platform was constructed, again using limestone fill. The process was undertaken a final time before the platform housed the structure that would come to be inhabited by its final occupants. Here, the rubble in the aftermath of destruction (limestone blocks) was used as the building blocks of reconstruction (see Reilly 2016a; Dawdy 2006a). While providing taphonomic clues, the material culture associated with these levels made maintaining discrete chronological control through stratigraphy rather difficult. The loose limestone fill failed to seal material culture in their associated place of deposition. Additionally, episodes of destruction and reconstruction could have disturbed particular contexts. As a result, a temporally diverse array of imported ceramics was found at all levels of excavation, including mid-nineteenth-century sponge-decorated, Scottish-made whiteware found at the very bottom of rubble fill at a depth of nearly two meters, while sherds of pearlware were recovered from the first level of excavation (0–10 cm).

Units excavated outside the structure's perimeter lacked the stratigraphic

TABLE 3.1. EXCAVATED BELOW CLIFF ARTIFACTS BY TYPE

Artifact category	Number	Percentage
Imported refined earthenware	748	20.84
Coarse earthenware	307	8.55
Glass	769	21.42
Nails (and fragments)	475	13.23
Metal	261	7.27
Shell	73	2.03
Bone	115	3.20
Small finds (buttons, plastic, etc.)	487	13.57
Plaster/cement	45	1.25
Charcoal	121	3.37
Tobacco pipe	33	0.92
Brick	156	4.35
Total	**3,590**	**100**

profile and soil depths found inside. Despite gradual soil changes in the units excavated along the pathway, no discrete stratigraphic levels were observed in the nearly 60 cm of excavated soil. In the detached kitchen, no recovered evidence points to cooking activities; no faunal remains (though they were found elsewhere in small numbers), charcoal, cooking vessels, or evidence of a hearth were recovered. The portion of the trash pit that was excavated returned late nineteenth- to twentieth-century artifacts associated with household use, such as ceramics and bottle glass. Finally, the units along the exterior of the foundation were shallow (the deepest reaching 45 cm) before reaching compact limestone, likely associated with the limestone fill encountered inside the structure; artifacts were minimal within these units. From the interior and exterior excavations, a total of 3,210 artifacts were recovered from the Norris household.

ASSESSING COMMUNITY LIFE BELOW THE CLIFF

A total of 3,590 artifacts were collected from Below Cliff. The data these material items provided speak to the dynamics of community life from the mid-eighteenth century to the time of the tenantry's abandonment in the 1960s and beyond. The items recovered were not extraordinary in terms of monetary value or prestige. They do, however, reflect the quotidian dimensions of life on the plantation landscape during and after the period of slavery. Table 3.1

provides a list of the materials recovered in absolute numbers and percentages. The assemblage is divided into groups reflecting common artifact types. A functional typology was avoided due to the significance of artifact reuse, a phenomenon discussed in more detail in the following chapter. Most types reflect a particular material, such as glass or metal nails. More broadly, the category for small finds encompasses a wide range of diagnostic artifacts whose specific function could be determined. These artifacts include clay tobacco smoking pipes, buttons made of various materials, twentieth-century plastic, clothing and other items of adornment, and pieces of slate boards and pencils.

The household items found below the cliff demonstrate that residents were engaged in local and international consumption practices. Ceramics and glass bottles from England and Scotland were found alongside water pitchers made in Barbados and marine shells from local crustaceans. Some items were manipulated and reused at the household level, such as a handle being applied to a tin can for use as a drinking vessel. Additionally, architectural signatures found below the cliff match common vernacular forms found across the island. All of these archaeological findings indicate a dynamic relationship among residents, their immediate neighbors, island society, and global consumerism. Despite firsthand accounts from island elites and visitors, historical scholarship, and twenty-first-century popular opinion that suggest an isolated Redleg population, the image of community life I present here is one that emphasizes inclusivity, involvement, and interaction based on specific choices made by community members. These choices are visible in the items they chose to produce, consume, use, reuse, exchange, and discard. They can also be seen in where and how residents build their homes. Finally, they can be seen in how residents manipulated and moved through the landscape.

The manipulation and navigation of the landscape speak to how people interacted, goods and information were passed, and people got from place to place. The narrow dirt paths used to explore the forested area below the cliff were oftentimes, according to former residents, the same pathways used and maintained by Below Cliff community members in decades and centuries past. Some have become overgrown and rendered invisible, but those that are still navigable reveal a circuitous network that connects individual houses, places of social gathering like shops, and main arteries that connected Below Cliff to neighboring villages, tenantries, and plantations. Without the formality of paved roads, these informal tracks were the primary means by which community members engaged with other Barbadians, from their kin in close proximity to those living beyond. Major highways literally cut into the limestone base of the island facilitated travel for people and commodities from the rural districts to the ports and towns. Unlike these roads, which were constructed and maintained by the enslaved under mandates from local vestries, roads and paths in places like Below Cliff were built and maintained communally, to facilitate inter- and intracommunal relationships.

The three pathways connecting Below Cliff to Clifton Hall Plantation on top of the cliff are most exemplary of this phenomenon. Hackleton's Cliff provides a daunting physical boundary between the acreages above and below the cliff. Like walls (Singleton 2015) or fences (Cobb and Sapp 2014), this imposing geological feature could easily serve to physically separate those living on either side of the divide—during the period of slavery this would mean poor white tenants living below and enslaved laborers living and working on top. These were sizable populations that would have been attuned to life on either side of the divide. Shortly after emancipation, the owner of Clifton Hall Plantation, Robert Haynes Jr., claimed over £6,000 for his loss of property, which referred to the 260 enslaved individuals who lived on the plantation (UCL Legacies of British Slave-Ownership Database: Claim No. 4281). With an estimated population of roughly 200 living below the cliff and 260 residing on top, a sizable population of racially diverse, nonelite individuals would have been living together, if separated, in a relatively small space.

Those living in this community were determined to stimulate movement up and down the escarpment to promote interaction and exchange. As one walks along the ridge of the cliff from south to north on the land of Clifton Hall, three entryways are encountered that were carved into the dirt and limestone when Below Cliff was still occupied—the Gates, Monkey Jump, and the Ladders (see Figure 3.2). Given that the field abutting Monkey Jump bears the same name and is situated next to the field named "Negro Yard," which was likely the location of the village for the enslaved (Handler and Lange 1978:45; see also Handler 2002), it can be deduced that these pathways existed prior to emancipation. One former resident recalls watching men return from work at the plantation by way of Monkey Jump while another continues to use the Gates to go up and down the escarpment to collect coconuts. With a lifespan of at least 180 years, these pathways point to the attempts by plantation residents to facilitate movement up and down the cliff that, during the period of slavery, would have brought tenants and the enslaved into daily contact (see Reilly 2016c).

The Gates, Monkey Jump, and the Ladders offered navigable, if somewhat treacherous, routes for residents to engage with the world outside of their own immediate community. For instance, community members would have climbed up the paths to go to work at Clifton Hall in the mornings, children would have used them to pay the monthly rent to the plantation manager (as relayed by former residents), and before the erection of St. Margaret's Church, residents would follow the paths to get to and from the parish church for services. Additionally, traffic would have likely flowed in both directions, and during the period of slavery, enslaved laborers would have traveled to Below Cliff via these pathways in order to socialize, exchange goods, or participate in any number of other activities. Tracks running down the hill out from Below Cliff served similar functions, connecting the tenantry to neighboring plantations like Newcastle to the southeast, Glenburnie to the east, and Forster Hall to the northeast. They also allowed direct access to the waters of the east coast, which served as fertile fishing grounds for many Below Cliff residents. Registries from St. Margaret's Church list fishing as one of the more common occupations for male community members. Oral histories from former residents also provide stories of the men returning to the tenantry after a day of fishing where they would dry their haul on the roofs of chattel houses.

Subsistence strategies extended to agricultural practices, also serving as the basis for small craft industries. Unlike the acreages on nearby sugar plantations where sugar cultivation occupied the majority of available land, Below Cliff was home to diverse land-use patterns. In Below Cliff, small fields of less than half an acre were once planted in cane that could be sold to neighboring plantations when harvested. Small garden plots outside houses grew provisions like yams, sweet potatoes, and other tubers. Most houses also had several trees in their yards for the growth of breadfruit, tamarind, bananas, plantains, and mangos; fowl, pigs, and cattle (if land for grazing was available) were also raised. These small-farming practices facilitated the cottage industries that included the cultivation and production of ginger, cotton, aloes, jams, jellies, arrowroot, and vegetables to sell locally and in Bridgetown markets (Watson 2000b:132; Handler 1971b:72–73, 81).

Evidence supporting the existence of cottage industries, market activity, and informal economies is found in the minutes of parish vestry meetings. Parishes across the island were responsible for collecting quarterly taxes from all individuals who operated as shopkeepers or hucksters (BDA D273). These individuals were not wealthy merchants but sold limited goods, both locally made and imported, in the parish of St. John. The internal marketing system on the island was a vital component of island socioeconomics that involved the enslaved, free people of color, and whites (see Handler 1974:125–130). Sunday had traditionally been the day reserved for marketing activity, and poor whites no doubt participated. More localized marketing practices, however, involved small shops and informal huckstering at the community level. It is, therefore, unsurprising that a list of taxed shopkeepers in the parish vestry minutes from April 1, 1896, includes many common surnames found in the Below Cliff community, such as Croney, Downey, Goddard, King, and Mayers.

Emphasized here are the diverse relationships forged among Below Cliff residents, their families, immediate neighbors, St. John residents beyond the boundaries of their community, the plantation landscape, broader island society, and local and global networks of socioeconomics. During the period of slavery, residents of Below Cliff were not restricted in their movements on and off the plantation. Even if prohibitive laws governing the enslaved that sought to curtail their movements were unsuccessful in severing ties between the enslaved and the world outside the plantation, Barbadian Red-legs could more freely engage with those in and around their community. Despite notions of isolation, this analysis of Below Cliff demonstrates that they took advantage of the opportunities that their legal and racial status afforded them.

Legal and racial classificatory differentiations between the enslaved or free Afro-Barbadians and poor whites resulted in inequities. For instance, poor relief was allotted only to poor whites, and poor whites were free to choose their occupations and places of residence—choices that were clearly circumscribed by economic circumstance. Yet the portrayal of community life presented here indicates that despite these differences, there was overlap in how these seemingly disparate groups lived their daily lives. Alterations to the physical landscape show that Below Cliff residents were invested in interacting with their neighbors above the cliff. The complex racial genealogies of former residents show that such interactions went well beyond economic exchanges—the nature of these were, however, complex and not entirely amicable. During and after the period of slavery, Below Cliff was a dynamic community that lived on the plantation landscape but functioned in ways that clashed with planter ideals about how a plantation society should function.

COMMUNITY CONTESTATIONS OF COLONIALISM

The following chapters detail the tensions between the realities of everyday life in Below Cliff and the desires, designs, and disappointments of island elites. These tensions operate at discursive and material levels, pointing to the power of colonial rule on the lives of subjects, as well as their responses that often failed to meet colonial designs and expectations (see Cooper and Stoler, eds. 1997; Delle 2014a). Archaeological studies of the plantation have aptly demonstrated that these spaces were home to the brutal implementation of the inhumanities associated with slavery and, simultaneously, the setting for resilience on the part of the enslaved to develop their own ways of life, resist planter control, and openly rebel against their enslavement. For poor whites living in rural Barbados, the rigid dichotomy and antagonisms were not as explicit or defined. The precarious place of poor whites in island society directly affected how their communities functioned and how they interacted with other Barbadians.

The image of the community presented here is one of seeming contradictions. Below Cliff was a poor white tenantry, but the racial identity of its residents was far from straightforward; the tenantry was abandoned in the 1960s, but it is still an active space of work and memory; residents were cut off from the broader plantation community due to an imposing geological feature, but they facilitated daily interactions with those around them; many Redlegs were impoverished and in need of poor relief, but the tenantry boasted diverse subsistence strategies and cottage industries; the Redlegs were categorized as white and poor, but they lived in a society dependent on white socioeconomic power. Each of these contradictions is based on inconsistencies from available sources. In other words, documents, oral sources, and archaeological materials can weave complex and conflicting narratives at the microlevel (Beaudry 2008; DeCorse 2008). Therefore, I mediate these superfluous contradictions to make sense of a minority that is seemingly out of place in a sugar and slavery society.

The historical archaeological methodologies undertaken to investigate the former tenantry of Below Cliff place marginal spaces and people at the center of the discussion. This focus comes with significant methodological challenges. In particular, it is difficult to trace a population that makes fleeting appearances in the historical record and struggled with economic hardship. The assemblage recovered archaeologically is not quantitatively vast, but when complemented by historical and oral sources, it provides intimate details of how the lives of Below Cliff residents were involved in race- and class-based negotiations on a daily basis. This is not to say that community members were always consciously aware of issues of race and class in their routine interactions with people and their environment. Along the same lines, these mundane items are in no way illustrative of direct resistance on the part of community members against the plantation system of industrial capitalism and race-based slavery. Rather, the data collected assist in building an interpretation of how a community functioned on the margins of the plantation landscape. When placed in the broader, transatlantic context, the lives Below Cliff residents lived demand alternative approaches to how race and class functioned in colonial plantation societies.

FOUR

SOCIOECONOMIC (IN)ACTIVITY

Of all the preposterous assumptions of humanity over humanity, nothing exceeds
most of the criticisms made on the habits of the poor by the well-housed, well-
warmed, and well-fed.

—Herman Melville (1922 [1854]:288)

I nhabitants of Below Cliff struggled with economic hardship. This reality
did not, however, prohibit them from making lives for themselves under
otherwise difficult circumstances. The lives those living under the cliff forged
were a complex amalgam of diverse economic activities that were sometimes entangled with broader modes of plantation production. These entanglements, as well as the economic activities that had ambiguous ties to the
plantation, represent choices made by residents concerning the most practical and desirable ways to subsist on plantation peripheries. These choices are
observable in close readings of the historical record, oral sources about daily
life below the cliff, and the mundane archaeological materials recovered from
excavated households.

Choices community members made were directly related to class positioning and economic limitations. As plantation studies have demonstrated
(Handler and Wallman 2014; Gibson 2009; Armstrong 1990; Delle 2014b),
enslaved laborers undertook diverse means through which to complement
the often-meager provisions planters provided. Poor whites implemented
similar strategies, but their status as free, nominally white, and strapped for
economic means demands an alternative approach to understanding their
position in plantation society. Through an examination of poor white class
positioning and economic activity, this chapter confronts the sharp critiques
that were leveled against poor whites by those far more fortunate. Paternalistic attitudes on the part of island visitors, administrators, and planters led to
condemnations of the Redlegs as well as a host of opinions about what was to
be done with them. Just as there was a lack of consensus among planters and
administrators on how the enslaved should be managed (see Newman 2013),
Barbadian authorities were ambivalent about the governing of and care for
the Redlegs. Vestry minutes suggest that many planters felt that it was their
Christian duty to support this struggling demographic. Others, however,
thought that the group's inherent laziness would prove relief efforts futile. In
general, the poor whites were portrayed as lazy and unwilling to participate
in the sugar industry or any other kind of profitable trade that contributed
to island society. This discourse contributes to the overarching portrayal of

the Redlegs as being marginal and isolated, cut off from broader Barbadian socioeconomics.

This chapter first unpacks this discourse to illustrate how authorities viewed the work habits and economic status of the Redlegs. These sentiments are then put into dialogue with findings from Below Cliff that describe the ways in which community members were connected to economic spheres. I suggest that their involvement in global and intimate economic networks stood in sharp contrast to elite conceptions of labor. This contrast follows Vinay Gidwani's (2008) notion of a "politics of work," whereby laborers choose their own level of involvement in capitalist modes of production, much to the chagrin of elite observers. By elucidating the tensions between historical accounts of the poor whites and realities observed in this case study, I provide more depth than a simple refutation of tired stereotypes and elitist condemnations of the poor. Rather, I illustrate that elite sentiments were based on particular logics surrounding labor and class; these logics, however, were not universal, often conflicting with the ways in which poor whites desired to live their own lives. These frictions relate to deep-seated expectations about labor in capitalist societies on the part of those tasked with monitoring its efficiency (Reilly 2015b).

In reality, Below Cliff residents were active participants in formal and informal economic networks—including networks that involved Afro-Barbadians—that allowed them to make the most of imperfect circumstances. I begin with a discussion of elite portrayals of poor whites and paternalistic strategies developed to deal with the "poor white problem," but I also place emphasis on the everyday lives of Below Cliff residents to understand attitudes about class positioning and economic status on their own terms, or least as interpreted from their possessions and recollections. The material culture recovered from Below Cliff was limited in terms of artifact count, which speaks to restricted consumption power. Theresa Singleton recently noted a similar limitation in her study of the enslaved laborers at a Cuban coffee plantation with a relatively similar period of occupation. In reference to a low artifact count, Singleton poignantly remarks that "a paucity of artifacts does not necessarily imply poverty, nor is it an index of an 'impoverished' culture" (Singleton 2015:183). Those living below the cliff may not have had access to the same material goods as those residing at the great house of Clifton Hall, but what they chose to produce, acquire, use, reuse, exchange, retain, and discard nonetheless reveals much about their lives.

"Nurtured in the Lap of Prejudice and Distinction": Elite Portrayals of the Poor Whites

Seventeenth- to nineteenth-century observers expressed specific sentiments about the laboring habits and general disposition of the poor whites. Examples of these attitudes abound, serving as the only documented descriptions of the Redlegs, thereby clouding any nuanced understanding of their history. Expanding on accounts first presented in chapter 2, other elite portrayals of the Redlegs were explicit in their observations. Henry Nelson Coleridge, the nephew of the bishop of Barbados, who visited the island in 1825, noted that the "greatest part of them [the poor whites] live in a state of complete idleness" (Coleridge 1826:272). In his *Barbadoes, and Other Poems*, Barbadian Matthew Chapman would brand the Redlegs as "idle and insolent" (Chapman 1833:96). During his visit to the island in the late 1840s, Dr. John Davy, in an account originally published in 1854, characterized the poor whites as "indolent and idle, ignorant and improvident, and often intemperate" (Davy 2010:66). Finally, a visiting doctor to the island in 1798, John Williamson, describes them as "tall, awkward made, and ill-looking fellows, much of a Quadroon colour; unmeaning, yet vain of ancestry; a degenerate and useless race as can be imagined" (Williamson 1817:27).

Williamson's passing comment about the phenotype of the Redlegs is intriguing and directly relates to the themes discussed in the final chapters of this book. For the purposes of the argument presented here, these comments illustrate that in the years surrounding emancipation there was a general perception of Redleg laziness that was well ingrained among the Barbadian elite and visitors. If we look to the period of the rise of slavery, we see glimpses of the origins of this discourse. In a 1676 letter from Governor Atkins to the Lords of Trade in England, Atkins would lament the condition of the former indentured servants, arguing that there was "no encouragement and no land for them, nor anything but hard service and small wages." He would further argue that "most come from Ireland and prove very idle; Three blacks work better and cheaper than one white man" (Sainsbury 1893:445). This suggests a long-standing discourse that cast the poor whites as idle due to their lack of participation in the island's dominant economic realm (see Watson 2000b).

Interestingly, the derisive comments concerning poor white idleness first appear at roughly the same time as the earliest recognition that they needed assistance. As early as 1655, minutes from vestry meetings reveal that planters took strides to assuage economic hardship among the poor whites through the allocation of poor relief (BDA D279, 1649–1682:6; see also Marshall 2003). Elites, planters, and authorities made attempts to better the condition of the "deserving poor" through "outright gifts (donations) and capital gifts (endowments) to extend poor relief schemes, to establish educational institutions, to educate select groups of the deserving poor, and to keep churches in good repair" (Marshall 2003:167).[1] While there were multiple motivations for these actions, religious duty certainly played a major role in compelling, and even forcing, residents to provide relief for the island's poor, evidenced in the parish vestry's responsibility in collecting and allocating poor relief funds from parish residents. To reiterate, this relief, however, was only extended to those identified as white, and "non-whites, whether slave or free, were deliberately excluded from participation" (Marshall 2003:167). The parish vestry minutes housed in the Barbados Department of Archives provides a rich resource from which to garner such elite attitudes toward the poor whites, attempts to improve their conditions, and the successes and failures of these attempts.

On June 25, 1655, we find the earliest reference to parish money being collected via taxes to support poor relief. The entry reads that "one pound of suggar p acre be leavyed this yeare for the repairing of the Church and the mantainance of the poore in the pish" (BDA D 279, 1649–1682:6). There is no indication of how this money is to be allocated or to whom. It is not until over a decade later in January 1667 that specific reference is made of a recipient of poor relief: "Ordered from the day above said that Dennis Fallin for his future relief be allowed him eighty pounds of suggar per month" (BDA D 279, 1649–1682:17). The surname Fallin suggests that this individual may have been from Ireland or of Irish descent, but no further information is provided as to why he received relief. It likely stands to reason, however, that only those deemed deserving through an inability to work (illness, injury, or otherwise) would be assisted. From its inception, however, poor relief was not provided on a community-wide basis.[2] Additionally, it is debatable as to whether assistance was actually granted to those deemed deserving of relief given that a 1675 entry notes that "severall persons are refractory in the payment of the said Leavey" (BDA D 279, 1649–1682:31).

Parish vestry minutes are not available for the parish of St. John for the eighteenth century until 1792, by which time the documentation of the poor relief was much more thorough and descriptive. By this time the vestry minutes provide detailed lists of the names of those who were receiving quarterly pensions and how much they were receiving. Through community engagement and the analysis of burial and baptism records for Below Cliff, it is evident that many of the surnames of residents receiving such pensions in the late eighteenth century correspond to the surnames of community members from the nineteenth century to the present. While social mobility was certainly a possibility (twentieth-century examples are well known around the island), this evidence suggests that many Redleg families struggled economically for several generations. For the period 1792–1820, surnames listed include Goddard, Gibson, Norris, Mayers, Ince, Fenty, Charge, Standard,

King, Downey, Marshall, Moore, and Bailey. The parallel in names suggests a minimal amount of relocation or social mobility of these families.

In fact, many of these names found in the poor relief registry correspond to households with known previous inhabitants found on the map in Figure 3.3. While the lack of relocation and social mobility likely has multiple contributing factors, the persistence of these names on such lists suggests limited success on the part of poor relief efforts. In fact, during his stay on the island in the late 1840s, John Davy noted that "some attempts, not I believe very vigorous or long continued, have been made to raise these poor whites from their degraded state, but hitherto without success" (Davy 2010:69–70). He briefly discusses relief efforts on the part of Joshua Steele, an avid supporter of industrial training and relief efforts, as well as government support, which raises doubts as to whether he was concerned with parish-based relief, but his observation about the success of such programs is nonetheless revealing.

Parish vestrymen were aware of the mixed results that their poor relief efforts were having on the poor white population. It is difficult to gauge how relief efforts were reformed on an island scale, but the vestry minutes from the parish of St. Philip (directly south of St. John) offer some insight into how the vestry attempted to reformat the pension system. An 1808 report was delivered to the vestry based on a study carried out by a vestry-appointed commission that investigated each individual case of poor relief to determine the legitimacy of the claim. In half of the 64 cases the commission concluded that the recipients of quarterly pensions were undeserving of the sums they were receiving. While they deemed some unable to work due to disease, illness, old age, or injury, many were said to be capable of some form of industry. Additionally, they determined that many women were having children in order to receive parish support. As they argued (BDA D 273, 1794–1835, Feb. 9, 1808), "Those who receive payment on account of Children, the Pension we consider acts to the discouragement of Industry by taking away the greatest of all Stimulus to exertion, the desire to support our Offspring and rather excites heedless and inconsiderate Poor, to contract Marriage and acquire Families, when they have neither established the means, nor possess the Industry to support them." Instead, the vestry decided, children were to receive clothing. In all, of the 64 individual pension cases, 32 (exactly 50%) were either severed from the poor relief system or received some form of decrease in the funds or services they had been allotted.

Of particular significance is the commission's assessment that poor relief was discouraging recipients from working or contributing to local industry. A similar assumption was expressed in an anonymously authored letter found in the Barbados Council Minutes roughly a generation later in 1847.

During that year the vestry of St. Joseph, the parish directly north of St. John, requested additional funds for poor relief following a severe drought that had evidently hit the poor whites particularly hard. The author, arguing against the allotment of extra funds, was highly critical of the poor relief system, which in the postemancipation era was still reserved for poor whites in an attempt to bolster their position against that of the recently freed Afro-Barbadians. He argued that such relief was the cause of Redleg idleness: "The very means adopted to raise them [the poor whites] above their fellows [Afro-Barbadians] has been the very means to work out their destruction and sink them to the very abyss of misery and woe, they are nurtured in the lap of prejudice and distinction, and thereby despise the means of earning themselves an honest livelihood" (BDA Barbados Council Minutes, 1847). Investigations into the poor relief system are telling of elite perceptions of the poor whites and of poverty in general. In essence, and starkly similar to the sentiments that persist in the twenty-first century, poverty was a self-fulfilling prophecy and a tautology; the Redlegs were lazy and in need of relief, which discouraged them from working and encouraged the cycle of idleness and poverty.

Entries concerning poor relief in the parish vestry minutes are representative of the ambivalent stance elites took on the matter of how to (or not to) assist impoverished parish residents. The parish vestry displayed a continued commitment to providing pensions for those deemed deserving. There were mixed feelings, however, as to who was deemed deserving and how this was to be determined. Ultimately, the record indicates that elites were unhappy with the poor relief system, judging it to encourage idle lifestyles and perpetuate the cycle of Redleg poverty. Comfortable with the adage that the poor whites were impoverished because of their own laziness, little is documented concerning how individuals and communities supported themselves or made their livings. Before turning to archaeological findings from Below Cliff, I first look to registries of baptisms, marriages, and burials in an attempt to elucidate how Below Cliff residents were defined occupationally in official records.

Planters, Laborers, Carpenters, and Domestics: Occupational Identity and Class Positioning in Below Cliff

The significance of parish registries of baptisms, marriages, and burials goes well beyond their genealogical value; these documents are integral in generating a semblance of local demographics, residence patterns, marriage practices, mortality rates, average ages, and occupational statuses, among other localized patterns and practices.[3] From the outset it is pertinent to again note the power dynamics inherent in the production (and use and interpretation) of official records; censuses and registries are prime examples of documents through which power is manifest (Cohn and Dirks 1988; Stoler 2009; Comaroff and Comaroff 1991). Following James Scott (1988), Michel-Rolph Trouillot's concept of "identification effects" views the census (among other official registries) as one of the "theoretical and empirical tools that classify and regulate collectivities" (2003:90). With this in mind, I focus on how occupational identities are understood, classified, and documented, and what these identifications reveal about how labor was conceptualized in Barbados.

Detailed registries for the parish of St. John begin in 1825, nine years before emancipation. Therefore, the registries reflect labor patterns among the poor white population during a period of significant transformations on the island. Following emancipation, it is possible to make informed assumptions about the identities of the formerly enslaved in the historical record. Additionally, in 1862 St. Margaret's Church opened its doors at the bottom of the cliff, which quickly became the religious institution of choice for Below Cliff residents, who made up a major component of the church's congregation. While the years represented in this sample are not necessarily indicative of patterns that were established in earlier centuries, given that the region was inhabited for a long period of time through a pattern of consanguinity, similarities in labor patterns are likely to be found throughout earlier generations. This also stands to reason given that the economic landscape remained committed to sugar production throughout the period of slavery and well into the postemancipation era.

Baptismal, marriage, and burial registries were organized in a standard and more detailed format in the parish of St. John (and across the island) beginning in 1825. Information expected to be provided included the name of the individual (first and last name), age (in the case of marriage and burial), names of parents (in the case of baptism and marriage), place of residence, and occupation or occupation of the individual's father. Despite standard organization, the recording of information was left in the hands of the reverends presiding over official ceremonies. Unfortunately, throughout the St. John and St. Margaret registries, information was sporadically recorded with several omissions and inconsistencies, making a holistic interpretation of the data impossible but nonetheless significant in gleaning partial understandings of labor patterns.[4] Given that occupation data is particularly scarce in burial and marriage records from St. John and St. Margaret's, only information compiled from baptismal registries will be considered here. Of the records analyzed from 1825 to 1965 there were 878 individuals baptized with a place of residence given as Below Cliff or Clifton Hall.[5] Of these 878 baptized children, occupations for their fathers (or, in select cases, the mother) are provided for 462 individuals, or roughly 52.6% of individuals. Of the occupations listed, laborer was the most common mode of employment of Below Cliff residents, accounting for 222 (or roughly 48%) of the 462 occupations given. Other common occupations listed were planters (small farmers), carpenters, fishermen, shoemakers, bookkeepers, and policemen.[6]

Distinct patterns are noticeable in each individual volume consulted, indicating that perspectives on employment changed with time and the individual recording the information. For instance, in the 1825–1848 baptismal registry for St. John, 67 (33.2%) of the 202 individuals registered had fathers who were described as planters. In sharp contrast, of the 262 individuals baptized at St. Margaret's between 1863 and 1965, only five (1.9%) are listed as planters. There is no clear explanation for this phenomenon, but there are a number of possibilities for the dramatic drop. It is possible that the change is simply representative of the nature of record keeping at the two different churches. This seems unlikely, however, since several different reverends were documenting baptisms at each location, and there seems to be no direct relationship between specific reverends and how occupations were documented. This could also reflect a shift in vernacular throughout the nineteenth century of how small farmers were documented. There may be some truth to this hypothesis, but the fact that the term *planter* still appears well into the twentieth century casts doubt on this suggestion.

I argue that as the period of slavery drew to a close, and as discourse concerning poor white idleness became more socially ingrained, changes took place in how authorities perceived poor white labor. Based on how individuals are listed in baptismal registries, it is possible, to a fair degree of certainty, to ascertain whether an individual was a formerly enslaved Afro-Barbadian. Following emancipation, many formerly enslaved Afro-Barbadians chose to be baptized in local parish churches (Welch 2013). These individuals were, therefore, listed as "adults," and when their children were baptized they were typically listed without a surname. Of note, of those individuals believed to be formerly enslaved Afro-Barbadians, none are listed as planters or having a planter father. This suggests that prior to emancipation and immediately in its wake, there was an explicit attempt to differentiate poor white labor and occupational identity from that of Afro-Barbadians, regardless of how their occupations differed in reality. The fact that formerly enslaved Afro-Barbadians were residing in Below Cliff following emancipation speaks directly to interracial interaction, the topic of discussion in the following chapter. At this juncture, however, we can briefly expand on what these labor patterns reflect about elite conceptions of labor and work.

The designation of *planter* may have been assigned to poor white small farmers whose labor needed to be explicitly distinguished from that of the formerly enslaved. Therefore, shortly after emancipation, when the labor of Afro-Barbadians and Redlegs was legally held to the same standard, the designation of planter nearly vanishes from the registries. More pertinent to our discussion of class relations, however, is the lack of specificity for the overwhelming majority of occupations given. Of the 462 occupations provided, 222 were listed as laborers and 72 were listed as planters, thus comprising roughly 64% of all occupations provided. Specific information about the labor being undertaken is lacking, so it is impossible to determine whether individuals work in the sugar fields, in the works, as mechanics on machinery, or any other of the host of "laboring" positions available in the region. Cast simply as laborers or planters, the roles of the poor whites are officially documented as being unskilled and even unnecessary in the case of those simply left out.

Additionally, patterns emerge when gaps are observed and analyzed in the registries. For instance, throughout particular date ranges when occupations are seldom listed, an occupation was far more likely to be recorded if the individual had a more skilled occupation, such as a carpenter, shoemaker, bookkeeper, fisherman, or police officer. Read as an artifact, the registry data reflect a particular ideology of capitalist labor where individual identities are attached to single occupations. Just as clocks (Smith 1994) or ceramics (Leone 1999, 2005) can be representative of the imposition of routine, order, possessive individualism, and discipline in capitalistic labor patterns (see also Glennie and Thrift 1996; Thompson 1967), so too can we view these registries as an attempt to order, classify, and identify individuals by their singular perceived role. Additionally, we can view the omission of occupations as a possible way of inscribing their livelihoods as out of sync with, antithetical to, or unimportant within the imposed order, taxonomy, and ideology of labor. It is then possible to trace the connection between discourses of poor white idleness and how labor was perceived and organized on the plantation landscape. In other words, Redlegs were portrayed as lazy or idle because their occupational identities frequently failed to meet authoritative expectations about productive and contributive forms of labor.

Even if derisive, observer accounts of plantation life were often more verbose in their descriptions of the work undertaken by the poor whites. John Davy describes their livelihoods in the 1840s as follows (Davy 2010:68–69):

> Those who possess a little land, or who rent a few acres, cultivate chiefly those crops which require least labour, and the smallest means, such as ground provisions, arrowroot, aloes, and perhaps a little cotton. I have seen

one of them at work on his ground in a manner not a little characteristic; a hoe in one hand, an umbrella in the other, which he held over his head, and a face cloth over his face. Some who have been taught to read and write, are engaged as book-keepers by the proprietors of the larger estates, with a pay of about six dollars a month, and board and lodging. Some are chiefly occupied in fishing, and that of a simple kind, by means of the casting net, and are to be seen exercising their skill on the shore, almost among the breakers, apparently at the risk of their lives. Some gain a livelihood as carters and grooms, and some as field labourers, a kind of occupation which, when slaves only were employed in field labour, would have been resisted by them as an insupportable degradation, and even now is only engaged in from necessity, and with good reason, for they are ill fitted for such work.

Rev. Nicholls, who was asked by Parliament of the economic and subsistence activities undertaken by the poor whites in 1790, reported that many worked as "carpenters, joiners, masons, coppersmiths, blacksmiths, shoemakers, taylors, and others; and also some of the poorer whites spin cotton for the lamps in the boiling houses; whites are also employed in the coasting vessels, and as fishermen" (HCPP 1790:334–335). These descriptions can be read in one of two ways: (1) as the single occupations of poor white Barbadians, as they are often listed in registries, or (2) any number of activities that individuals undertake to make a living (see Handler 1966). The latter is more likely in settings like Below Cliff where community members could, for example, harvest crops from their provision grounds in the morning, fish in the afternoon, and assist in the construction of a neighbor's house in the evening.

As is evident from this discussion, the official registries are laden with power structures and particular capitalistic and individualistic logics that can mask the nuances of communal economic activities. Despite the fact that those recording this information were not members of the plantocracy, parish priests were central figures within the political infrastructure, especially since the established church held considerable power on the island. Although significant, these interpretations are based on a top-down official record that contains purposeful and significant silences (Trouillot 1995). Following Ann Laura Stoler, the colonial archive can be treated "both as a corpus of writing and as a force field that animates political energies and expertise, that pulls on some 'social facts' and converts them into qualified knowledge, that attends to some ways of knowing while repelling and refusing others" (Stoler 2009:22). Some forms of knowledge were repelled and refused in the production (and, in some cases, the interpretation) of the historical record—in this case, concealing the dynamics of everyday life that failed to neatly comport with simple categorization.

INSTABILITY AND THE BARBADIAN CHATTEL HOUSE

Alternative readings of historical sources provide glimmers of how communities like Below Cliff survived on a tumultuous landscape for several centuries. Of the harsh stereotypes leveled against the poor white population, observations of poverty did have some level of validity. Simply alleging that Redleg community members lived in poverty, however, does little to explicate or understand the realities of economic hardship, or the strategies employed to counter their effects. With that in mind, before delving into how the archaeological record lends itself to an interpretation of poor white relations to capital and other informal networks, I turn to the relationship between the physical environment and vernacular architecture; where and how Below Cliff residents chose to build their houses was constrained by plantation geography, the availability of affordable land, and restrictions posed by volatile geology.

The location of former households throughout the forested region below the cliff was determined by the visibility of articulated limestone foundations. Limestone is ubiquitous across the island, and large boulders and small fragments are abundant below Hackleton's Cliff due to frequent rockslides. Rockslides can be unpredictable, but the onslaught of heavy rains, especially during powerful hurricanes, increases their likelihood. Despite the bounty of limestone noted in the region, some of which was collected and carved for use as groundsels, there were few examples of complete walls. In most cases, as is still the favored construction technique for boarded houses on the island, limestone was placed underneath the walls as needed to support the structure, rather than contiguously around the entirety of the perimeter. Additionally, as house sites became abandoned, the former foundation stones were frequently reappropriated for use at a new site. In some cases, housing platforms appear to be haphazardly constructed, uneasily supporting houses that, especially in the more hilly regions, could seemingly collapse with the slightest disturbance.

Ephemerality was, and is, a central characteristic of this form of vernacular architecture, making its roots and physical vestiges sometimes difficult to trace. Not surprisingly, similarities in the vernacular form of houses found below the cliff can be seen in those built by Afro-Barbadians. The histories of these vernacular forms, however, are largely treated separately. In Barbados, as on other islands, former villages for enslaved laborers are often located on long-abandoned and dangerous hillsides, in fields that have been deep plowed for the production of sugar, or buried under housing or tourist development.

Figure 4.1. Example of the vernacular form known as the Barbadian chattel house. (Courtesy of Lynda Lewis)

While the histories and specifics of the domestic forms for the enslaved have been traced (see Handler and Bergmen 2009; Watson and Potter 1993, 2001), poor whites have largely been omitted from these discussions. To remedy this omission, I suggest that poor whites and Afro-Barbadians used a similar, if not the same, architectural form—the chattel house—to cope with unstable environments, land and labor policies, and socioeconomic hardship. However, these forms were developed under different circumstances.

The chattel house is said to have origins in the postemancipation era (Fraser and Kiss 2011; Watson and Potter 2001:53–57). The 1840 Masters and Servants Act gave rise to plantation tenantries for the formerly enslaved on which residents constructed their homes and worked for wages on the plantation. An important caveat, however, was that they did not own the land on which their homes rested. If residents were evicted or chose to move, they would be able to disassemble the boarded walls and have community members assist in carrying the walls to a new housing platform. In their most basic forms, chattel houses were "a movable two-room cabin, approximately 18 by 10 feet in dimension and built on a loose rock-pile foundation" with a hipped roof (Watson and Potter 1993:376) (Figure 4.1). As residents accumulated enough capital or as families grew, additional rooms could be added onto the original structure. As evidenced by the environment found below the cliff, however, such architectural forms were also practical in recognizing the ephemeral nature of housing structures due to rockslides. If a rockslide damaged portions of a boarded house or disturbed the immediate landscape, it was relatively easy for community members to move the structure to a new location. This is not to suggest that poor whites were the first to build chattel houses on the island or that they developed the vernacular tradition. A claim of origins would be far less significant than highlighting the ways in which nonelite populations developed strategies to mitigate their respective circumstances of hardship.

Evidence of such household ephemerality abounds below the cliff. One of the most articulated limestone foundations was found at the Norris household, described in the previous chapter. The remains of the foundation that once supported the home sit atop a raised platform consisting of a mix of earth and rubble limestone. The remaining foundation stones demarcate a structure that had dimensions of 6.6 by 3.9 meters (or 19.8 by 11.7 feet), slightly larger than the specifications outlined by Watson and Potter. Oral histories confirm the chattel house form of the Norris home, but little was known about the previous household(s). A rubble pile under the housing platform, however, suggests that there was at least one previous structure in the same location. Although the orientation of the previous foundation is difficult to assess due to the state of disarticulation, it appears that there would have been a slightly different orientation and positioning than the stones representing more recent occupation. A plan view map of the Norris household (see Figure 3.5) illustrates the existence of a well-articulated foundation wall below the surface and slightly to the northeast of the structure. Additionally, limestone rubble to the foundation's northeast and northwest may be the ruins of an even earlier foundation. It is possible that a rockslide damaged the previous structure and altered the immediate landscape in such a way that the new structure had to be reoriented to sit flat on the new platform surface. The distinction here between rubble and ruins is important, where the former bears negative connotations of lacking form while the latter is more commonly assigned an aura associated with a particular function or meaning (Gordillo 2014:9–10). Both, however, speak to ruin as a process and verb, suggesting the persistence and afterlives of these structures. This suggests a commitment on the part of residents to remain in this particular location. Perhaps the occupants had a particular attachment to the location through either family ties or a relatively fertile yard area in which to grow crops, or, more likely, residents had few or no alternative places to live.

Excavations reached surprising depths in the units within the interior of the Norris's former home. As excavations reached 30 cm in depth, it became abundantly clear that previous rockslides or the material detritus of such events played a major role in the taphonomic processes of the site. While soil consistencies varied slightly from unit to unit, Level 1 (0–10/15 cm) contained the most recent occupation layer in loamy dark brown/black soil that transitioned to a compact clay soil, which may have been the floor surface found under the boards of the previous occupation phase. Level 2 (15–30 cm) was a compact, claylike deposit. While these stratigraphic layers were rather straightforward, excavation and interpretation proved difficult once the loose rubble layer appeared in Level 3 (30 cm). Depths of 30 to 80 cm were dominated by limestone rubble from smaller-sized stones (diameters from roughly 5 to 10 cm) toward the top of the context to larger stones (diameters from roughly 10 to 20 cm) closer to 80 cm. Trowels were often abandoned as stones were removed by hand. From 80 to 110 cm, soil returned, replacing the loose limestone and indicating another habitation layer. From 110 cm to bedrock (the depth of which varied depending on the unit, but it was roughly hit between 190 and 200 cm) limestone rubble reappeared, ultimately leading to tremendous boulders (well over 100 lbs.) at the bottom of excavation units before reaching bedrock. Excavations persisted, despite difficulties, due to the fact that material culture was found throughout each of these contexts, with imported ceramics frequently found wedged between loose limestone fragments. In fact, two sherds of sponge-decorated whiteware were found resting atop the bedrock directly underneath a tremendous boulder at the base of one of the units.

The stratigraphy suggests at least two separate destruction or (re)construction episodes evidenced by the two thick layers of limestone rubble (see Figure 3.6). Additionally, the presence of material culture throughout the limestone layers suggests that residents may have been piling trash as well as limestone to level the housing platform following a slide or storm in order to rebuild or replace a boarded chattel house. The rubble layers also pose an interpretive conundrum given that stratigraphic integrity may be disturbed. For instance, within the limestone fill layer between 30 and 80 cm, small fragments of plastic were uncovered. These twentieth-century bits of material culture were inconsistent with the early to mid-nineteenth-century imported ceramics, and their presence may be due to the fact that the limestone layer was not capped, allowing materials to literally slip through the cracks and become imbedded in deeper contexts. For this household, there is no evidence to suggest a gap in habitation. As such, it appears that following the destructive consequences of a rockslide or other instances of destruction, residents simply began the rebuilding process at the same location.

Other house sites in the tenantry reflect a similar ephemerality but with significant gaps in occupation periods. The last house site to be excavated was the former home of Gorringe and Hampden Gibson (referred to as the Gibson household in chapter 3). Excavation units placed on the exterior of the foundation were similarly littered with limestone rubble, but not to the degree or depth found in the Norris homestead. Despite the abundance of limestone rubble, a change in soil color signaled a new stratigraphic context after roughly 30–40 cm (depending on the excavation unit). Surface and Level 1 finds date to the mid to late nineteenth century and twentieth century based on the presence of plastics, ironstone, and whiteware. In Level 2, few imported ceramics were recovered with the exception of barley-patterned white salt-glazed stoneware sherds dating to the mid-eighteenth century. These sherds were uncovered in the same context as five cross-mending sherds of a green, lead-glazed coarse earthenware flatware (Figure 4.2). The presence of the white salt-glazed stoneware in a stratigraphic lens directly beneath a mid to late nineteenth-century context suggests that the house site had been abandoned at some point in the mid to late eighteenth century and reoccupied roughly a century later. The absence of evidence is not necessarily evidence of absence, but a clear stratigraphic division and temporal break in represented imported refined earthenwares suggests a gap in occupation.

Evidence from these house sites suggests that rockslides or other destructive events like hurricanes were an everyday threat to the lives and well-being of Below Cliff residents. This archaeological evidence in conjunction with the oral histories collected from former residents sheds light on the often-undocumented realities of life in unstable environments (Reilly 2016a). There are two such documented cases of individuals potentially being injured by rockslides. The vestry minutes of St. Philip reveal that in January 1826, John Thomas Goddard needed to have his arm amputated, "occasioned by the crush of a large stone" (BDA D273, 1794–1835). In July 1897, a similar incident occurred in which a woman was badly injured by falling rock in the parish of St. John. She was taken to her home in Glenburnie to await medical treatment, meaning that she may have sustained her injuries in the nearby area below the cliff (BDA D279, 1896–1901). Living with an unstable environment presented real dangers to residents who oftentimes lacked the means to move elsewhere. Of course, economic factors were not the only forces that compelled families to stay or go. Given the rich kinship networks that existed below the cliff, familial considerations certainly weighed heavily in processes of place-making and developing a sense of home. However, living on this unaccommodating landscape proved less than desirable on a number of levels.

CONSTRICTED CONSUMPTION

Observing taphonomy in the archaeological record provides a window

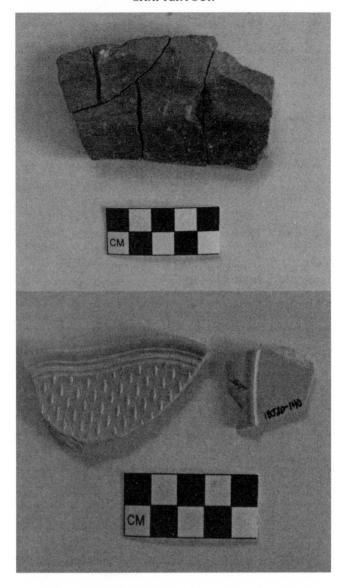

Figure 4.2. Cross-mended coarse earthenware base sherds from a shallow bowl or platter (*top*); white salt-glazed stoneware decorated with a barley motif (*bottom*). Sherds recovered from the Gibson household. (Matthew C. Reilly)

into how community residents coped with environmental instability, using the rubble of destruction as the building blocks of reconstruction (Dawdy 2006a). Similar strategies are also observable in the banal material culture of everyday life. In brash economic terms impoverishment is associated with a general lack of access to resources, amenities, services, and a certain quality of life. States or degrees of impoverishment are therefore of interest to archaeologists because they have explicit material correlates. Despite a relative lack of material goods consumed, used, and discarded at sites inhabited by those struggling with poverty when compared with sites occupied by those with access to more resources, those materials that *are* present reflect how economic limitations affect residents' access to goods, their consumption choices, how materials were used, how they were repurposed, and how they enter the archaeological record. Here I explore both presences and absences, or what individual and groups of artifacts reveal about the realities of hardship with which Below Cliff residents coped. In recognizing the reality of material inequality, I tacitly avoid allowing poverty to define the individuals being discussed. A balance is needed in which the structural roots of inequality are openly critiqued while those who suffer from such inequities are not essentialized or victimized by condemnations often extended toward the poor (Orser 2011; Spencer-Wood and Matthews, eds. 2011; Rimmer et al. 2011; Reilly 2016b).

I first turn to one of the most ubiquitous forms of material culture traditionally found at historical archaeological sites: ceramics. Ceramic analysis has long been linked to interpretations of socioeconomic class. Most notably, George Miller (1980, 1991) developed his CC index to classify English-made ceramics on a scale of market value in order to interpret the general socioeconomic positioning of those who consumed and used the goods (see also Spencer-Wood 1987; for consumer culture see Mullins 2012). This approach has been critiqued for being economically deterministic, eschewing consumer tastes and symbolic meaning (Camp 2011:17; Cook et al. 1996), and additionally for its failure to account for market availability (Brighton 2001). The latter is particularly significant when considering an island colony at the southeastern extreme of the Caribbean region. As its economic significance waned at the turn of the nineteenth century, market availability may have played an increasingly important role in consumption.[7] Despite the shortcomings of the CC index, the reality of limited means reminds us that economic standing severely hinders one's options when consuming goods.

In total, 1,055 ceramic sherds were collected from the three households excavated. This is a relatively small number considering the excavations undertaken. To reiterate points made earlier, however, the scarcity of material culture should not stand as a simple correlate to poverty. Rather, the ceramics present need to be properly contextualized in order to adequately interpret what the absences and presences reveal about the consumers and users of these items. Of the 1,055 sherds 307 were coarse earthernwares and 748 were imported refined earthenwares (see Table 3.1).

The coarse earthenwares have yet to undergo XRF or neutron activation analysis, and it is, therefore, difficult to assess whether these sherds definitively represent locally made or imported vessels. Diagnostic sherds, however, reveal that locally made vessel forms are present (more on these vessels will be provided in the following chapter). Additionally, the fact that only 21 of the 307 coarse earthenwares recovered were readily identifiable as industrial wares (those used in the industrial process of sugar production, like cones and drip jars) suggests that Below Cliff residents were actively participating in local markets to acquire domestic wares, rather than repurposing industrial sugar wares at any large scale. This may suggest that Below Cliff residents had restricted access to industrial wares due to their limited involvement in the plantation economy. In terms of cost, locally produced goods would generally provide a more affordable alternative to imported ceramics (see Scheid 2015 for a discussion of local ceramic production; for locally produced ceramic markets in Jamaica, see Hauser 2008).

The imported ceramics, which constituted roughly 71% of the total ceramic assemblage, were entirely produced in Britain (England and Scotland) and ranged from white salt-glazed stoneware (only found in small numbers at the house site of Hampden and Gorringe Gibson) to twentieth-century decaled porcelaneous stoneware. The ephemerality and frailty of the landscape dramatically affected the condition of the wares found. Hampden and Gorringe Gibson's house site had likely been occupied by a family at some point in the mid to late eighteenth century and, as a result, common late eighteenth- and early nineteenth-century wares like pearlwares and creamwares were entirely absent. The Norris homestead had a similar assemblage, with no creamware and only minimal pearlware sherds recovered (23 total sherds). Additionally, few large sherds were recovered. The overwhelming majority of sherds recovered are small in size, seldom measuring more than 5 cm in length (Figure 4.3). It is possible that the rocky and unstable environment caused significant damage to ceramics before and after deposition. The ceramics collected from the excavation units placed within the walkway adjacent to the former home of the Norris family displayed similar signs of breakage, likely due to frequent foot traffic and trampling.

The variety of imported ceramics reveals interesting consumption patterns and choices in addition to illustrating the occupational periods of the households. While a small amount of pearlware was present (roughly 3.5% of the total imported ceramic assemblage), the majority of the assemblage has manufacture dates from the 1820s onward, with a preponderance of whiteware,

Figure 4.3. Sample of transfer print whiteware sherds recovered from various households in Below Cliff. (Matthew C. Reilly)

yellowware, and ironstone (in total, accounting for 84.4% of the total imported ceramics). Surface collections from a household just northwest of the Norris household, said to be occupied by relatives of the Norris family, revealed an abundance of decaled porcelaneous stoneware dating to the twentieth century. When considered as a whole, the limited sample size of ceramics indicates that the tenantry households were primarily occupied in the decades leading up to emancipation (1810–1830) through the mid-twentieth century, a date range that complements those provided through historical and oral sources. However, a lag between ceramic manufacture dates and occupation period may exist due to market availability and the fact that those with limited economic means may have held on to household goods for longer periods of time. Despite these caveats, the rough chronologies likely hold water. Archaeological evidence has yet to confirm if the community was inhabited prior to the mid-eighteenth century, but clues from the historical record do seem to hint that mid-seventeenth-century occupation was possible.

Interestingly, there was a significant amount of Scottish sponged-ware sherds. This ware type is roughly contemporaneous with its English-made counterpart, with production beginning in the 1830s. There are, however, noticeable differences in the decoration between the two. First, the color

Figure 4.4. Sample of sponge-decorated whitewares manufactured in England (*left*) and Scotland (*right*). (Matthew C. Reilly)

schemes differ, with blue being the favored color on the English version and maroon and dark green frequently appearing on the Scottish. Additionally, the Scottish version typically has a black annular band around the rim of the vessel. The differences also extend to the application of the decoration. As can be seen in Figure 4.4, the decoration is more crudely applied in the case of the Scottish wares. Typically, the colors run outside of their designated boundaries and appear rather sloppy when compared with the English sponged decoration (Cruickshank 2005; Kelly 1999). The differences in decoration allowed for a distinction to be made between the two types of sponged-ware. Of 88 sherds decorated with the sponge technique, 46 were readily identifiable as Scottish. One sherd even had a maker's mark reading "Glasgow." Of the 748 imported ceramic sherds recovered, 11.8% were identified as being decorated using the sponge technique, with 52.3% of these wares being of the Scottish variety. It is likely that several of the undecorated sherds belonged to vessels bearing sponged decorations along with rim sherds that solely displayed a black annular band. It is therefore fair to say that sponged-wares make up a substantial portion of the ceramic assemblage in Below Cliff. Unfortunately, as noted by Webster (1999:60), many of these Scottish wares were frequently unmarked, making it difficult to readily assign place of manufacture. While the specific site of production may be difficult to determine with any certainty, the sponge technique and its appearance can be reliably associated with Scotland. As Webster notes, "Although sponge-printed wares were made by many English potteries, particularly in Staffordshire, the technique of sponge-printing has always been particularly identified with Scotland" (Webster 1999:68).[8]

More pertinent to this discussion, these Scottish wares were less expensive than English alternatives. Despite the lack of specific market values, Webster categorizes these wares as belonging to the "bottom end of the ceramics market" (Webster 1999:60). In considering Stephen Brighton's argument surrounding market availability (2001:20–21), it does not appear as if Below Cliff residents or Barbadians in general lacked access to English-produced whitewares (including sponged-wares). At the risk of generalizing due to a lack of quantitative data, whitewares are ubiquitous artifacts throughout the island, often littering the ground surface in fields and urban areas. It is therefore unlikely that Below Cliff residents had difficulty getting their hands on such relatively affordable vessels. While we may posit that local taste was a prerequisite for the purchase of Scottish wares, a more likely explanation is that limited economic means hindered consumption choices and that residents frequently chose the more affordable option. Scottish sponged-wares were also found during surface collections of a mid-nineteenth-century tenantry inhabited by the formerly enslaved at the Mount Plantation, St. George, in 2011 (Finch et al. 2013; Finch 2015). As noted by Jonathan Finch (2015:204), preferences for certain patterns or motifs can be indicative of consumer choice in such contexts (see also Wilkie and Farnsworth 2005), but it is equally likely that limited economic means constricted the choices of inhabitants of tenantries like Below Cliff.

MAKING ENDS MEET THROUGH ARTIFACT REUSE

In addition to limiting consumption power, economic hardship is also pertinent to discussions of artifact reuse. Indeed, limited means can be indicative of individual and group attempts to remain "independent and self-sufficient" (Gray 2011:68). In acknowledging the economic circumstances that led residents of Below Cliff to reuse particular materials, it is also necessary to laud their ingenuity while carefully avoiding assumptions about functionality. In Below Cliff artifact reuse is best exemplified when glass shards and tin can fragments are complemented by evidence from oral sources. In total, 769 glass shards/bottles were collected. Significantly, of these 769 shards and whole bottles, 478 (roughly 62%) were collected from the surface or within the first level of unit excavation.[9] Based on limited stratigraphy, as well as the machine-made production method on the complete bottles collected, more than half of the glass recovered was manufactured in the late nineteenth and twentieth centuries.

Despite few diagnostic shards from deeper contexts, it is still possible to generate some initial interpretations about consumption and, in considering oral sources, how glass items were reused. Most glass was from bottles produced to hold beer, wine, mineral water, soda, pharmaceutical products, and spirits (Figure 4.5). Condiment and ointment jars along with mineral water and soda bottles were predominantly found on the surface, some with decals still present. Decals and production techniques indicate that most were twentieth-century bottles. Scattered Banks Beer bottles, the national brand of beer that began production in 1961, suggests that even after the tenantry was formally abandoned, the wooded area was used for small-scale agriculture or any number of other purposes. Dates associated with manufacturing methods of select bottles overlap with those garnered from imported ceramics, but many of the diagnostic shards represent more recently manufactured bottles. When present, seam lines indicated nineteenth- and twentieth-century mold production techniques.

Of the pre-mid-twentieth-century glass, a preponderance of beer, wine, and liquor bottle glass is of particular interest. In total, bottle glass composed roughly 87% of the entire glass assemblage, the overwhelming majority of which likely being from alcohol bottles.[10] Alcohol bottles can naturally lead to conclusions about alcohol consumption, and poor whites, like most Barbadians, certainly drank. Such an interpretation, however, must be carefully weighed with the evidence at hand and the proper social context. In general, stereotypes of alcoholism often went hand in hand with idleness. An anonymous author recollected his experiences in Bridgetown prior to 1805, and of the poor whites he notes (*Sketches and Recollections* 1828:27): "Few of [the poor whites] have been well educated, or bred to any business or profession; or, if they have, they are too proud or indolent to follow it. . . . In no other colony is the same number of unemployed whites to be met with as in Barbados. Many of them differing little in dress and mode of life from their slaves. Some, indeed, cultivate their lands, raise stock, and sell fruits and vegetables, by which they earn a livelihood; but the majority prefer billiards, smoking, and drinking, to any useful employment." While stopping in the Scotland District during an island tour in 1837, Thome and Kimball would similarly comment that the poor whites "live promiscuously, are drunken, licentious, and poverty-striken,—a body of the most squalid and miserable human beings" (Thome and Kimball 1838:57). Alcohol was widely available and consumed by Barbadians (Smith 2008:118), and, as Frederick Smith points out, alcohol had a number of important social functions, but there is nonetheless a strong correlation between idleness and drunkenness in attitudes expressed about the poor throughout the Anglo-Atlantic world during this period. As Smith (2008:81) notes, "temperance was closely linked to middle-class notions of respectability," even if patent medicines were high in alcohol content and alcohol consumption was widespread among all classes.

Figure 4.5. Glass artifacts from Below Cliff. Leaded glass tumbler base and black glass beer bottle base (*top left*); sample of pharmaceutical glass and stemware (*bottom left*); full Black & White Scotch whisky bottle (*right*). (Matthew C. Reilly)

These attitudes reflect particular logics about acceptable modes of work and proper/civil forms of behavior. The high quantity of glass from alcohol bottles could then support the stereotype of high alcohol consumption among Barbadian Redlegs, and, to a degree, the consumption of alcohol was quite likely. In considering oral sources provided by local residents, however, an alternative interpretation that combines alcohol consumption and bottle reuse is equally plausible. A complete Black & White Scotch whisky bottle was recovered from the trash pit adjacent to the Norris household (see Figure 4.5). The company started production in 1884, and this particular bottle was produced between 1890 and 1910. Given the expense of this imported item and the ubiquity of rum consumption on the island, the presence of such a bottle might seem a bit odd. Despite its 1890–1910 production date, a former resident of the household, now in his seventies, remembered the bottle as being used as a container for water throughout his childhood. Given its distinct features and its association with the household, there is little reason to doubt a former resident's claim that the bottle was used to collect and hold water. While the nature of this particular bottle's acquisition by a member of the Norris family is speculative, it is possible that as a gardener at Clifton Hall, the male head of household acquired it from a manager or the owner following the emptying of its initial contents. Additionally, it is possible that a community member had purchased or stolen the bottle for a special occasion. Regardless, in conjunction with oral sources, the archaeological record suggests that items were used for very long periods of time and for purposes outside their original functions. It should also be noted that, archaeologically, a similar phenomenon of bottle reuse has been suggested by Paul Farnsworth (1999:127) in the Bahamas and John Chenoweth (2017:132) in the British Virgin Islands on sites associated with enslaved populations.

During a trip through the woods with another former resident for the specific purpose of documenting oral histories, we spotted several shattered alcohol bottles found resting underneath large stones. According to the former resident, the limestone had at one time functioned as a dripstone, with the alcohol bottles collecting the water that had been naturally purified after passing through the porous rock. In his study of alcohol-related bottles in Barbadian caves, Smith (2008) has suggested that these spaces were inconspicuous locales in which the enslaved gathered to consume alcohol and plot rebellion. More specifically, he posits that early nineteenth-century alcohol bottles recovered from Mapps Cave in the parish of St. Philip may have been associated with the planning of the rebellion of 1816 (also known as Bussa's Rebellion) that began in the same parish. While Smith's hypothesis is certainly plausible, it might be equally plausible that alcohol bottles had been placed in caves to collect water from dripstones. Alcohol consumption was pervasive across the island, but so was the need for efficient water procurement, especially in the years prior to standpipes that pumped water to local residents and on an island that generally lacks fresh water. In short, the use of glass bottles below the cliff need not be an either/or scenario. Alcohol may have been readily consumed by community members who then reused the bottles for water procurement, storage, and consumption.

Of the 769 shards only 39 were identified as being from glassware/stemware vessels. Vessels represented include at least two tumblers along with a possible decanter, the shards of which accounted for nearly 25% of the glassware shards recovered. The shortage of drinking vessels sparked questions regarding the use of relatively common household items such as cups and glasses. Answers came through the solicitation of local residents and analysis of metal artifacts. The tropical climate poses challenges for the recovery of metal artifacts, and this proved to be the case during excavations in Below

Cliff. Few metal artifacts were collected at depths greater than 30 cm, and those that were recovered from the first 30 cm were severely corroded, small, and difficult to identity. It was, however, possible to identify small fragments of tin cans based on rims and the thickness and shape of the fragments. The tin can fragments were initially given minimal consideration beyond their function as containers for canned goods until conversations with community members. Collected oral traditions confirmed that tin cans were frequently reused as drinking vessels (Figure 4.6). This repurposing of tin cans was common across the island, as tin handles were hafted to cans to allow for seamless transport and drinking.

There is no direct evidence of smithing in the Below Cliff tenantry, making it impossible to definitively conclude that tin can fragments are directly associated with drinking. Given the oral sources, however, it is highly likely that such material reuse was taking place to some extent. The revelation that tin can fragments were reuse items illustrates the significance of collecting oral traditions and speaking with local community members throughout the archaeological process (for more on the significance of oral sources see DeCorse and Chouin 2003; DeCorse 2013:12–16; Jones and Russell, eds. 2012). For members of the Below Cliff community, innocuous bits of tin represented the quotidian ways in which those with limited means used the items at their disposal to cope with their circumstances.

My discussions with local residents further proved essential in analyzing and interpreting a diverse assortment of buttons recovered from households, particularly the Norris homestead. In all, 96 buttons were recovered, with all but five being found in Levels 1–3 of the Norris home, from deposits dating from the mid to late nineteenth century to the mid-twentieth century. These buttons also came from units within the interior of the household. Buttons were diverse in terms of material (bone, ceramic, plastic, shell, and metal), size (ranging from 9.4 mm in diameter to 20.2 mm), color, and decoration (Figure 4.7). Of the 96 buttons, there is not a single matching pair despite the fact that multiple buttons were recovered from single contexts within the interior of the household.

The large number of buttons found in these household units, combined with evidence from the historical record, suggested that one of the inhabitants could have been a seamstress. In 1826, Coleridge, a visitor to the island, would disparagingly comment on the idleness and backwardness of the poor whites, noting that "the women who will work at all, find employment in washing and mending the clothes of the negroes" (Coleridge 1826:274). In an interesting juxtaposition to other contexts of slavery, the heightened presence of poor white women facilitated their roles as seamstresses, a mode of employment

Figure 4.6. Fragments of tin cans likely repurposed as drinking vessels recovered from Below Cliff (*top*); examples of tin cans refurbished as drinking vessels on display at the Springvale Eco-Heritage Museum, St. Andrew (*bottom*). (Matthew C. Reilly)

commonly held by enslaved women elsewhere (see Jordan 2005; Galle 2004; Wooderson 1930; Heath 1999). A former resident of the Norris household was unsurprised by the diversity of the buttons that had been recovered, but he quickly pointed out that no one in his home had been a seamstress, at least not

Figure 4.7. Assortment of ceramic, plastic, bone, shell, and brass buttons recovered from Below Cliff households. (Matthew C. Reilly)

when he had been living there during his childhood. The mending of clothes may have been taking place, but such activities, as discussed above, do not necessarily neatly comport with monolithic occupations.

Rather than associating the buttons with a single activity or occupation, this childhood resident noted that community members had long worn button-down shirts while working. The wear and tear caused from physical labor frequently caused the loss of buttons or the widening of the holes through which the button fit. With extra buttons being in high demand, local shops sold packages of buttons of various sizes. Accordingly, as shirt holes began to widen due to wear and tear, button size increased in order to securely fasten the shirt closed. Considerations of economic limitations, therefore, inspire an alternative reading of buttons that focuses more on labor than on adornment, ethnicity, or style. Buttons can certainly serve as a symbolic representation of the consumer's "knowledge of current styles as well as their ability to participate in the market economy" (Galle 2010:25), but we should consider their more banal functions and how variation in style, size, and decoration may serve a purpose that is linked to economic limitations. Far from displaying wealth or the most current styles, button consumption in Below Cliff was an

economic decision on the part of residents who found it more practical to buy
new, larger buttons than discarding a worn shirt. Just as in contexts of slavery
in which buttons can be linked to the labor of enslaved washerwomen (Jordan
2005:225–226), the diverse assemblage of buttons from Below Cliff is representative of labor activities. Contrary to notions of consumption in which
consumers display their wealth and fashion sense, buttons can also be harsh
reminders of economic hardship (see Reilly 2016b).

Impoverishment was endemic across the plantation landscape. Despite
ingenuity and perseverance, nonelites residing on plantations, both enslaved
and free, were confronted with the material manifestations of economic inequities on a daily basis. As mentioned, however, simply labeling the Redlegs as
poor or destitute is a vapid exercise that ultimately explains little about how
they lived their daily lives or how those daily lives differed from those of their
enslaved or free Afro-Barbadian neighbors. The archaeological evidence presented here certainly speaks to the realities of impoverishment but also provides more nuanced insights into consumption choices made by residents and
frequency of material reuse. Additionally, oral sources allowed for alternative interpretations that would have been overlooked without the insights of
community members. In short, the data gathered shed light on the everyday
realities Below Cliff residents experienced, the choices they made, and the
practices employed to cope with a harsh environment and difficult economic
circumstances. To conclude, I place this archaeological data in conversation
with elite portrayals of poor white economic inactivity. To facilitate this dialogue, I ask how the lifestyles of the poor whites as seen through the archaeological evidence intersects, if at all, with elite perceptions about labor and the
role of the poor whites in local production and economic spheres.

ECONOMIC FRICTIONS AND AMBIVALENT OCCUPATIONAL IDENTITIES

One of the many transformations that occurred during the sugar revolution
was the development of a rigid correlative between people's racial identity,
their legal status, and their socioeconomic function within the burgeoning
sugar industry. As indentured servitude slowly began to fade as a significant
form of bound labor, those who came to be known as the Redlegs or poor
whites were physically, economically, socially, and conceptually severed from
the island's dominant production industry. Thus, we see the logic of the
development of a discourse of poor white laziness, idleness, and isolation.
This discourse is visible in how elites and visitors described the poor whites
and how they categorized them in official documents. These portrayals and
categorizations, however, seldom provide a realistic description of how communities such as Below Cliff functioned on a daily basis or within broader

Barbadian economic spheres. In this final section I suggest that spaces such as Below Cliff were arenas for an entanglement of the hypercapitalistic production processes of the plantation and an informal or moral economy at odds with elite ideologies of labor and acceptable occupational identities.

Historical data gathered from official registries provide some clues as to the diverse occupations of Below Cliff residents. When complemented with archaeological and oral sources, however, we see that such registries are limited in what they are able to express. By categorizing individuals in single-occupational identities (carpenter, bookkeeper, shoemaker, fisherman, etc.), these documents fail to account for the multioccupational nature of many Below Cliff community members. In speaking with former residents and descendants of former residents, it became abundantly clear that, out of necessity, most community members were small farmers, fishermen, carpenters, seamstresses, *and* general laborers, a phenomenon similarly noted by Jerome Handler (1966:269) in his ethnographic study of small-scale cane farming on the island in the 1960s. Additionally, rather than solely relying on wage labor (as is expected within a capitalistic framework), community members operated in a semimoral economy, assisting neighbors in farming, carpentry, and other daily household tasks under the assumption that such practices would be reciprocated. In observing a moral, or what he calls a "second," economy in urban Côte d'Ivoire, Sasha Newell notes that "transactions did not typically produce as much financial gain as one would imagine, and such profits tended to be immediately diffused back into the network in any case. Instead, the economy was dominated by social investments and the maintenance of social relations" (Newell 2012:96). While not completely counterintuitive to capitalistic networks or processes, in Barbados such an economy would have appeared at odds with a capitalist plantation system in which labor was harnessed for the explicit purposes of profit accumulation. Such a tension would lead to participants in these moral economies being marked as isolated from island socioeconomics by elites and administrators.

One former resident who spent her childhood and early teens growing up in Below Cliff had her baptism recorded in the St. Margaret's registry in the year 1941. Her name can be found alongside that of mother and father, now both deceased. In this entry, her father is described solely as a "laborer." When presented with this information, she found it rather perplexing. The designation of "laborer" was typically associated with someone who cut cane, and she was adamant that her father had been a gardener at Clifton Hall Plantation. Additionally, she fondly remembered her father planting crops in the yard areas of the house, raising pigs and fowl, cultivating a small patch of sugar cane that he harvested and sold to Clifton Hall, going fishing when time permitted, and assisting with household maintenance and carpentry around the community. A cousin of this former resident, himself a child of Below Cliff, was equally surprised when his own father was similarly referred to as a "laborer" in his baptismal entry.[11] Former residents of Below Cliff and current residents of the neighboring communities harbored drastically different perceptions of work and occupational identity from those who were responsible for keeping official records. It would surely be difficult to find an individual who would disagree with the assessment that such community members "labored," but how they identified themselves and others in their community was far more complex.

To explicitly counter claims of Redleg idleness and laziness, time spent excavating Below Cliff and interacting with local community members made it abundantly clear that subsisting and maintaining one's home was a full-time job that required constant attention. Additionally, this responsibility was shared by community members. Mrs. Fenty, an elderly woman who lives in the community next to the forest that used to be Below Cliff, recalls the sight of community members carrying the boards of a house up the road to reassemble the structure at a new location. The task would frequently take the better part of a day and enlisted the services of 10 to 12 able-bodied community members. The former member of the Norris household recalled a similar scene when his aunt decided to close her shop, and the structure was downgraded from a two-story to a one-story structure. Leslie Layne, then a senior member of the Below Cliff community known for his expertise in carpentry, directed operations as boards were removed one at a time, allowing the structure to slowly be lowered down to rest comfortably atop the limestone foundation.

As would be expected from such vernacular architectural styles, nails were a common artifact encountered during excavations. In total, 475 ferrous metal nails or nail fragments were recovered along with 18 cuprous nails, tacks, and fragments. During excavations it was noted that most of the nails were coming from portions of interior units that bordered foundation walls, indicating that many of the nails were likely used on the boards of the home. Given the assortment of nail material, as well as the range in size, it seems that residents were not particularly selective in the nails used to keep boards in place. Metal hardware was also used to keep hurricane shutters closed, contributing to the list of household architectural features that needed to be maintained and/or replaced (Figure 4.8). Given the tropical environment and the unstable landscape, it is likely that occupants frequently had to tend to rusted nails, rotting boards, broken latches, and general repairs. It is not surprising that a wide variety and proportionally high quantity of nails were recovered.

Figure 4.8. Brass tacks and nails recovered from the interior of the Norris household (*top*); ferrous metal shutter latch, possibly used to secure windows on the first floor when the shop was closed (*bottom*). (Matthew C. Reilly)

Christopher Matthews has noted a shift that occurred in building construction, deconstruction, and maintenance as capitalist processes developed in American contexts. Referencing James Deetz, he notes that in early colonial society "builders revealed aspects of the shared corporate culture that tied together those living in early colonial communities," continuing that "this work was part of the larger circulation of value within a community" (Matthews 2010:64). Conversely, following the shift to capitalism, contrary to the "shared corporate culture," he argues that "when builders completed the work [of building a home], their relationship with homeowners was complete" (69). I agree with Matthews's assertion that the onset of capitalist modes of production involved specific divisions of labor, as well as divisions in the sociality of communities based on socioeconomic class (for the division of labor on the plantation landscape see Delle 2014b; Singleton 2015). However, such transformations do not take place wholesale across the landscape. Shifts in community and laborer relations were gradual processes. Furthermore, some transformations in community relations may have never taken place. In essence, while forms and processes of hypercapitalism (most evident in the processes of sugar production) were taking place on the plantation above the cliff, a moral economy or form of "early" capitalism was concomitantly coexisting below the cliff. Labor transactions between poor white wage laborers and plantation management may have ended with the compensation for work performed, but in communities like Below Cliff, these transactions were part of a broader moral economy that intimately tied residents to one another, even after specific tasks or jobs were completed.

The entanglements and frictions between these two economic schemes can be seen in the individuals who participated in each system in various capacities. As bookkeepers, watchmen, distillers, boilers, and cane cutters, some Below Cliff residents would have been directly implicated in sugar production as wage laborers. As producers and consumers of locally grown crops, participants in the local fishing industry, or neighbors assisting in the maintenance of a house or its moving, their lives below the cliff were a marked departure from the cane fields and works on the plateau above. Long associated with "peasant communities," moral economies have been interpreted as alternatives to or active resistance against the state and/or capitalistic processes (see Scott 1976; Fafchamps 1992; for peasant communities in the Caribbean see Trouillot 1988; Mintz 1974; Slocum 2017). Presented as noncapitalist, moral economies support community networks that provide affordable goods and services based on individual and community needs, rather than free market pricing. Despite its anticapitalist underpinnings, Below Cliff evidence suggests that moral economies and capitalist networks need not be diametrically opposed or mutually exclusive (see Hauser 2008). As participants in both forms of economies, Below Cliff residents carved a unique niche for themselves within Barbadian socioeconomics, resulting in their being historically ostracized from the very processes that they were an integral part of.

This chapter has presented a particular discourse of poor white idleness that was developed by elites and island visitors after white laborers were no longer needed in large numbers on the plantation. Physically and conceptually severed from integral roles in sugar production, the Redlegs were cast as lazy and the cause of their own destitution. Archaeological evidence illustrates the material manifestations of Redleg economic hardship, but it also points to specific instances of ingenuity through artifact reuse. Additionally, in considering local economic systems, specifically the existence of a semimoral and intimate economy, we see the frictions between the capitalist processes unfolding atop the cliff and those taking place below. We can, therefore, view the discourse of idleness as a failure of elite ideologies of labor to understand multioccupational identities or modes of production and subsistence that fell outside the purview of explicitly capitalist processes. Thus far, however, we have only considered the relationship between elites and those living below the cliff as well as the intimate relationships between poor white community members. Their role within the plantation economy, as well as alternative social and economic practices, involved other actors, specifically enslaved and free people of African descent. These individuals, after all, made up the overwhelming majority of the population on an island defined by sugar and slavery. The next chapter considers these interactions to place the poor whites within the broader framework of Barbadian society.

FIVE

"A NUMEROUS RACE OF MULATTOES"

(De)Constructing Racial Barriers

> Their [the poor whites'] history is far more akin to the history of the blacks [than it is to the white elites], with whom they share centuries of marginalization, discrimination, oppression and poverty.
>
> —Karl S. Watson (2000b:131)

> Who knows who had "close relationships" with whom in plantation societies?
>
> —Stuart Hall (2017:17)

The previous chapter argued that elite ideas about labor conflicted with how poor white residents of Below Cliff made lives for themselves despite economic hardship, a harsh environment, and a physically and conceptually strained relation to sugar production. These themes speak to issues of class relations and frictions between two coexisting modes of economy operating atop and below the cliff. Despite spatial separation, these systems often worked through and with one another. In plantation societies like Barbados, however, class relations and formation processes are inextricably linked to those of race, and violently so. Notions of racial identity and their relation to class status began to develop in Barbados in the seventeenth century even before the island transitioned to a sugar and slave society. Throughout the period of slavery, however, these notions continued to be interpreted, reinterpreted, transformed, deconstructed, and reconstructed in local contexts. This chapter explores the degree to which Below Cliff residents interacted and intermixed with their enslaved and free Afro-Barbadian neighbors within the confines of their tenantry below the cliff and in neighboring communities. Through this analysis it is possible to interrogate the very racial categories that were essential to Barbadian and Atlantic-world socioeconomic hierarchies and structures.

The rapid technological and economic developments associated with the sugar revolution demanded a reorganization of labor practices and colonial governance as the population of Africans in Barbados skyrocketed in the mid-seventeenth century. Religious, national, and ethnic differences eventually gave way to phenotypic hierarchies as race-based slavery became wedded to Atlantic-world socioeconomics (Mills 1997). This transition is visible in seventeenth-century Barbadian laws that "sought to divide the laboring class into two separate and unequal groups, 'Christians' and 'Negroes'" (Rugemer

2013:442; see also Handler and Reilly 2017). Throughout the seventeenth century, categories such as white, black, slave, servant, Christian, pagan, English, Irish, Scottish, and African were significant markers of difference that placed individuals along a socioeconomic spectrum that was constantly in flux and susceptible to negotiation, even if white elites did their best to ensure that hierarchies remained rigidly in place.

In her study of Irish and Africans in seventeenth-century Barbados, Jenny Shaw argues that throughout the seventeenth century diverse groups were able to manipulate elite ideologies about difference through cooperative acts of resistance as well as other methods of contesting hierarchies. She concludes that "as the seventeenth century drew to a close the ability to counter elite ideologies appeared to collapse altogether" (Shaw 2013:185). This appearance, however, may be a product of the ways in which the historical record was produced rather than a realistic indication of social life on the island. Indeed, such ideologies (elite or other), particularly those about race, are always in a state of becoming (Stoler 2002; Monahan 2011). It is certainly the case that by the close of the seventeenth century elite ideas about racial hierarchies had been made more rigid and become manifest in local governance, codified into colonial law, and visible within island socioeconomics. Ideologies concerning race, racial identity, and racial difference, however, were continuously being contested, interrogated, and complicated from the seventeenth century up to the present. Additionally, it is imperative that we bear in mind that the appearance of these ideologies and their presence in the historical record reflect the desired state of affairs in Barbados and elite attempts to make them realities. As Ann Stoler highlights, colonial ideas surrounding race involve "how people identified the affinities they shared, how they defined themselves in contexts in which discrepant interests, ethnic and class differences, might otherwise weaken consensus" (Stoler 2002:25). It is situated in these weakened contexts that we encounter the fragility of colonial categories and "the exclusions they enabled" (Stoler 2002:8). With this in mind, along with the brutalities and violence of the race-based system of slavery, I turn to the localized setting of Below Cliff to examine the success and failures of broader ideologies of racial hierarchies and identities.

Race, Poor White Racial Purity, and Cultural Pluralism

The Caribbean region was plagued by race-based slavery for nearly four centuries. Plantation labor exploitation continues in new permutations, making it self-evident that race-based dispossession is a complex sociopolitical issue that had, and continues to have, significant bearing on everyday life for millions of people (see, for instance, Martínez 2007). It is naive, however, to assume that racial politics and classificatory schemes were similar throughout the region, or that preconceived notions of how race functioned in United States history, for example, were prevalent and practiced in other American contexts. Sidney Mintz argues "that the perception of race differences by the majority, which has so consistently shored up the operation of racial oppression in the United States, simply has not functioned in the same ways in Caribbean societies" (Mintz 1974:21). Rather, he argues, in the Caribbean region, "the operation of racial bias has generally been more subtle and more complicated" (21). While blanket arguments concerning the general white over black nature of social structures and colonial infrastructure may hold water (see Jordan 1968; Mills 1997), local context is needed if we are to make specific claims about the nature of race relations and racial identities in a particular island setting.

Since the earliest years of English settlement of the island, Barbadian elites and colonial officials sought to account for the island's population in broad racial terms. Although population figures are unreliable for this early period, collection and interpretation of these sets of data by Dunn (1969, 2000 [1972]), Handler and Lange (1978), and Handler (personal communication) all illustrate that seventeenth-century demographics were calculated using different but related terms. For instance, demographic breakdowns were based on place of origin (Africa or Europe),[1] legal status (slave or free), religion (Christian or other), and phenotype (white or black). The numbers themselves are not of immediate significance for the purposes of this argument. Rather, it is evident that from early on the population was categorized in broad racial categories that were heavily determined by one's place of origin. This phenomenon would persist throughout the period of slavery and well into the postemancipation era. Jerome Handler has argued that Barbados was a unique case among Caribbean colonies in that there was not a complicated matrix of racial identities. Rather, the Barbadian system was similar to the American "one drop rule" whereby if one had an ancestor of African genealogy, it was impossible for that person to ever be considered fully "white" (Handler 1974:68–69). In other words, African genealogy was more determinate of one's racial identity than skin complexion.

This system stood in marked contrast to more complex and subtle racial typologies established in other Caribbean territories. For instance, M. L. E. Moreau de Saint-Méry's eighteenth-century (1797) description of Saint-Domingue documented and elaborated on 11 distinct racial categories that were used in the French colony. Furthermore, we know that these categories and concepts were fluid and transformed over time, such as in Spanish Puerto Rico where categories like "mestizo" and "criollo" shifted in meaning, covering place of birth and genetic ancestry throughout the early colonial period (Schwartz 1997). Despite shared imperial parentage with Barbados, the Jamaican racial taxonomy was slightly more complicated. Borrowing from the Spanish, who had previously controlled Jamaica until 1655, Edward Long describes at least four terms for people of mixed ancestry, including mulatto, sambo, quadroon, and mestize (Long 1774:260–261; see also Jordan 1962:192). In short, legal and social racial taxonomies varied across Caribbean contexts.

In lieu of the subtle and genetically fractal taxonomic scheme, Barbadians relied on a more simplistic model of racial identity whereby individuals were categorized as white, black, or mixed (mulattoes). During his visit to the West Indies in 1833, Captain Studholme Hodgson commented that "he who is ambitious of entering into what is designated *good society* in the West Indies, must especially be prepared to exhibit an undoubted pedigree of three generations of *white* ancestry" (Hodgson 1838:58, emphasis in original). Conversely, he sarcastically remarks, "but woe, woe to the unhappy wretch, if among his ancestors can be numbered one in whose veins flowed some of the African blood" (59). These passages reveal the inextricable links between race and class in Barbadian society as well as strict adherence to notions of racial purity. Despite the fact that Hodgson would go on to enumerate the racial categories and their characteristics as relayed to him by a woman at a gala (62), the presence of African blood was the most significant element of one's racial identity. This schematic, however, was not necessarily clear cut, and discrepancies often arose. Such discrepancies are informative of the porousness of racial categories and the fluidity of racial identity. I explore such issues throughout this chapter as they pertain to individual identity in addition to the interaction of individuals across these supposedly definitive racial identities.

By the close of the seventeenth century there was an apparent crystallization of the association of plantation labor with black skins. Slavery had become synonymous with Africans, and Europe was no longer being tapped as a major resource for procuring plantation laborers.[2] Slave codes around the Atlantic world ensured that there was legal support for the treatment and ownership of black bodies, heightening the significance of one's racial identity. Painted in broad strokes, ideologies of racial identities and hierarchies seemed impervious to contestation and negotiation. These ideologies were dependent on a lucid and pragmatic classificatory scheme through which to determine one's racial identity. Adherence to what Michael Monahan (2011) refers to as the "politics of purity" allowed for a simplistic schematic that placed individuals within the categories of black or white, thereby determining an individual's place in Barbadian plantation society.

The development and success of these ideologies was contingent on constant maintenance of these racial boundaries. It is therefore unsurprising that from the seventeenth century to the present the poor whites have often been portrayed as isolated and racially pure. During the course of a parliamentary commission on the state of the slave trade and colonial commerce, Barbadian Governor Parry would comment in 1789 that the "lowest class of white inhabitants . . . live all separate from each other, either as tenants on detached pieces of land belonging to the plantations, or as occupiers of little parcels of ground, appertaining to themselves" (HCPP 1789:17). Again turning to traveler accounts, it is significant that the white phenotype of the Redlegs was frequently an observation deemed worthy of comment. In his 1806 *Notes on the West Indies: Vol. II*, George Pinckard would note the entirely European appearance of several poor whites he came across while passing their cottages in the island's Scotland District. Despite their European appearance, he also noted that they identified as being "true Barbadians" (Pinckard 1806:131–139). Henry Nelson Coleridge, a short-term visitor to the island, similarly commented on the phenotypic attributes of the Redlegs during his stay on the island in 1825. He noted that their perceived racial arrogance was "in virtue of their freckled ditchwater faces" (Coleridge 1826:274). These commentaries reveal that the racial status of the poor whites was dependent on phenotypic appearance in conjunction with their free legal status. Direct links are constructed between the Redlegs encountered in early nineteenth-century Barbados and their European ancestry. In short, despite a legal reliance on ancestry, pale complexion often equated European ancestry and white identity, while dark complexion was linked to enslavement and African descent.[3]

Similar to the discourse of Redleg laziness, portrayals of the Redlegs as being racially pure and arrogant permeate twentieth-century and contemporary literature. Peter Simmons (1976:22) suggests that miscegenation was first observable only in the 1970s, particularly in the urban context, which, he argued, would eventually lead to the decline of the traditional Redleg identity. Conversely, one year earlier, Thomas Keagy would assert that "although the whites live in close associate with the blacks, and resemble them culturally, they have maintained their racial pride and opposition to racial admixture, and, therefore, their homogeneity" (Keagy 1975:20). Barbadian historian David Browne expresses similar sentiments, claiming that the poor whites "were so proud of their racial purity that they resisted assimilation into the mainstream of Barbadian society, especially with the black population" (Browne 2012:16). Irish journalist Sean O'Callaghan's overtly vicious assessment of the contemporary Redleg population bluntly states that the Redlegs "look down on the blacks and have never intermarried with them"

(O'Callaghan 2000:207). The literature discussed illustrates prolonged commitment to a binary model of racial identity. In addition to racial identities being enamored with imaginations of purity, we see a stark social separation of these apparently disparate groups. Presented here is evidence that interrogates the rigidity of Barbadian racial identities as well as the perceived social distinction between Afro-Barbadians and poor whites.

Before proceeding, however, addressing particular ambiguities about "cultural" identity, as it pertains to the poor whites and Afro-Barbadians, helps in contextualizing the significance of racial markers on the island. The rhetoric employed by the above authors makes no mistake in explicitly identifying the Redlegs as being purely of European descent and, therefore, white. The ambiguity emerges, however, when confronting the "cultural" identity of the poor whites.[4] Despite racial distinctiveness, based on the data compiled for this book, it appears that little separates Redleg culture from that of Afro-Barbadians, though many Barbadians might reasonably suggest otherwise. Indeed, many Barbadians are quick to point out the distinct dialect of white Bajans. To be clear, however, the similarity noted here extends to the material culture produced, consumed, used, and reused, forms of vernacular architecture constructed, dietary practices, and other quotidian practices— not their legal status or social standing. The realities of living in a highly racialized plantation society cast a shadow over daily encounters and interactions in terms of how individuals identified themselves and viewed others. Despite the omnipresence of racial discourse that permeated everyday life on the island, cultural transmission was facilitated in locales where poor whites and Afro-Barbadians came into contact. In fact, in a sociohistorical analysis of the Redlegs, Karl Watson (1970:86–87) employs concepts like creolization and acculturation to suggest that poor whites adopted the lifeways of Afro-Barbadians, a truly novel interpretation of an acculturation process that throughout the twentieth century assumed African adoption of European cultural traits, whatever such generalizations may have meant.

Contact and transmission between Afro-Barbadians and poor whites could lend itself to interpretations grounded in M. G. Smith's model of plural societies in the Caribbean. Borrowing the model of plural societies from an economist, Smith developed the notion of cultural pluralism to approach the cultural diversity he observed in the British West Indies in the 1950s. Smith acknowledges the importance of contact between cultural "units" and even points to the commonality of racial mixing, particularly in the form of "Negro-white" miscegenation (Smith 1965:11), but he nonetheless argues that "in a culturally divided society, each cultural section has its own relatively exclusive way of life, with its own distinctive systems of action, ideas and values, and social relations. Often these cultural sections differ also in language, material culture, and technology" (81). Invaluable to Smith's analysis is the existence of definitive cultural "units," a framework that neatly coincides with historical renderings of Barbadian poor whites. Smith's approach had an enduring impact on sociological and anthropological research in the Caribbean, but it is invoked here to demonstrate the problematic nature of these essentializing categories and to suggest that individual members of these "units" destabilized these groupings in manipulating and constructing their physical and social landscapes.

VERNACULAR LANDSCAPES

The built landscape of Caribbean plantations reveals the manifestations of ideologies of racial and economic order. The landscape atop the cliff, where sugar production was the raison d'être, contrasted sharply with the activities and spatial organization found below. In attempting to make sense of this contrast, John B. Jackson's concept of the "vernacular landscape" is useful but in need of revision. Jackson, applying the architectural trope of the vernacular to the broader landscape, defines a vernacular landscape as "one where evidences of a political organization of space are largely or entirely absent" (Jackson 1984:150). The deficiencies in Jackson's concept are linked to its dependence on modern notions of evolutionary progress. The connotation here is that vernacular landscapes are developmentally behind those that are politically arranged and, therefore, lacking a "purposeful continuity" (151). There is, however, a silver lining in Jackson's term, as it neatly comprises how space can be produced in ways not entirely harnessed by capitalist processes, coloniality, or political governance. Rather than being unaffected by political organization, my usage of the term relates to spaces that have an emic logic that rests outside colonial sensibilities of order and organization, despite being affected by them. These landscapes make sense to community members who use the space at their disposal and manipulate its features to suit their needs, despite structural limitations (see also Hauser and Armstrong 2012). The vernacular landscape of Below Cliff was one that was created by those who held little power on the plantation landscape but were nonetheless able to navigate its contours to facilitate desired social, economic, and kinship networks.

For the portions of the wooded area that were explored and documented below the cliff during archaeological research, interesting household patterns associated with kinship and social networks were observed. Additionally, an analysis of the broader Clifton Hall Plantation landscape affords significant interpretations about the interaction of individuals below and above the cliff.

In general, the Below Cliff landscape would have appeared disorganized and erratic to planters and other elites. As illustrated by James Delle (1998, 2014b) in his analyses of Jamaican coffee plantations, the plantation was a space in which the state of nature was to be ordered, controlled, systematically organized, and rigidly managed to maximize labor efficiency and profit (see also Armstrong and Kelly 2000; Lenik 2011; Bates 2015; Hauser 2015). While the natural landscape, disasters like storms and earthquakes, and acts of resistance on the part of the enslaved were all contributing factors to the successes and failures of elite attempts at organization and control, a particular logic to plantation organization was undeniably anchored by power relations and order. This was reflected not only in the great house, the works, and fields but also in the villages the enslaved inhabited.

Douglas Armstrong's analysis of seventeenth- and eighteenth-century Jamaican villages for the enslaved illustrates a particular attempt by planters to organize, surveil, and control laborers through the establishment of linearly arranged slave quarters with standardized architectural forms usually situated in close proximity to the works, overseers quarters, and the great house, depending on topographic variables (1990; Armstrong and Kelly 2000). Not unique to Jamaica, such laborer organization finds correlates in other American settings such as Mulberry Row at Thomas Jefferson's Monticello (Kelso 1997:51–81) and Cuban coffee plantations in which the village was sometimes confined within imposing walls (Singleton 2015). At Seville Plantation, however, Armstrong and Kelly argue that the second village, established in the closing decades of the eighteenth century, reflected a dramatic transformation in which Afro-Jamaicans "had an opportunity to define social boundaries within the village on their own terms" (2000:386). Rather than showing characteristics of planter-mandated organization and construction, the village and houses "not only exhibited well-defined and expanded house-yard compounds, but they also show considerable variation in the specifics of house design, construction and alignment" (387). Armstrong and Kelly suggest that this later village reflects Afro-Jamaican social behaviors and practices that entail particular forms of social interaction, small farming practices, household organization, and spatial organization.

In turning to the spatial organization of Below Cliff depicted on the maps found in Figure 3.3 (as well as the photograph in Figure 3.2), we see stark similarities in how tenantry space was organized to that of self-organized villages for the enslaved, from the overall landscape to the layout of house-yard areas. A far cry from the linearity and rigid boundaries that were characteristic of planter-dominated and designed plantation spaces, this tenantry appears to be disorganized and haphazardly constructed. Households are grouped in small clusters, and, although it is tenuous to project such patterns into the past, in the decades before the tenantry was abandoned, these clusters were associated with kinship networks (nuclear and extended families). For instance, members of the Norris family recall how they were related to each of the families that resided in close proximity to their places of residence. Additionally, like the late eighteenth-century village in Seville, Jamaica (Armstrong and Kelly 2000:380), the environment played a major role in determining household positioning and orientation based on local topography (a crucial consideration in Below Cliff) and trade winds. In terms of spatial use, visible changes in vegetation in the area today indicate previous spatial functionality in the past. For instance, khuskhus grass was planted to prevent erosion and to mark the boundaries between household plots, vestiges of which are still visible today. Additionally, parcels of tall grass and other weed-like small bushes found adjacent to residential platforms were areas that were once meager sugar fields worked by local residents who sold their harvest to neighboring plantations.

The presence of these small sugar fields may have been a modification to the landscape of Below Cliff, as Handler (1966) notes that between the 1940s and 1960s, small-scale sugar production accounted for roughly 15% of the island's total sugar growth. Combined with provision agriculture, these farming techniques would have been undertaken by poor whites and Afro-Barbadians to make modest incomes from market sales. Directly southeast of the foundation of the Norris homestead is the faint outline of a semicircular stone wall. Given the architectural styles typical of the area (and island as a whole), the articulated wall was initially believed to serve as part of the structural foundation. Oral histories reveal that the articulated stones had once served as a retaining wall for a small provision ground in which sweet potatoes and yams were grown. Additionally, to the southwest of the household are the small ruins of three walls of a square. These stones are the traces of what were once several pigpens. During its use, the pen's fourth wall, often a piece of corrugated metal, served as a gate. Finally, the northwest stones of the foundation extended beyond the perimeter of the household in a southwestern direction. This extension served as the backing foundation/wall for the household's detached kitchen. Excavations inside and surrounding the detached kitchen revealed few artifacts, confirming assumptions that such areas were frequently swept clean during occupation. Few faunal remains were recovered and no indications of burning or burned material were noted, but the function of the feature was confirmed through oral sources.

In returning to landscape and spatial observations made at Seville, Armstrong and Kelly note similar uses of space when Afro-Jamaicans expressed their autonomy in the late eighteenth-century village. In discussing the activities undertaken in the surrounding household areas they suggest that (Armstrong and Kelly 2000:382) "the yard activities should include exterior kitchen and food preparation areas, gathering areas, animal pens, and gardens. With the exception of specific activity areas, such as hearths and planted garden beds, the yard area should be relatively artifact-free because of repeated yard sweeping, with increased artifact frequencies at the edge of the house and along the perimeter of the cleared yard." This description is strikingly similar to the spatial layout of households below the cliff and the associated activities that took place within such spaces. Historical evidence also points to these practices taking place in Barbados contemporaneously with the inhabitation of the Seville village in Jamaica. Transcriptions of interviews that were part of a parliamentary committee report on the slave trade and commerce in the American colonies describe observations Barbadian elites made about the practices of poor whites. In 1790 Rev. Nicholls was asked by Parliament whether "white people even labour in the open air in the island of Barbados." His response, quoted in chapter 2, was in the affirmative, with specific references to the poor whites, claiming that "those who are called tenants, being men who serve in the militia for a small allotment of land, and persons in similar circumstances as to the quantity of land they occupy, do commonly work in their grounds with their negroes, if they have any, or else cultivate the whole with their own labour; that ground is commonly in provisions, not in canes" (HCPP 1790:334–335). Rev. Nicholls's assertion that the grounds were not in sugar cane aligns with Jerome Handler's (1966) research on small-scale cane farming, which illustrates that such practices were more prominent beginning in the early to mid-twentieth century. Therefore, it is likely that subsistence agriculture as well as cash-crop farming were common features of life below the cliff throughout its occupation, with small-scale sugar farming picking up during the twentieth century.

A final example of how community members engendered and resided in a vernacular landscape relates to the ways in which they promoted movement through their community. Three pathways were used by former tenantry residents to climb from the bottom of the cliff to the top (two of which are still safely navigable today). Conversations with local residents revealed that the entry points were called the Ladders, Monkey Jump, and the Gates (from north to south). Monkey Jump also corresponds to the sugar field located adjacent to the entryway. The field directly south of Monkey Jump is called Negro Yard, which, as research has shown, often indicates that it was the location of a former village for the enslaved (Handler and Lange 1978:46; Handler 2002). While a lack of plantation maps makes it difficult to confirm the names of these fields during the era of slavery, field names across the island generally demonstrate strong continuity. Therefore, entrances/exits to and from Below Cliff likely facilitated the interaction of poor whites and Afro-Barbadians before and after emancipation.

Additionally, given that Below Cliff was situated far out of sight of the great house and works, it also would have been possible for the enslaved to traverse the pathways down to the community below. By law, the enslaved were prohibited from leaving the plantation without permission, but, since Below Cliff was technically part of Clifton Hall Plantation, this peripheral community offered a potentially permissible context for interracial interaction and sociability. In the postemancipation era, interactions persisted, which is one explanation for why many Afro-Barbadian families chose to reside in Below Cliff shortly after emancipation, as confirmed through baptismal registries. The organization of the plantation landscape was largely determined by top-down models that implemented strategies for control and efficiency. At its peripheries, however, community members were able to manipulate their landscape to build an infrastructure that conflicted with designs that privileged the industrial production of sugar.

The experiences of Afro-Barbadians and poor whites were dramatically shaped by the landscape, which was in turn shaped by its inhabitants. These interactions fostered relationships that frequently would have led to cultural exchange in the form of architectural techniques, agricultural practices, food preparation, dietary preferences, innovation in artifact reuse, and spatial organization, to name a few of the characteristics identifiable in the archaeological, historical, and oral record. As pointed out, this degree of interaction was noted by Barbadian historian Karl Watson, who suggests that the Redlegs "illustrate the process of acculturation, for they were the white group closest to the Negroes and farthest away from continuing English cultural influences, and could therefore be expected to show the highest degree of acculturation" (Watson 1970:87). This assertion is significant, especially given the context within which it was made. At a time in which the cultural characteristics of African Americans were hotly debated following the publication of Herskovits's theories of acculturation (1990 [1941]), and shortly before the intercessions of Mintz and Price (1992 [1976]), Watson suggests that in the context of Barbados, acculturation was turned on its head; here, Afro-Barbadian culture was transmitted seemingly whole cloth to poor whites.

Interestingly, the evidence recovered as part of this study does not necessarily suggest a directionality for cultural influences. In other words, there is evidence of cultural similarities, but directionality and influence are rather ambiguous. In returning to the classic work of Mintz (1974), however, we are reminded of the significance of local contingencies and circumstances as well as the transformative nature of culture, especially within oppressive conditions. Therefore, while it is certainly in our interest to explore the degree to which particular traits or practices were carried from a distant homeland such as Africa or Europe, the quest for distinct "Africanisms" may obfuscate local transformations that have less to do with cultural origins and more with the nature of everyday life on the plantation landscape (Mintz 1974:26–28). To be clear, I am not suggesting that particular cultural traits and practices from Europe or Africa failed to make the journey to the New World, or that observing them is a frivolous endeavor. Rather, an approach that focuses on local transformations (see Armstrong 1998, 2003) privileging not original cultural forms but the building of vernacular landscapes and their associated practices of everyday life allows for a more holistic examination of how supposedly disparate groups interacted. I seek to remove focus from the concept of cultural (as well as racial) distinctiveness and further explore the degree to which historically specific cross-racial/cultural interaction was responsible for the emergence of particular ways of life observable in Below Cliff.

Coarse Earthenwares and Integrated Markets

The argument developed earlier concerning the development of a vernacular landscape hinges on the possibility of providing evidence of nonelites interacting in substantive ways. Similar architectural forms and spatial organization is circumstantial, hinting at influence and transmission but not necessarily integrated networks of interaction. By complementing spatial evidence with excavated material, however, a more comprehensive picture of Afro-Barbadian and poor white interaction emerges. The objects discussed here, coarse earthenwares,[5] are ubiquitous across the island landscape, especially given the use of sugar cones and drip jars that were essential to the production of sugar. Industrial earthenwares such as sugar cones and pots have been recovered from domestic sites in Barbados (Armstrong and Reilly 2014; Finch 2013; Agbe-Davies 2009), but the wares discussed here were produced specifically for domestic use, argued to be representative of Redleg participation in local markets.

The production of earthenware has a rich history in Barbados dating back to at least the mid-seventeenth century and has been the focus of several anthropological and archaeological studies (see, for example, Handler 1963a, 1963b, 1965; Stoner 2000; Finch 2013; Loftfield 2001; Siedow 2014). Historical sketches by Jerome Handler indicate that "in former days [likely referring to the seventeenth through nineteenth centuries] pottery-making was primarily a plantation based industry, in which pots were made that were used in the manufacture of Muscovado sugar" (Handler 1963a:129). Despite the use of wooden containers and imports from England for sugar cones, locally made wares were essential to the production process beginning sometime between 1650 and 1680 when islanders began to properly fire locally made vessels (131–133). The origins of cottage pottery industries are more difficult to trace. Handler highlights the significance in local Sunday markets, suggesting that by the early eighteenth century locally made ceramics were a common craft good found for sale or barter (139–140). While these markets were predominantly forums for the enslaved and their descendants (Mintz 1974; Handler 1963a; Hauser 2008), evidence suggests that poor whites were also active participants in the context of Barbados. As noted by Handler, "These markets served as vehicles through which the personal produces of the slaves were exchanged among themselves and with others, e.g., poor-whites, on a cash or kind basis" (1963a:139–140). Based on comments made by an attorney at an estate owned by Codrington in 1741, it is evident that some of the impediments to converting the enslaved to Christianity were perceived to be "the attraction of marketing activities on Sundays and the bad influence of poor whites" (USPGA 1741: Vol. B8, Item 51).

Poor white participation in markets extended beyond the realm of production and included the selling of goods as well as the consumption and use of locally made ceramics. Hucksters were mobile vendors who often sold goods at "the great market" in Bridgetown, but others serviced the rural areas, purchasing and providing goods for plantation residents. During the period of slavery, free people of color and white Barbadians had the opportunity to serve as shopkeepers or merchants in the rural districts, a practice later afforded to all those with the necessary capital following emancipation. It was through hucksters and shopkeepers that residents of Below Cliff would have had access to the mass-produced wares arriving from the British Isles in addition to those goods made available through cottage industries. The hucksters and shopkeepers were conduits that connected not only consumers with local and global goods but also people across the plantation landscape. The spread of diverse goods across the island was facilitated by these racially diverse individuals, representing market intimacies that brought people into contact on a regular basis—contact that refuted spatial boundedness and isolation. Thanks to the availability of oral sources from select community members that had spent their childhoods below the cliff, it was confirmed that one of the excavated domestic sites, the Norris household, had been a two-story structure that housed a family on the second floor and a small shop on the first. Goods sold included cooking necessities like oil, butter, flour, and sugar as well as imported items like buttons, ceramics, and textiles.

In addition to the details about shops provided by local residents, shop-keepers in Below Cliff are also found in the minutes of parish vestry meetings and registries. For instance, in 1896 the vestry taxed 61 shopkeepers in the parish of St. John (BDA D279), five of whom (George Goddard, William King, Edward Marshall, Lucretia Mayers, and Mary Small) are also listed as Below Cliff residents in local baptismal registries (SMR: Baptisms 1863–1891). The acquisition and sale of goods was not dependent on gender, or on racial identity, intimating that exchange involved racially diverse men and women. Despite legislative attempts to restrict the abilities of free people of color and the enslaved to participate in marketing activities, "in most cases the practices they were designed to control continued" (Handler 1974:127). Illegally acquired goods were also commonly bought and sold, leading one plantation's attorney to note in 1741 that white hucksters were "often worse than the Negroes, by receiving all stolen goods" (see Handler 1974:125). Therefore, these exchange networks brought Barbadians of all racial identities together in illicit, sanctioned, and intimate activities.

In addition to market spaces fostering interracial interaction, the production of marketable goods like ceramics was an undertaking that involved those identified as black and white. Historical data illustrates the immigration of English potters to work on Barbadian plantations in the seventeenth century (Handler 1963a:133–135), and Handler's ethnographic work in the Chalky Mount potting village of the Scotland District reveals that Afro-Barbadian potters referred to white potters who potentially initiated the island's cottage industry (142). While he explicitly highlights the indeterminate nature of these oral traditions, it is significant that Afro-Barbadian potters openly refer to the craft being practiced across racial lines, despite the fact that it had become an exclusively Afro-Barbadian craft in the village of Chalky Mount at the time of Handler's ethnographic research (1963a:142). Ceramic production was also undertaken by enslaved African and Afro-Barbadian men and women on a number of plantations, including in the parish of St. John at nearby Codrington College (Stoner 2000; Loftfield 2001; Farmer 2011; Finch 2013; Scheid 2015). As far as can be discerned from the historical record, oral sources, and walking surveys, there was no potting operation in Below Cliff or at Clifton Hall Plantation, meaning that locally made ceramics had to be brought into the community.

Preliminary data concerning the ceramic assemblage were presented in the previous chapter, but, to reiterate, coarse earthenwares accounted for 28.5% of the ceramic sherds collected. Only 7% of the earthenware sherds were readily identifiable as industrial wares (sugar cones or pots), indicating that Below Cliff residents were consuming and using domestic ceramics rather

Figure 5.1. Sample of coarse earthenwares, likely produced locally, collected from Below Cliff. (Matthew C. Reilly)

than reusing the wares produced on and for the plantations. It is also possible that limited access to plantation materials led to a diminished presence of industrial wares. Despite the fact that these wares could be reused for domestic purposes, it is clear that Below Cliff community members were far more likely to acquire wares specifically designed for domestic use.

Unfortunately, similar to the condition of the majority of the imported refined sherds discussed in the previous chapter, most of the coarse earthenware sherds were small body fragments with few diagnostic features. There were, however, select distinguishing features about the sherds (Figure 5.1). For instance, glazes of various colors were not uncommon decorations, appearing on the interior and/or exterior of 34.5% of the earthenware sherds. Glazes were primarily lead-based and colorless, displaying the color of the paste. Colored glazes were also present on select sherds, including yellow, light green, olive green, and brown. To eliminate the possibility of very recently produced ceramics being represented, glaze color schemes were compared to those used by local potters. Based on the strong local tradition of potting in the Scotland District community of Chalky Mount, the art form has been passed down across several generations. Despite the fact that the craft has declined over the past half century, select third-, fourth-, and fifth-generation potters still work in the community. The wealth of knowledge passed down includes old techniques and forms that make potters familiar with traditional methods as well as changing styles. More recent decorative patterns (those used in the last 20 years) include bright floral colors as well as a specific drip technique. Potters from Chalky Mount confirmed that the glazes on Below Cliff ceramics had not been used in several decades, but they nonetheless recognized the clay composition and vessel forms as wares that were likely made on the island. In general, the variety in glaze prohibits any particular interpretation of consumption preferences or function beyond the retention of liquids for hollowware storage vessels.

Select base, rim, and shoulder sherds provide clues as to the various forms of vessels represented below the cliff. Analysis revealed that 44.5% of the sherds could be identified as hollowware vessels. This is in keeping with the popular vessel forms Handler documented during his fieldwork in Chalky Mount as well as the forms commonly used across the island. The most popular vessel forms (though diminishing in quantity produced at the time of Handler's fieldwork) were monkeys (typically used to keep water cool), goglets (pitchers), and conarees (used for storage and food preparation) (Handler 1963a:146–147). Based on the descriptions, all of these vessels are hollowwares. Diagnostic sherds recovered indicate that several of these regularly produced hollowwares were consumed and used by Below Cliff residents. For instance, the three cross-mending rim sherds seen in Figure 5.2 likely represent the mouth of the vase-shaped goglet. Additionally, the large fragment of a hollowware base, also found in Figure 5.2, represents the common form of a monkey jar, a vessel only made today in limited quantities by Chalky Mount potters for consumers interested in purchasing "traditional" wares.

Sherds from large bowls and storage jars (conarees) indicate food storage and preparation techniques indicative of cooking one-pot stews. Stews could be made using a variety of protein sources. While faunal remains were limited (115 animal bones, or roughly 3.21% of the entire assemblage), fish vertebrae were present. Many community members fished, and oral histories relay that in the late afternoons, fish could often be found on the roofs of households where they would dry in the tropical sun. Starches were also dietary staples, the most common associated with the poor whites being breadfruit. A traditional Barbadian folk song, "Backra-Johnnies—Da Redleg Song," mentions the affinity of poor whites to breadfruit, noting "Dey love de breadfruits to dey hearts" (Marshall et al. 1981:43). Few remaining breadfruit trees can be found in the woods below the cliff, though it is still common to find a breadfruit tree in the yards of most Barbadians (regardless of racial identity) throughout the rural districts. Breadfruits were commonly roasted or could be used in stews. Sitting on a step behind where his childhood home once stood during a trip into the woods, one former resident nostalgically recalled his mother cooking stews and roasting breadfruit in the rear detached kitchen

Figure 5.2. Coarse earthenware sherds of hollowware vessels and re-creations of the full vessel forms. Rim and base sherds of a hollowware vessel with a wide opening at the mouth (*top left*); conaree jar, used for the storage of salted meats, produced by potter John Springer in Chalky Mount, St. Andrew (*top right*); base and body sherds of a monkey jar, used for the storage and cooling of water (*bottom left*); monkey jar produced by potter John Springer in Chalky Mount, St. Andrew (*bottom right*). (Matthew C. Reilly)

before the prepared meal would be portioned out into ceramic bowls. The food preparation and cooking practices along with dietary staples of poor whites relied on the consumption of locally produced vessel forms that further provide evidence of their interactions with Afro-Barbadians.

Although tenuous, based on the limited sample size and number of units excavated, it is possible to sketch a preliminary hypothesis that Below Cliff residents had previously been far more committed to the use of locally made earthenwares than they were in the final decades of the tenantry's inhabitance. Although the preponderance of loose limestone made it difficult to discern stratigraphy inside the Norris household, the three units excavated in the pathway to the northeast of the household provided some clues to changing consumption patterns. Stratigraphic layers within these units were discerned through subtle changes in soil color, transitioning from a black loam on the surface to a lighter brown claylike soil approaching bedrock. Excavations were therefore undertaken in roughly 10-cm levels depending on soil change. A large majority of sherds (both refined and coarse earthenwares) were recovered from the surface and within the first 10 cm of excavation. The second and third levels of excavation revealed a noticeable decrease in the number of sherds of each category recovered. Of interest, however, was the increasing proportion of coarse earthenwares from the first to the third level. The percentage of coarse earthenwares increased from 16.7% in the first level, 25% in the second, and 37.3% in the third. The lack of discrete stratigraphic changes makes it difficult to argue for such a relationship with any certainty, but, if stratigraphic principles hold, it appears that Below Cliff residents had previously been more committed to acquiring and using what were likely locally made earthenwares.

The reasons for this shift may be multiple, but they likely include an increasing availability or affordability of imported ceramics and a decline in cottage pottery industries around the island. Interestingly, however, the ratio of coarse-to-refined earthenwares is far higher for materials collected from Below Cliff than roughly contemporaneous sites for enslaved and free Afro-Jamaicans. Using the Digital Archaeological Archive of Comparative Slavery (DAACS) (Artifact Query 1:January 15, 2016), comparisons were made between materials recovered from Below Cliff to contexts associated with Afro-Jamaican laborers at six archaeological sites (Good Hope Estate, Seville, Mona, Papine, Montpelier, and Stewart Castle) in addition to data available from Drax Hall (Armstrong 1990) and Marshall's Pen (Delle 2014b:158). When possible, specific contexts that were roughly contemporaneous with Below Cliff were selected for comparison, as in the case of Drax Hall (Armstrong 1990:136–137). I have categorized all imported and refined earthenwares together in a single category. This includes delftware, stonewares, refined redware, creamware, pearlware, whiteware, and ironstone, among others. Coarse earthenwares include all wares that *could* have been locally produced. This taxonomic system includes DAACS's category for Caribbean Coarse Earthenware and coarse redwares. Without the use of XRF or neutron activation analysis, it is difficult to assign place of manufacture for these wares with any degree of certainty. In general, however, it is possible to make a preliminary sketch of how readily laborers were consuming imported refined earthenwares over coarse wares, including those that were locally produced. For the broader comparison with Jamaican sites, the general category of coarse earthenwares was used instead of differentiating between industrial

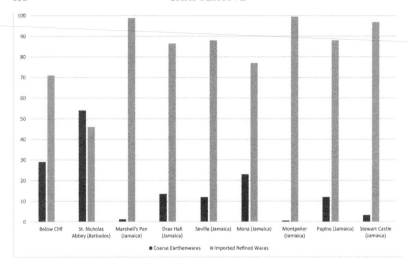

Figure 5.3. Percentages of ceramic types recovered from early nineteenth-century plantation sites in Barbados and Jamaica. (Matthew C. Reilly)

sugar wares and domestic wares, a subdivision that becomes important in analyzing the Barbadian data. In all, for the Afro-Jamaican contexts selected, coarse earthenwares represented 11.5% of the total ceramic assemblage, with the highest proportion recovered from shovel test pits at the Mona Village (23%) and lowest (0%) coming from two Montpelier households (Figure 5.3).

The only data from a Barbadian context available through the DAACS database comes from the 2014 excavation season directed by Frederick Smith at the worker's village at St. Nicholas Abbey Plantation in St. Peter. Here we see a striking difference in the proportion of coarse-to-refined wares. Of the 1,701 ceramic sherds recovered, 917, or roughly 54%, were identified as coarse earthenwares. This is a marked contrast to sites in Jamaica, perhaps indicating that nonelite Barbadians, including the enslaved and poor whites, had greater access to local wares or preferred these wares over those imported from the British Isles. The percentage of coarse wares found at St. Nicholas Abbey is significantly higher than that of Below Cliff, but ceramic typologies play a role in how these figures can be interpreted. On closer examination of the data for the coarse earthenwares, the overwhelming majority of sherds are listed as unidentifiable or placed in a general utilitarian category. While select sherds are specifically identified as sugar molds or drip jars, many of these ambiguous hollowwares could very well have been from industrial sugar vessels. The distinction between industrial and domestic wares is extremely important in determining how plantation residents gained access to such goods. Industrial wares, including sugar cones/molds and drip jars, were, in all likelihood, coming directly from the plantation, while domestic wares were those purchased from markets or through hucksters/local shopkeepers. In taking this caveat into account, the actual percentage of coarse earthenwares for domestic use is likely lower than 54%, therefore making the percentage of industrial wares found at St. Nicholas Abbey higher than that found below the cliff. For Below Cliff, the overwhelming majority of coarse earthenwares recovered were determined to be manufactured for domestic use based on vessel form, sherd thickness, and glaze.

Noting that imported ceramics come to dominate assemblages by the late eighteenth century due to their affordability and availability, Armstrong (1990) and Delle (2014b) attribute these market forces to the tremendous drop in the presence of coarse earthenwares. Figure 5.3 demonstrates that Below Cliff community members, who certainly had access to imported refined earthenwares, were still consuming domestic coarse wares, many of which were locally produced, at rates higher than Afro-Jamaicans and possibly even laborers (enslaved and free) at St. Nicholas Abbey. Of course, assemblages vary based on individual households and communities, and house sites around Jamaica demonstrate considerable variability in the ratio of imported to locally made goods (see Reeves 2011:193–200). Furthermore, production and consumption patterns were undoubtedly different in Jamaica and Barbados, as well as across sites on each island. Nonetheless, it is significant that during a period in which imported refined earthenwares from the British Isles were becoming ubiquitous across plantation sites, including in Barbados, poor whites in Below Cliff were still demonstrating a commitment to coarse wares, many of which were locally made and acquired through community-member involvement in racially diverse economic networks. For Barbados, it is likely the case that those who were forcefully tethered to the plantation landscape had more access to industrial wares, but all nonelites, regardless of racial identity, were committed to markets dealing in coarse earthenwares.

"Until They Conform to What Has Been Desired of Them": Re-creating Space

If, as the archaeological data and vernacular landscape suggest, Afro-Barbadians and poor whites were interacting socially, exchanging goods, and sharing cultural practices, planters and other elites would have likely been keenly aware of such transgressions of the racial order. How they reacted to these encounters reveals much about elite attitudes toward interracial relationships. Additionally, it is revelatory of the ways in which nonelites re-created space to facilitate encounters that befit their social and economic networks. This tension between elite and nonelite conceptualizations and uses of space is visible in the historical record and raises significant questions about the salience of racial separation and categories.

At a meeting on the first of November, 1806, members of the vestry for the parish of St. John discussed how seating was to be arranged for services at their church. They detailed the names of several families who owned or rented pews (the overwhelming majority of whom were owners of local plantations) and turned their attention toward available seating. It was determined "that the South Gallery be appropriated for the reception of the poor of the Parish, the pew No. 15 for the reception of the Coloured people, and that the Girls of the Female School of Industry be seated on the Western side of the Organ loft" (BDA D279).[6] Therefore, given that most pews were owned/rented by local planters, the concern over seating was raised specifically about poor whites and free Afro-Barbadians. Discussions surrounding seating assignments in parish churches were common, and an incident in the parish of St. Michael in which free people of color sat in the section reserved for whites reveals that the vestry did not take such situations lightly (see Handler 1974:167–170).

Months later, on August 3, 1807, the minutes read, "Whereas the southern Gallery in the Church has been comfortably and decently fitted up for the Reception of the Poor of the Parish during Divine Service, and that said Poor obstiately [sic] refuse to sit there, Ordered that the Churchwarden withhold from such as shall hereafter continue to refuse to occupey [sic] the said Seats, their quarterly Pensions until they conform to what has been desired of them" (BDA D279). The minutes provide no further details, making the entry open to interpretation. Given the vestry's attempts to circumscribe the seating arrangements of poor whites and free people of color, it would seem that their frustration with the poor whites not sitting in their designated seats may be associated with where they were *choosing* to sit. It is unlikely that the poor whites would be allowed to sit in the pews owned or rented by planters. One can hardly imagine the outrage of a planter arriving for Sunday services to find a poor white tenant seated in his reserved seat. It is more likely that the poor whites were seating themselves in close proximity to, or even alongside, free people of color. While this interpretation is speculative, it stands to reason that the policing of the color line in domestic, social, and official spheres extended to religious services, especially those where planters were present. It then stands to reason that planter outrage would ensue following the commingling of poor whites and free people of color.

The threat put forward by the vestry is also worthy of discussion. As described, poor relief was doled out only to those deemed worthy of such charity. Additionally, the vestry was responsible for establishing the parameters with which recipients were obliged to comply. Failure to comply with vestry requirements could result in removal from the pensioners list (see Marshall 2003; Reilly 2016a). Apparently, poor white refusal to sit within the designated area of the church was sufficient grounds to withhold quarterly pensions. If the interpretation of poor white and Afro-Barbadian commingling is warranted, we see a complicated relationship involving the policing of racial boundaries and the ideologies associated with charity and poverty. The impoverished condition of the Redlegs was a sufficient cause for almsgiving, but such charity was not unconditional. As evidenced from these cases found in St. John, maintaining distinct boundaries between the poor white and Afro-Barbadian population was of greater significance than providing relief for those (whites) in need.

Given that laborers were no longer tethered to their immediate plantation domain through enslaved status, interracial interaction reached new levels in the postemancipation era. By no means did planters or other officials go to great lengths to document such changes, but they are nonetheless visible in the historical record, directly speaking to how places like Below Cliff changed as a result of emancipation. Full emancipation in 1838 brought significant changes to plantation organization. Villages for the enslaved were abandoned as tenantries were established near plantation boundaries. The Masters and Servants Act of 1838 attempted to ensure that the formerly enslaved would be contractually attached to the plantation whose owner had formerly owned their bodies (Newton 2008:229). For poor white militia tenants, the disbandment of the militia meant that former members were now expected to pay rent. At Clifton Hall a new tenantry was established on top of the cliff at the southern boundary of the plantation, now referred to by the plantation's name, Clifton Hall. Along with the villages of Church View and Newcastle, these small villages/tenantries today make up the broader Below Cliff community, or those local community members with ancestry or personal links to the former tenantry.

The tenantry of Below Cliff was inhabited well before emancipation, but the dramatic change brought on by the abolition of slavery brought several newcomers to the community. Baptismal records indicate that following emancipation several formerly enslaved Afro-Barbadians were living in Below Cliff rather than the newly established plantation tenantry on top of the cliff. Forty-six of the 176 individuals baptized between 1838 and 1848 (roughly 26%) can be readily identified as formerly enslaved Afro-Barbadians. These individuals are either listed without last names, described as "adults" instead of given a last name, and often have the first name of a single parent with an occupation of laborer or domestic (BDA RL1/26). These characteristics are strong indicators that such individuals were formerly enslaved rather than being poor whites. In each of these 46 cases Below Cliff is listed as their place of residence. It is unclear if tenants were choosing which tenantry in which to reside or they were being allotted parcels by plantation management. The former, however, is more likely, given that racial divisions among the laboring population was a central facet of Caribbean plantation society, making the latter option questionable. Less expensive rent may have been the impetus for residents to choose Below Cliff as their new home. The possibility of long-standing relationships between Afro-Barbadians and poor whites, however, needs to be considered.

"A Numerous Race of Mulattoes": Policing and Penetrating Racial Boundaries

Interaction has thus far been presented as being a phenomenon taking place between two disparate groups. Ample evidence for cultural exchange and socioeconomic interaction counters persistent stereotypes about poor white isolation, but the reification of racial categories remains problematic. The categories of white and black were fundamental to the functioning of plantation society, but, as Anna Agbe-Davies notes in her study of seventeenth-century Virginia plantations, "social barriers were not a given and needed to be policed" (Agbe-Davies 2015:73). In Barbados, legal attempts were made to preclude the movement of the enslaved across the plantation landscape, but, as this study demonstrates, interaction between groups was not only possible but also part of everyday life. It is therefore a worthwhile endeavor to critically engage with how racial barriers were policed and interrogate the successes and failures of these attempts. If interaction between poor whites and Afro-Barbadians extended into the realm of sexual liaisons and relationships, how stable were racial categories in peripheral locations like Below Cliff? In other words, how salient was the division between white and black?

The lack of clarity of the divisions along lines of race and class was seldom taken lightly by administrators, and in colonial contexts governance associated with sex and marriage sought to remedy the disorder of intermixtures (Loren 2012; Voss 2012). Barbados was no exception, and while there was no official law forbidding interracial marriages, they were extremely uncommon due to the "force of social convention" (Handler 1974:201). Social convention certainly speaks to colonial designs of order, but their transgressions represented unintended consequences of the "effects of empire" (Scaramelli 2012:145). Intermarriage may have been uncommon, but that says little about the degree to which people interacted and intermixed across racial lines

(Handler 1974:210–211), thus blurring the colonial ideal of rigidly separated racial populations. Marginal spaces on the landscape like Below Cliff were ideal settings for these transgressive behaviors, but they leave ambiguous material signatures and limited representation in the historical record.

Historical scholarship touching on racial intermixing in Barbados is rather limited, seldom being the explicit focus of research projects (Handler 1974; Bush 1981; Beckles 1993).[7] A notable exception to the lacunae of such analyses is Cecily Jones's (Forde-Jones 1998; Jones 2007) investigation of poor white women and the mapping of racial boundaries in nineteenth-century St. John (again, the parish home to Below Cliff). Jones's research exposes how elites attempted to monitor and maintain racial boundaries. Through her analysis of the St. John parish vestry minutes, Jones argues that relief provided by the parish to poor white women was a "consequence of the colonial authority's attempt to incorporate disenfranchised poor whites in general, and poor white women in particular, into a white ruling-class cultural sphere that rested on an ideology of white supremacy" (1998:10). There is a strong parallel between this argument and philosopher Lewis Gordon's reading of Charles Mills's conceptualization (1997) of the racial contract. Gordon suggests that the "project of whiteness took the form of historic agreements drawn upon between elite whites explicitly and less powerful whites tacitly at each stage of European humanity's conquest and colonization of the rest of the world" (cited in Mills 2010:214–215). White supremacy and solidarity were ideological adhesives that maintained order throughout the Atlantic world and characterized the "white over black" infrastructure of slavery. I suggest, however, that it is dangerous to assume that such an ideology affected all members of society in the same way. While the significance of racial hierarchies would have cast a shadow over daily interactions on the plantation landscape, they could also be challenged and transgressed, revealing fissures in the rigid separation of racial groups.

Despite the lack of Barbadian legislature that explicitly prohibited interracial marriages or progeny, evidence suggests that such relationships were discouraged and, therefore, seldom appear within the historical record. We do, however, have evidence that the interacting and intermixing of whites and blacks caused distress among island elites, specifically planters whose labor pool was contingent on the functioning of the system of racial slavery and, after emancipation, racialized wage labor. While the scope of this argument makes it difficult to explicate the nuances of racial norms in Barbados from 1627 through the twentieth century, it is possible to gain a semblance of these ideologies through how they became manifest in the historical record in the decades surrounding emancipation, a period during which Below Cliff was a dynamic and active community. Interestingly, evidence of these ideologies illustrates elite desires for racial purity and distinction as well as their frustration when instances of interracial commingling were taking place, thus suggesting the limited success they had in imposing these ideals at the local level.

When racial intermixture is discussed in contexts of plantation slavery, it is usually in instances of the sexual exploitation of enslaved women at the hands of overseers or planters. As in other slave societies, Barbadian planters and managers frequently wielded their power over their property through the rape of the enslaved. Michael Craton has noted that domestics were particularly vulnerable to such attacks, even going as far as claiming that "many female domestics were little better than prostitutes" (Craton 2009:44–45). In one of the earliest documented instances of such a relationship in Barbados, Morgan Godwyn described "a mulatto child" born of a "father being of the Scottish nation, and the other his domestic slave" (Godwyn 1680:113–114). It is unclear whether the child was a direct result of rape, but in all such cases, power asymmetries between the parties is tragically self-evident, giving credence to the notion that consent is impossible under slavery. Such brutalities were common enough for Special Magistrate John Bowen Colthurst, first introduced in chapter 2 with regard to the island's militia, to express his disgust over how this travesty affected the compensation planters received following emancipation in 1834. In September 1836 he commented that "these planters are also receiving the full compensation for their own bastards, begat by themselves or by their rascally white underlings, by slave women, who because the mothers were slaves, were the moment they were born, themselves, slaves by law!!" (Marshall 1977:75). It is impossible to provide quantitative data on the preponderance of enslaver/enslaved (forced) relations and the resulting mixed-race progeny, but the fact remains that such individuals would be born as enslaved or, in the postemancipation period, be identified as being of African descent.[8]

Despite the preponderance and harsh reality of these exploitative events, alternative forms of interracial relationships frequently commented on by elites and observers fomented between poor whites (servants and wage laborers) and the enslaved. While the extent to which such relationships involved marriage is difficult, if not impossible, to discern, sexual relationships as well as mixed-race children often received the scorn of commenters. As with relationships between planters and the enslaved, relations between laborers of different racial identities were often plagued by the abuse of power. Within the Parliamentary Papers are found comments by an anonymous planter in 1788 attributing the "Natural increase of Negro Slaves" not only to their "promiscuity" but also to "the lascivious abuse of authority in white servants, over the immature and unprotected females" (HCPP 1789:27). Despite the decline in use of indentured labor in the late seventeenth century, it appears the use of white labor was common enough by the late eighteenth century to draw comment as it pertained to the violent effects on the slave population.

The power dynamics inherent within plantation slave society allowed the sexual exploitation of enslaved women to continue almost unabated throughout the period of slavery. This does not, however, eclipse the fact that relationships could have developed between laborers of diverse racial identities, much to the chagrin of planters and other elites. For instance, in an 1824 report, plantation manager Alleyne would comment that "whenever I have discovered any attempts on the part of the white servants to form connections with the females of the estate, I have invariably discharged them" (Anonymous 1824:104). In 1798, Wood, a manager responsible for Newton Estate, would write the owners in England providing an "Annual summary of the condition of your property." In this letter Wood describes his frustration in his failed attempts to control the enslaved women. He writes, "They all of them either have or have had white husbands, that is, such men who keep them. Mary-Thomas, since I came here [i.e., took up managing Newton Plantation] got into a connection with the bookkeeper. I ordered him immediately to be disciplined. She was with child by him and delivered . . . in May last of a boy" (Newton Manuscripts [NM] 523/381/1). Again, power asymmetries certainly plagued such relationships, but the possibility of enslaved women actively pursuing such relationships should not be immediately discounted. Despite the best efforts of island elites and management to patrol racial boundaries, it is evident that relationships developed with resulting offspring complicating the island's binary model of racial identity.

A generation later Mary Thomas of Newton Plantation, along with her children, appears again in the records of Newton Estate. In 1815, Robert Haynes, a prominent Barbadian planter who also happened to own Clifton Hall, commented in a letter to Lane, the owner of Newton, that there had been difficulties in dealing with Mary and Kitty Thomas and her three children. The women had been such trouble that Polly Kitty Williams, daughter of Kitty Thomas, was sold for a black girl of "equal value." Commenting on the difficulties faced in dealing with Polly Kitty Williams, Haynes notes that "since her birth she has never as much as turned over one straw for you, she is as white as either of us and in fact I could not find an occupation for her" (Watson 2000a). In his interpretation of this passage Karl Watson argues that the racial identities of these women illustrates that in contrast to the United States, which harbored a more rigidly defined racial taxonomy (i.e., the "one drop rule"), Barbados was home to "a more flexible attitude which allowed shifts in racial classifications to take place over several generations," a stark contrast to the assertion discussed earlier in this chapter made by Handler about racial politics on the island. I agree with Watson's assessment to an extent given that Haynes noted the ambiguity in the race of these women and their children. Despite the acknowledged phenotypic variation between these white women and other enslaved laborers, however, given that these pale-skinned children were born to enslaved women, they, too, were enslaved. Under Barbadian law, therefore, their white appearance could not alter their status as slaves and, thus, a black racial identity. Haynes's only reluctance is in their white *appearance*, not their imposed *identity*.

In looking more closely in the region surrounding Below Cliff, instances of interracial relations between poor whites and Afro-Barbadians persisted well into the postemancipation era. Additionally, in some cases, the genders of such relationships were reversed, involving black men and white women. Although such instances are difficult to track in the historical record, they are nonetheless significant in the parishes of St. John and St. Philip. Additionally, given the nature of the parish records, we simultaneously see elite attempts to police and prohibit such commingling. Woodville Marshall's (2003) research on the Carpenter Trust of St. Philip is particularly revealing of elite attempts to police racial boundaries and laborers actively behaving otherwise. The Carpenter Trust was established in Richard Carpenter's 1662 will, which stipulated that deserving members of the poor (white) community were to receive specific allotments of muscovado sugar and small parcels of land on which to reside. The parish vestry was responsible for carrying out the parameters of this trust each year and determined who qualified as deserving members of the poor community. The trust is still active today, but discrepancies surrounding the allocation of funds have troubled the charitable resource since its establishment. For instance, throughout the nineteenth century, women were frequently evicted from trust lands for immoral behavior (as determined by the vestry). One such "immoral" act that was grounds for eviction was a white woman giving birth to a mixed-raced child, which occurred in April 1873 when a Mrs. Bascom was discovered to have "lately had a coloured child" (Marshall 2003:186). Despite the charitable nature of the trust in providing land and financial support for those deemed worthy, Marshall has argued that "eviction from Parish Land [parcels allocated to the deserving poor whites] and removal from the pensioners' list were obviously the main weapons used by the Vestry in their long war against the undeserving poor" (186). As evidenced here, one aspect of this war was the struggle to maintain what elites believed to be racial purity among the "white" community.

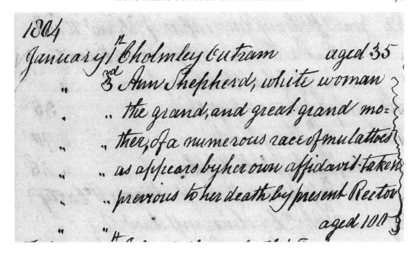

Figure 5.4. Burial record for Ann Shepherd in the St. Philip Church burial registry (BDA RL1/25, 108). Records accessible at https://www.familysearch.org. (Matthew C. Reilly)

Remaining in the parish of St. Philip, an entry in the burial registry during the final decades of slavery reveals an individual instance of a transgression of the line that divided nonelites along racial lines. On January 3, 1804, Ann Shepherd's burial was registered with a peculiar note beside her name. Shepherd's burial record (Figure 5.4) reads, "Ann Shepherd, white woman the grand, and great grand mother [sic], of a numerous race of mulattoes as appears by her own affidavit taken previous to her death by present Rector— aged 100" (BDA RL1/25:108). Shepherd's burial entry is unique for a number of reasons. Being 100 years old at the time of her death was certainly novel in early nineteenth-century Barbadian society. Additionally, it is odd that she is specifically identified as being a "white woman." Given that it was uncommon for the enslaved or free people of color to be recorded in parish registries during the period of slavery, it is strange that Shepherd was explicitly identified as being white. Furthermore, the five-line note that accompanied her entry is peculiar given that the overwhelming majority of entries were simply listed with their name, date of burial, and age at time of death. Perhaps Shepherd's old age warranted the extra space in the registry and the inclusion of these personal details, but the exact reasoning is unknown. Regardless, Shepherd's affidavit suggests that she desired to be identified as a white woman and the matriarch of a kinship network that comprised "a numerous race of mulattoes." Additionally, the entry is clear in noting that this information was "by *her own* affidavit" (emphasis added). This assertion suggests a semblance of pride felt by Shepherd, not only because of her large family, but also because of the fact that they were a mixed-race clan.

o

Below Cliff and other such vernacular landscapes around the island were far from racial utopias in which inhabitants and those that operated in their networks were immune to the realities of racism and racial violence that permeated all aspects of Barbadian society. Racial tensions would have been palpable, and, even if seldom discussed, they still affect island socio-economics. The argument put forward in this chapter does not suggest that members of the Below Cliff community actively resisted racial ideologies or explicitly combated planter strategies of spatial organization. Rather, under the circumstances of life on the plantation, they manipulated and created a landscape that facilitated socioeconomic networks across racial lines. Having mixed-race children should hardly be attributed to desires to irk the plantocracy. Below Cliff boasted a geographical space in which degrees of autonomy could be expressed through choices of social interaction, cultural and material exchange, and intimate relationships. Racial categories and identities, especially those that were imposed, mattered a great deal (and still do); they could, however, be transformed and embodied in ways that challenge assumptions about the salience of categorizations. Through a reliance on essentializing categories there is a subtle danger involving the terms that were (and are) necessary to produce ideologies of distinction and separation. The historical and contemporary use of determinant identity markers such as white and black reify the supposedly pure nature of these categories, thus creating challenges for interrogating their stability, historical deployments, and shifting meanings (see Monahan 2011).

It can be argued that the limited data showcasing instances of poor white and Afro-Barbadian interaction may be exceptions rather than the rule, but these exceptions are nonetheless important in recognizing alternatives to plantation modernity. If these practices and behaviors deviate from colonial ideals or norms, then the legitimacy of those norms need to be questioned. The consumption of cottage-industry monkey jars, poor whites sitting alongside Afro-Barbadians in church, and similarities between poor white and Afro-Barbadian architecture, dietary practices, and use of space are rather innocuous and unassuming occurrences. They can be described as forms of "residence" (Silliman 2014), or ways of living in and through repressive structural governance. At the same time, regardless of their quotidian nature, they are nonetheless powerful in challenging the central ideologies that underpinned and anchored plantation modernity.

SIX

ALTERNATIVE MODERNITIES
BELOW THE CLIFF

Modernity is not one, but many.

—Dilip Parameshwar Gaonkar (2001:17)

Fred Watson was born in Bath, St. John (located a few short miles southeast of Below Cliff), in 1926 and currently lives in a small village due east of Below Cliff. Having spent his life in the rough waters off the island's east coast, he has an intimate knowledge of local fishing practices, the fishing industry, and rural life in a region with a diverse racial population. On a summer afternoon in 2013 I showed him the photograph of Redleg fishermen (see Figure I.2) as he quietly stitched together a fishing net alongside his wife in their chattel house. Watson commented that he had never seen it before but softly and quickly responded that "this is a family photograph." With brief hesitation, he was able to point to and identify by name most of the individuals pictured. At nearly 90 years of age, he was then able to explain the kinship networks that tied together the men pictured. Connecting past and present, he then rattled off a list of descendants who still live in the area.

The photograph is widely known among island history buffs and those interested in family genealogy. It is also callously circulated on the web as evidence of what has become of the seventeenth-century "white slaves" who were sent to Barbados. I have also encountered individuals who trace their ancestry to one or more of the men in tattered garments. Until my conversation with Fred Watson, however, I had never heard this remarkable early twentieth-century photograph referred to as a "family photograph." Represented are members of the Watson, Goddard, King, and Haynes families, surnames popular among the Redleg population for several generations who are still present in St. John. Fred was able to identify several of his father's and mother's brothers who were pictured in the photograph, including his mother's brother, Simeon Goddard, found on the lower left, and his father's brother, Joe Watson, found in the center of the back row. Each of the familial connections pointed out by Fred was later confirmed using registry data from St. Margaret's Church. The revelation that the photograph depicts an extended matrilineal kinship network was made more significant by the realization that the phenotypes of the men pictured indicate that this network involved Afro-Barbadian as well as poor white ancestries.

More remarkable yet was Fred's connection to the Norris household, the primary site of archaeological investigation in this book. Fred's sister, Clarine Watson, was the mother of a childhood resident of the household, making this gentleman the nephew of Fred Watson. This member of the Norris household, whose pale skin warranted his involvement as an interviewee in documentaries about the Redlegs, as well as being the subject of a local newspaper story titled "The Last White Cane Cutter," is of mixed-race ancestry—a fact that he openly acknowledges and willingly discusses. Of particular interest is the language he uses in discussing color and racial identity. Following my discussion with Fred Watson, I inquired about this former resident's mother. He quickly produced a framed black-and-white photograph of his mother, likely taken when she was in her thirties. Despite the age of the photograph, as well as the quality of the coloration, it was evident that his mother's complexion was rather dark. As I looked at the photograph I heard the quiet but confident statement "she a dark woman." This language was in keeping with how former inhabitants of Below Cliff households were described by community members. For instance, when walking by the ruins of the Bradshaw residence, I was once told by a former resident that the patriarch "was a dark fella' who worked in a shop."

Many Below Cliff community members chose to use the terms "dark" and "light" on a sliding spectrum when referring to the racial identity of an individual, past or present.[1] This vocabulary was new to me as an outsider and also sidesteps conventional terminology used in the scholarship of race, even if this lexicon is still saturated with the politics of racial epistemologies and colonial logics. Dark and light are ambiguous terms that not only problematize hard-lined categories like white and black but also challenge social norms about how race is perceived and structurally monitored. Throughout this book, I have favored the use of traditional vocabulary, but the insight community members provided should make abundantly clear the multiple and complex conceptualizations of race. The effects of racialization are conspicuous across the Barbadian landscape. Despite their shortcomings, the faulty categories of white and black had unparalleled impacts on the lives of plantation residents. Offered by members of this community, however, is an alternative to the traditional ways in which the experience of modernity is conceptualized. In this closing chapter I bring all of the threads of the conversation together to suggest what might be gained through an archaeology of alternative modernities.

Conceptualizing Alternative Modernities

The tangible consequences of modernity are ubiquitous features on the

Barbadian landscape. They include vast (though diminishing) sugar fields, opulent and decaying plantation great houses, and rows of deteriorating chattel houses inhabited by descendants of the enslaved. Despite observable and significant variation between and within islands, these symbols, scars, ruins, monuments, and memorials of modernity characterize the past and present of the Caribbean. A recognition that the experience of modernity is varied, however, is not enough. Modernities are multiple and contextually articulated. This case study of the poor whites illustrates the complex relationships between planters, administrators, enslaved and free Afro-Barbadians, and poor whites inhabiting the plantation landscape. In Below Cliff, a space cast as marginal, a particular way of life was developed that was out of sync with traditional understandings of Caribbean modernity, but it was nonetheless modern—even if those who made this modernity a reality were conscripted (Scott 2004).

The concept of alternative modernities has roots in the late 1990s/early 2000s, but it was short-lived within anthropological literature (Gaonkar, ed. 2001; Knauft, ed. 2002; Holston 1999; Taylor 1999). This relatively small yet compelling body of literature leads with the premise that modernity is inescapable given the onset of globalization spanning the past five centuries. Even in the face of resistance to processes of modernity, it stands to reason that the whole of the world's population has been affected by its forces in some fashion. While modernity as a concept has been vastly critiqued along the lines of its association with progress, development, capitalism, colonialism, liberalism, and general inequality, Knauft notes that approaching modernity "as a differentiated and variegated process" (Knauft 2002:3) demands local analysis given that "the way people engage the ideologies and institutions of a so-called modernizing world provides a valuable vantage point for understanding contemporary articulations of culture and power" (4). Localized engagement with how historical actors responded to modernizing processes can therefore reveal how alternative modernities are engendered as a result of these contentious relations.

Such an ambiguous and subjective perspective rooted in academic pluralisms has its critics. Knauft has suggested that the recent scholarly preference for pluralizing concepts and forces has resulted in an "adjectival softening" that ultimately weakens academic insight (Knauft 2002:35). This can be due, in part, to an adherence to extreme relativism, whereby localized difference, diversity, and exceptionalism diminish the significance and analytical merit of broader processes such as colonialism, capitalism, power, and modernity at large. Using a different point of departure, but ultimately arriving at a similar point, John Kelly (2002) argues that modernity's sublime character, like that of civilization, demands that we abandon the term as a central analytic of the social sciences in favor of the grotesque to approach, and adequately oppose, the detrimental forces of modernity. A similar relativism and lack of a lucid engagement with the more consequential applications of power and subordination became a point of critique of postprocessual archaeology in the early 1990s, a movement that owes much to a general fascination with the emergence of postmodernism (see Trigger 2006:529–548; Harvey 1990). While this critique is understandable, engagements with intimate, regional, and global instantiations of power ultimately assuage concerns that extreme relativism can temper the ability of local analyses to be more broadly relevant. Throughout this book I remained keenly aware of institutional, material, and discursive structures that operated on multiple scales in an attempt to speak to broader experiences in the colonial and capitalistic Atlantic world.

A more germane critique, which also presents suggestive avenues of conceptual development, comes from David Scott's (2004) reading of C. L. R. James's *The Black Jacobins* (1963). In his analysis of the plantation as an inaugural space of modernity, Scott positions the Haitian Revolution's romantic and tragic hero, Toussaint Louverture, as a conscript of modernity whose place within processes of modernity made the possibility of an alternative a reality. Scott argues that "the idea of alternative or subaltern modernities operates by constructing a normative expectation of resistance or overcoming." Scott continues, "Imagined in this way, what is obscured is the extent to which the transformed terrain on which these creative responses are being enacted is itself positively constituting (or rather, reconstituting) these subjects, their new objects of desire, and the new concepts that shape the horizon of that desire" (Scott 2004:114–115). He finds nothing particularly disheartening about such interpretations but finds the underlying model of repression and resistance misguided (115): "I am urging, therefore, that we need a way of describing the regime of slave plantation power in which what is brought into view is less what it restricts and what resists this restriction, less what it represses and what escapes or overcomes this repression, and more the modern conditions it created that positively shaped the way in which language, religion, kinship, and so on were reconstituted." While burdensome and oppressive, Scott suggests we view the forces of modernity as opportunistic in their capacity to generate the conditions for the very ability to engender alternatives. In this sense, we see the positive, productive power of modernity that gives rise to its own multiplicity.

Despite Scott's focus on plantation slavery, his approach is applicable for analyses of all conscripts of modernity. Additionally, although Scott's appeal is phrased as a critique of alternative modernities, it is evident that it conveniently doubles as a subtle champion of its central tenets—namely, that despite the ever-present and imposing forces of modernity, those affected are active participants in reconstituting the nature of such forces and associated ideologies due to their envelopment in such processes. The settlement and development of the Barbadian colony brought into contact a host of individuals from all walks of life (mostly coerced), who, for better or for worse, would play a role in the processes of modernization that overtook the island. As such, it was their very situatedness within such modernizing processes that offered the power of possibility. Presented with these possibilities, actors responded in multiple ways, from direct resistance to a host of alternatives that not only provided counterforces to processes of modernity (not necessarily synonymous with resistance) but also altered their nature.

These processes, as they unfolded with the advent of European expansion, have been separated into two conceptually related categories by Trouillot (2003): social modernization and cultural modernity. Despite the fact that the two are inextricably linked, Trouillot argues that "the distinction becomes necessary inasmuch as it illuminates specific historical moments and processes" (2003:37). Social modernization can be viewed as those forces associated with the expansion and development of capitalism, colonialism, the state, industrialization, and so forth—what Trouillot labels the "creation of place." Alternatively, he describes cultural modernity as having to do "with those aspects and moments in the development of world capitalism that require the projection of the individual or collective subject against both space and time" (37). In other words, we can characterize cultural modernity as how individuals or collectives experience the processes of modernization and develop ways of being in the world that affect and are affected by such processes. Trouillot's approach to modernity seamlessly allows for, if not demands, the creation and existence of multiple, varied, and alternative modernities.

Despite Trouillot's eloquent argument illustrating the five-century time depth of global processes of modernization, the literature on alternative modernities has thus far inadequately come to grips with the significance of this historicity. A central trope of globalization studies argues that global interconnectedness and the effects of modernity are more strongly felt in the contemporary than any time in the past due to consolidated geographies and technological innovation. While this may be the case, it in no way diminishes the significance of these processes in the past or their influence on the present. It is crucial that we address the nature of modernities in the past and how they are perceived, portrayed, denied, or repressed in the present. For if modernity or social modernizing forces have their roots in European expansion with the onset of colonialism and capitalism (as many scholars of and from the

Caribbean have argued), alternative modernities have similar roots. There are, however, inherent challenges associated with unearthing the alternative.

Reverting back to the literature discussed in chapter 1 (Fischer 2004; Buck-Morss 2009; Linebaugh and Rediker 2000; Trouillot 1995), we see that the denial of particular pasts in favor of the metanarratives of modernity serves as the crux for recognizing how and why particular alternatives emerged and were subsequently suppressed. For the Haitian Revolution, Fischer (2004) suggests that in addition to the radical resistance that became manifest in the violent rebellion, the aftermath of the revolution spawned a cultural, creole modernity that burst at the seams and sought to spread across the plantation landscape of the New World. In turn, the nature of this alternative modernity—its philosophical underpinnings, associated ideologies, and politico-economics—was vociferously denied on a global scale through an international rejection of the state's sovereignty, a refusal to believe that a black state could properly function, and an overall closed-mindedness to Afro-Caribbean cultural sophistication. Not only was the event of the Haitian Revolution "unthinkable" even as it transpired (Trouillot 1995:70–107), but also the ensuing alternative modernity that emerged was quickly, quietly, and purposely disavowed (Fischer 2004), making the event and its aftermath a "nonevent" and reclaiming plantation slavery as the metanarrative of Caribbean modernity.

In a similar fashion, although not couched in the rhetoric of modernity or its alternatives, Linebaugh and Rediker (2000) present the hidden, revolutionary Atlantic history that once was or could have been in their *The Many-Headed Hydra*. The volume destabilizes teleological metanarratives of Atlantic-world historiography, presenting instances where capitalism faltered due to individuals and groups who sought more egalitarian modes of subsistence, where racial divisions took a back seat as actors recognized mutual suffering and oppression across racial lines, and where colonial and capitalist power was continuously contested across the oceanic realm by a motley hydra that sought to alleviate its own suppression. In one sense the authors are suggesting the "hewers of wood and drawers of water," or the working classes of the Atlantic world, were responsible for amassing modes of resistance based on their particular experiences, leading to certain expectations of futures outside of the modalities and negative instantiations of modernization. In other words, their expectations are representative of Koselleck's (1985) "futures past," realities that failed to come to fruition that cause obstacles in how we perceive and comprehend histories that never were or occupy a different "problem space" (Scott 2004, 2013) than our contemporary scholarly purview allows.

Slated in terms of resistance or subordination, such conflict and struggles limit the ways in which local entanglements of people, structures, ideologies, and landscapes can be dissected and interpreted. While not being dismissive of instances of direct resistance, we need to be cognizant of less violent and more nuanced reactions to modernity and modernization on the part of those affected by such processes and how these reactions reconstituted these circumstances. These processes are also indicative of a dynamic dialogue between those who are responsible for imposing the forces of modernization as well as those called to be subordinates and participants in its schematics. Additionally, I recognize that the binary model of dominant and dominated implied here is an infinitely complex power structure based on any number of individual identities. These dynamic, nuanced, and power-laden relationships are immersed within processes of modernization that provided the necessary conditions for their alternatives.

To return to Barbados, those living below the cliff, in addition to the entirety of the Barbadian population, were invariably affected by processes of modernization and cultural modernity in a number of ways. In this sense, following Talal Asad, David Scott (2004:98–131) argues that those living in the Caribbean, particularly the enslaved, were conscripts of modernity. Whether planters, merchants, administrators, enslaved, or small farmers, those living in plantation society were enveloped within processes of modernization but were, nonetheless, essential to the development of localized incarnations of modernity. If, however, as Trouillot (2003) posits, modernity and its global sprawl have their roots in late fifteenth-century European expansion, then the development and its alternatives have similar ontologies. Keeping Dawdy's critique (2010) of modern exceptionalism in mind, this approach is, therefore, contextualized within the Caribbean experience of colonization. Despite the successes of particular metanarratives of modernity receiving salience while concomitantly silencing others (Trouillot 1995), unfurling the nature of these alternatives reveals much in terms of how historical actors responded to imposed conditions and thus transformed their very character.

With these theoretical musings in mind, the question on which this final chapter rests is, what constituted the alternative modernity found in places like Below Cliff? Thus far, I have illustrated historical, semiethnographic, and archaeological data suggesting past and present ways of life below the cliff that call into question traditional interpretations of poor white relations to capital and local socioeconomic spheres as well as the nature of racial identity and categories. Limited historiography, in addition to contemporary perceptions of the poor whites, seamlessly coincides with broader narratives of Caribbean modernity that have trouble locating the place of white labor in the broader framework of sugar and slave societies, thus failing to interrogate

the rigidity or porosity of racial boundaries. In this final chapter I engage
with these alternative modernities as they emerged and developed in the St.
John area of Barbados. Additionally, this research poses serious questions
about the nature of historical archaeological inquiry and suggests the need to
assess strongly held disciplinary convictions and goals as the discipline moves
forward.

Capital Relations and the Politics of Work

Plantation capitalism was regimented, refined, profit-oriented, exploitative,
and demanding—characteristics that most viciously affected the enslaved. At
Clifton Hall Plantation, poor whites resided below the cliff and were seen
as inconsequential to the functioning of the agro-industry. The relationship
between Below Cliff residents and processes of capitalism was, therefore,
contentious. Data suggest that poor white economic systems, networks, and
means of subsistence did not neatly comport with capitalist modes of production that defined plantation labor and industry. In short, contrary to discourses of isolation and idleness, poor white residents of Below Cliff were
not ostracized or severed from the capitalist mode of production associated
with production on the plantation. Rather, for both men and women, some
worked as wage laborers at Clifton Hall, some were subsistence farmers, some
held skilled positions in the community, some were fishermen, and others
supported themselves and their families by any means necessary. The complicated relationship between Below Cliff residents and capitalist processes
demands an approach that views historical actors not as passive subjects to
totalizing forces of capitalism or as explicitly resistant insubordinates to such
forces. A more nuanced approach carefully articulates the tensions between
poor white ways of life and capitalism.

The approach taken here owes much to Vinay Gidwani's (2008) Marxist interpretation of rural labor transformations in western central India as
read through Marx's *Grundrisse* (1973). Gidwani provides trenchant readings
of, and facilitates critical dialogue between, more orthodox Marxists such
as David Harvey (2006 [1982]) and culturally informed Marxism stem-
ming from postcolonial theory and subaltern studies like those of Dipesh
Chakrabarty (1992, 2000). These readings inform his observations of
changes in local labor patterns at the hands of the multiple shifts and forms
of capital. His geographical and ethnographic methodologies present informants who illustrate the ability of laborers to cause interruptions to or barriers for the fluid motion of capital. In a jarringly similar fashion to the way
in which poor whites are described, Gidwani presents laboring interlocutors
who choose to relate to changing terrains of capitalist production on their

own terms, thus transforming their structures. As Gidwani points out, such modes of existence do not necessarily have to take the form of explicit resistance to capitalist processes; instead, they can do so partially. "Ajibhai [one of his interlocutors] is not mounting a frontal assault against capital—an individual in any case does not have that kind of capacity—but he is producing a crisis in one molecular point through which capital as value must pass. Call it a counterforce. It is resistance in *that* sense" (Gidwani 2008:213). Rather than being viewed in terms of dominance or resistance, Gidwani views instances of these counterforces to be representative of his distinction between the politics of labor and the politics of work.

Using Marx's interpretation of the use value of labor as a point of departure, Gidwani suggests that a politics of work involves individual or group acts of labor that are not harnessed by capitalist modes of production (Gidwani 2008:212–216): in other words, labor that has not been conscripted by capital for profit accumulation but labor that is nonetheless productive for alternative purposes. In this formulation, work can be viewed as "*not-objectified labor*" and be conceived of "*positively*" as "the *possibility* . . . of multiple actualizations or becomings" (196; emphasis in original). The archaeological evidence, in conjunction with a reading of the now-forested landscape, suggests that Below Cliff residents developed modes of subsistence and economic systems that parallel Gidwani's "politics of work." While wary of succumbing to the pitfalls and perils of the archaeological analogy, countless examples of a twenty-first-century politics of work can be found in present-day Barbados, including among those identified as Redlegs. These examples can be viewed as inflections of the politics of work that very likely mirror economic relations and activity in the past. For instance, the Fentys, an elderly couple who are part of the broader Below Cliff community, live in a two-story walled house along the windy road in Church View leading down to Martin's Bay. In discussing life below the cliff, the husband and wife recalled "simpler" times (when select relatives still occupied Below Cliff) when informal and moral economies were the dominant means by which local residents made a living. Despite their nostalgia, their current means of subsistence reflects the persistence of such economies in the wake of substantial transformations in the broader capitalist economy.

I frequently visited with the Fentys after I had concluded excavations for the day. More times than not, I found Mrs. Fenty conducting household chores or in the kitchen preparing fish or vegetables. Her husband was still active in the yard areas and was seldom in the house when I approached. On various visits I arrived as he was painting the house, pruning the fruit trees, retrieving ripened breadfruit from their tree, picking ackees (known as guineps elsewhere in the Caribbean), and tending to the bananas. These fruits were consumed by the Fentys and shared with family and neighbors. Additionally, every Tuesday they would climb into their worn Volkswagen hatchback and sell a batch of bananas at a local market. These subsistence and market activities consumed much of their time and, in general, had provided them with what they believed was a comfortable life. In conjunction with these subsistence and informal economic activities, the Fentys, along with their friends and relatives, took part in various forms of wage labor from work on the plantation to various jobs they acquired in Bridgetown.

A combination of wage labor and informal community economies is a standard feature across the rural landscape. In the Below Cliff area, I frequently came across a member of the Gibson family who worked as a mechanical technician on construction vehicles. He spent most mornings, evenings, and weekends tending to his banana fields and maintaining his home. His brother undertook odd jobs around the community, from collecting and hauling coconuts to painting. Fred Watson, now retired after a storied career in education, spends his days making fishing nets and casually fishing. These various economic activities are the methods and matrices through which members of the extended Below Cliff community lived their daily lives. There was little, if any, noticeable difference between the economics networks of those considered to be poor whites and Afro-Barbadians. Rather, the difference lies in how each group's industriousness has been perceived in the past and present. As tangential or temporary participants in the plantation economy, the labor habits of the poor whites were perceived to be lackadaisical or nonexistent. It is then important to recognize not only the inadequacy of such historical renderings of labor but also the realities of the alternatives that were manifest in the forces of modernity.

This discussion of the politics of work smoothly lends itself to the discussion of the proposed archaeology of alternative modernities. Residents of Below Cliff developed particular strategies within a regional capitalist system that allowed them to survive and subsist, despite impoverished conditions and a harsh landscape, on their own terms. These terms did not necessarily adhere to abject resistance to or passive compliance with capitalist production, an unfortunate trap that has plagued some Marxist archaeological interpretations of the past.[2] While the forces of capitalism and its influence on the lives of working-class individuals are ubiquitous in the archaeological record, particularly following the changes associated with the industrial era of the mid-nineteenth century (see, for example, Shackel 2009), interpretations of resistance often assume a particular intentionality on the part of individuals or groups that runs the risk of turning a blind eye to more nuanced reactions to capitalist processes and transformations. Rather, the alternatives observed in Below Cliff involved modes of work that benefited those undertaking the work, their families, and community members in addition to forms of employment in which they sold their labor on the plantation. Despite unrelenting discourses that have projected the poor whites as homogeneously idle for several centuries, archaeological, archival, and semi-ethnographic evidence suggests that the socioeconomic structures established and engaged in by tenantry residents were at odds with capitalist notions of labor and industriousness.

The ongoing dialogue between poor white modes of work and elite conceptions of proper labor reveals itself in the vestry minutes that condemn and punish perceived idleness, the parish registries that identify and mark individuals with particular occupations of acceptable labor, and the volatile landscape that had been deemed "rab" land. Yet, work on this same landscape produced the necessary foodstuffs to sustain a population and provided the means through which to acquire the materials consumed, used, reused, and discarded by Below Cliff residents. The spatial arrangement of households below the cliff also bespeaks an array of economic activities that include garden plots for provision crops, small parcels for sugar production, animal pens, and detached kitchens. The creation of a vernacular landscape seen in the carving of entrances/exits up and down the cliff also indicates that community members were facilitating intra- and intercommunity interaction that had economic dimensions. Dismantling inept stereotypes that cast the Redlegs as lazy does little analytical work in establishing how and why such discourses were produced and how they affect and are affected by the realities of poor white socioeconomic networks. Their world was one dominated by sugar and slavery—a modernity within which they were conscripted to reside, survive, and interact with other individuals and groups on the landscape. Despite a degree of shared phenotypic character with plantation management, parish officials, island administrators, and planters, the everyday lives of poor whites marked a distinctly and alternatively modern manner of living on the plantation landscape. In addition to how they coped with the realities of poverty and ways of life that constituted counterforces to capitalist processes, the poor whites developed and sustained unique relationships with an Afro-Barbadian population from whom they were portrayed as being genetically, physically, socially, and legally isolated and distinct.

Making and Unmaking Race

Incorporating race and racial identity into this consideration of alternative modernities requires a subtle and imaginative engagement with culture and ideology in interpreting the presented data. Additionally, given that race, class, and gender are inextricably linked, the previous discussion of class and relations to capital is folded into considerations of racial relations, identities, and genealogies below the cliff. A dialectic involving elite ideologies about racial identity and distinction operated in conjunction with cultural encounters and nuances among nonelite plantation residents across the color line. The transformations that occurred as a consequence of these relations represented the emergence of an alternative racial modernity. Data suggest that Below Cliff residents, and potentially poor whites in general, were not entirely or purely white, not quite black, but nevertheless categorized in stark terms of racial identity.

The previous chapter illustrates that relations between poor whites and Afro-Barbadians were, and still are, complex, to say the least. The establishment of an agro-industrial plantation system inflicted unparalleled constraints on interracial relations in the form of legislation restricting the movement of the enslaved on and off the plantation, parish vestry policies that set behavioral and moral standards for the receipt of poor relief, a labor system in which, in general, black bodies were owned and white bodies were legally free to sell their labor, and the development of ideologies that viewed blacks and whites as being racially separate, distinct, and socioeconomically unequal. This last point is certainly not unique to Barbados, and despite spatial/temporal heterogeneity, there are underlying similarities in the broader imperial power structures and processes of Othering (Stoler 1995, 2002; Said 1978).

Informed by cultural anthropological and philosophical literature on race and whiteness (Hartigan 2005; Tyler 2012; Monahan 2011; Pierre 2013), the data presented throughout this book have suggested that ideologies surrounding race have drastically constricted the ways in which race and racial identities are perceived, produced, reproduced, and transformed in the past and present. The landscape of Clifton Hall Plantation facilitated commingling between the enslaved above and the poor white tenants below the cliff. Data from baptismal registries suggest that these relationships forged during the era of slavery may have provided the impetus for formerly enslaved Afro-Barbadians to reside in the poor white tenantry following emancipation. Cultural exchanges are visible in the material record, as seen through similarities in domestic architecture, usage of household and yard space, consumption patterns, and markers of socioeconomic status. In short, despite modern ideologies of racial distinctiveness and social isolation along lines of color, evidence from Below Cliff reveals that in this peripheral space not only was interracial interaction possible, it was also likely common.

While the available evidence only allows for brief glimpses into the nature of these complex relationships, it is likely that they were often contentious and far from equitable. At the close of the apprenticeship period in 1838, Thome and Kimball familiarly commented on the degraded, degenerate, alcoholic, and idle state of the poor white population (1838:57): "They [the poor whites] will beg of blacks more provident and industrious than themselves, or they will steal their poultry and rob their provision grounds at night; but they would disdain to associate with them. Doubtless these sans culottes[3] swell in their dangling rags with the haughty consciousness that they possess white skins. What proud reflection they must have, as they pursue their barefoot way, thinking on their high lineage, and running back through the long line of their illustrious ancestry, whose notable badge was a white skin." The passage bears significance in not only describing hostile relations of poor white and Afro-Barbadian but also in illustrating how, in some cases, modern ideologies associated with racial hierarchies explicitly affected these relations. The authors express a sense of distance from the subjects they are describing. As outside observers they appear to be describing relations between two distinct racial groups—distinct from each other as well as from themselves. John Hartigan (2005:38–39) argues that such a portrayal of the Redlegs reflects a self-reflexive anxiety on the part of the authors who, despite a shared phenotype with the poor whites, who were apparently proud of their white skins, are implying that without appropriate moral attitudes toward industriousness, hygiene, and etiquette, all whites are in danger of degenerating and joining the ranks of the poor white race.

In addition to the processes of Othering that distance the authors from the poor whites, they explicitly draw racialized and class distinctions between the poor whites and Afro-Barbadians to ensure that they are identified as racially pure and distinct demographics. Furthermore, by depicting relations between them as hostile, the authors reify the disparity between the groups. What is implied is a performative element to the class and racial identities of all parties involved (Jackson 2001). If, as this passage suggests, poor white and Afro-Barbadian relations were characterized by racial conflict and disdain, it would suggest the success of modern ideologies of racial hierarchies in being determinate of racial relations. As Hartigan suggests (2005), however, these ideologies often essentialize and reduce more complex cultural phenomena to reflections and reifications of these ideologies. Here again, examples from the present-day extended Below Cliff community provide insight into these complex racial relations.

On one of the occasions when I walked through the woods of Below Cliff with a member of the Norris family, he described his relationships with Afro-Barbadians while he was growing up in the tenantry. He explained that he socialized, went to church, and attended school with Afro-Barbadians and that, for the most part, they got along. He did, however, comment that "they had names for me and I had names for them" before summating that "it didn't really matter, we all got on as friends." His comments are significant on multiple levels. First, we should not assume that the Afro-Barbadians to whom he was referring felt similarly about these relationships. After all, race relations were often contentious and violent in sugar and slavery societies. At the same time, he openly acknowledged the daily social encounters between poor whites and Afro-Barbadians, something long denied in the historical record. Additionally, we see the influence of ideologies that projected an island society that was entirely divided. It is unsurprising that racial animosities would foment in such an environment, especially given the island's history. While significant, however, such ideologies were not entirely constitutive of racial relations.

The third participant in our conversation that afternoon was the grandson of this former Below Cliff resident, himself considered an extended member of the Below Cliff community. This young Barbadian regularly joined us on trips into the woods as well as on visits to speak with other community members. He explained that he was interested in learning more about his family's history, even feeling a strong connection to his grandfather's childhood home. His ancestry lies on both sides of the racial divide described by Thome and Kimball. Such an interracial identity is not uncommon in the area and, using the racial terminology encountered throughout the region, it became evident that in most families there were various shades of "dark" and "light" complexions. The examination of complex and interracial kinship networks presented at the start of this chapter, in conjunction with historical data, illustrates that the youngest generation of community members is the most recent in a long lineage of interracial families that resided in Below Cliff and surrounding areas.

These assertions about the prominence and persistence of racial intermixing are based on qualitative and limited quantitative data. Informal encounters with poor white families revealed the degree to which individuals were aware of, and openly acknowledged, their diverse racial genealogies. Of the many families that I came to know over the course of my fieldwork and encountered on a nearly daily basis, each kinship network included some degree of European and African ancestry. For the middle and upper classes of island society, families are starting to come to grips with their own diverse racial ancestries as well. Andrea Stuart's semiautobiographical *Sugar in the Blood* (2012) traces her dual family lineage, from an early English small farmer whose descendants eventually rose to prominence as planters, to enslaved Afro-Barbadians documented through planter exploitation of enslaved women (see also Morrison 2010). Her work takes several creative liberties in developing a tale of seventeenth-century adventure in a jungle wilderness, but it simultaneously generates thought-provoking questions about family genealogies in the post-colonial Caribbean.

Stuart presents an honest account of her personal identity crisis in discovering her ancestry among the enslaved and the enslavers (for the relationship between genetic and genealogical studies for people of African descent, see also Nelson 2016). Anthropologist Katharine Tyler (2012) introduces similar co-conversationalists in her ethnographic study of middle-class whiteness in England. She interviews diverse interracial families, each with Afro-Caribbean ties, who view this lineage as being essential to their own racial identities. She confronts and contests binary notions of black and white through an interpretation of the dynamic relationship between biological and cultural notions of race. For instance, one of her interviewees, Emily, is presented as "a White woman who is the mother of five children who self-identified as Black" (Tyler 2012:184). Interestingly, Tyler privileges the biological/phenotypic racial marker by stating that Emily *is* white as opposed to her self-identification as black through her marriage to an Afro-Caribbean man. These complex dynamics are essential in providing a framework through which to "disrupt the binary folk racial categories of 'Black' and 'White'" (195). Additionally, the dialectic between biological and cultural conceptions of race (see Gravlee 2009) inform racial identities at multiple scales including the colonial, national, and local individual level.

In acknowledging that race is a relational object (M'Charek 2013), I also recognize that these complex racial identities and relations have been produced, reproduced, and transformed for centuries throughout the Caribbean region. Racial formation processes are therefore essential to the analyses undertaken throughout this book, but when race is framed as a "master category" that, as suggested by Michael Omi and Howard Winant (2015:106, emphasis in original) in their classic study on racial formations, "has become the *template* of both difference and inequality," the fissures and fault lines that challenge that template can be overlooked in favor of the structural and historical rules. The consequences of racial formation processes are real and materially evident, but narratives that have the potential to disrupt the potency of racial categories are equally important. Indeed, people living in spaces like Below Cliff were required to negotiate their place in a hostile and complex plantation society to individually grapple with their own feelings about race and their own racial identities based on unique genealogies. These negotiations illustrate the inadequacies of colonial categories despite attempts to make distinctiveness a reality. Ann Stoler (2002:8) reflects on this paradox, arguing that racial categories "were fixed and fluid, precise and protean, received and malleable, all at the same time." Uncovering direct evidence of these complex racial identities in the past is a difficult task. As illustrated in the previous chapter, such instances are rare but informative, as in the case of Ann Shepherd who proudly proclaimed her interracial kinship network in an affidavit before she died in the early nineteenth century. In considering the fact that interracial unions and miscegenation were discouraged during and after the period of slavery, it becomes apparent why such examples of interracial individuals and kinship networks are difficult to find in the historical record.

Despite purposeful silences, oral and genealogical evidence coupled with select historical examples illustrates that Below Cliff and other spaces of poor white inhabitance have been, and are, home to racially diverse individuals whose interracial ancestries destabilize binary models of white or black identity. In some ways, these realizations make this book less about a specific Barbadian subpopulation than the complex historical and present-day relationships that gave rise to how this group is understood in relation to other seemingly disparate groups. In referring back to David Scott's (2004) arguments surrounding the circumstances of modernity, we see that the plantation landscape provided the setting for historical actors to formulate their own versions of modernity. In this case, processes of modernization associated with the plantation infrastructure engendered a socioeconomic setting in which diverse cultural groups confronted one another on a daily basis. Despite the significance of racial ideologies that sought to separate poor whites and Afro-Barbadians—ideologies that were fundamental in the racial violence witnessed through African chattel slavery—in peripheral locales, these ideologies often proved ineffective in policing and maintaining racial boundaries. These circumstances gave rise to an alternative modernity in which racial identities were not based on pure categories of black and white, but were undone (Jackson 2001:231), engendering complex interracial genealogies with which individuals had to negotiate within the power structures of plantation society.

Thinking through and with Things

To situate this broader conversation of alternative modernities, I take one final and brief look at the things that constitute the archaeological assemblage and material realm of Below Cliff. Archaeologists create the archaeological record (Hamilakis 2007:14), and these materials are imbued with meaning, revealing the networks of relationships between people and the world around them, including things, other people, and their environment.

The items recovered from Below Cliff are no exception. Their agentive qualities and ability to act on those who interact with them are based on how they reflect the complex relationships between residents, their possessions, the immediate environment, families and neighbors, other plantation inhabitants, the plantocracy, power structures, broader island society, and world markets. The material dimensions of these vestiges contain memories (Olivier 2011) that provide clues as to how the individuals procured, used, reused, and discarded these items. How these individuals internally perceived these relationships is inaccessible, but we do have some semblance of how individuals negotiated these relationships through interpretations of the material record.

Excavations uncovered a diverse range of material possessions ranging from the mundane to the intimate. Just outside of the northeast house foundation of the Norris household the remnants of the plastic packaging for a set of men's undershirts was recovered directly below the forest brush. Within the structure's foundation the worn rubber sole of a shoe appeared at a shallow depth below the surface. Given the unrelenting tropical climate, harsh environment, and hard work necessary to subsist, such personal adornment items were likely in need of constant maintenance or replacement. The quantity and diversity of buttons that were originally thought to be associated the workings of a seamstress spoke more to the struggle to maximize use out of garments. The presence of alcohol bottles can be reasonably associated with the social and political functions of alcohol consumption—drinking was a ubiquitous activity across all sectors of Barbadian society. In the context of Below Cliff, however, it can also be argued that such vessels were essential for the collecting of rain water that had been filtered through dripstones. These are innocuous items that held memories for former residents who interacted with them. They also represent the intimacies of everyday life in less-than-ideal conditions.

The residents of Below Cliff experienced economic hardship. Interpreting the archaeological assemblage required constant filtration through a lens that recognized the realities of hardship. This was equally the case in interpreting the stratigraphy observed. Excavations were particularly challenging in deep units filled with loose limestone. The unstable side walls not only provided methodological challenges but also caused disturbance within the stratigraphic layers. Despite limited amounts of pearlware uncovered between depths of 30 and 80 cm, sherds of sponged-ware (of the English and Scottish variety) were recovered from depths of 200 cm. It is difficult, if not impossible, to relate particular items to discrete occupational periods. In proper perspective, however, these frustrations are miniscule in comparison to those experienced by residents who had to deal with the consequences of living in an unstable environment. The absence of straightforward stratigraphy and a paucity of material culture are reminders of the ever-present effects of limited access to capital.

Despite the hardships with which residents coped, the materials recovered illustrate poor white inclusion in broader networks of market consumption. Given that Barbados was an English colony, the preponderance of British-made ceramics is unsurprising. The range of wares present in the assemblage illustrates that Below Cliff residents were actively consuming imported ceramics from the mid to late eighteenth century until the abandonment of the tenantry in the mid-twentieth century. Additionally, the high proportion of Scottish-made sponged-wares demonstrates that affordability was a heavy determinant in consumption practices, despite market availability. While imported wares were available and affordable, coarse earthenwares, some likely locally produced, composed a considerable proportion of the overall ceramic assemblage. The vessels represented by sherds recovered from Below Cliff suggest that residents were primarily using hollowwares for the purposes of storage, preparation, and consumption of food and drink. Residents carefully weighed their options and, when making particular purchases, considered item function, reuse value, availability, and affordability.

These broad interpretations of material types recovered during excavation provide intimate insights into how Below Cliff residents coped with circumscribed means and interacted with the world of people and things around them. But is this assemblage unique to this particular tenantry, the poor whites, or all working-class Barbadians? These are important questions that can be addressed through research that uses this limited sample for comparative purposes. In synthesizing this data, my overall findings are sympathetic to studies that take seriously how impoverishment affects the record of the past (Spencer-Wood and Matthews 2011; Rimmer et al. 2011; Reilly 2016b). Additionally, when considering the complicated racial identities of those living below the cliff, it raises poignant questions about the archaeological interpretive process and the practices and politics of categorization.

The negotiations of personal and relational identity described here took place in the intimate settings of one's psyche and in the household. Expanding outward, they also took place on intra- and intercommunity levels. The intimacies of daily life necessitate tools that are amenable for such analyses and interpretations. Archaeology has long proven its utility in circumventing the limitations of the historical record and in implementing interdisciplinary strategies to provide unique insights into community life. The case study presented in this book demonstrates the analytical depth of interpretation that can be reached in studying a single community through the use of archaeological, historical, and oral sources. Despite the strength of these methodological strategies, the arguments presented raise pointed questions about the implications of archaeological interpretation and its rootedness in contentious politics. In bringing this discussion to a close, I raise questions regarding some of the fundamental underpinnings of archaeological method and theory to suggest new and fruitful directions for future research.

UNMAKING THE MODERN

The project, like most, faced many methodological and theoretical challenges that inspired considerable transformations in research strategies and thought processes. Excavations proved effective in gathering material culture associated with domestic life, and I had the good fortune of developing relationships with local community members who provided crucial oral histories about their own families and everyday life in Below Cliff. Problems emerged, however, when I attempted to interpret material culture from households that I could no longer definitively say were inhabited by poor whites or Redlegs. As I developed more comfortable relationships with community members, I began to chart genealogies to better understand the individuals who inhabited the homes that were receiving archaeological attention. This led to the realization of the diverse racial genealogies of those who had lived in the households excavated. While I could only speculate about the genealogies of those who had lived in these homes in previous generations, as well as those of neighboring households, it was clear that the ruins of Below Cliff and their associated material culture were not the vestiges of a homogeneous poor white community. As scientists, archaeologists rely on categories and types. What should we do when things or people just do not fit?

Archaeological interpretation still hinges, in one way or another, on the "pots to people" analogy. The phrase encapsulates the basic and rudimentary questions asked of an archaeological assemblage. Whose stuff was this? Who made it, used it, reused it, and discarded it? What did it mean to them and what does it mean to us? What can we say about the identities of these individuals? The underlying logic is that through multiple lines of evidence, it is possible to say something substantive about people in the past (and present) based on their associated material culture. This practice transcends paradigmatic shifts within the field and remains a fundamental component of research agendas. Archaeologists have rightly recognized the infinite diversity of human cultures across space and time, but many have still been largely committed to the idea of collective cultural groups. This is particularly true in contexts in which identity politics have been forged from centuries of racial violence and dispossession. For the Caribbean, Edward

González-Tennant (2014) has argued that this has the result of "coloring" sites of heritage, whereby specific sites have been, and can only be, associated with a particular racial group. This may be due to an innate characteristic whereby "humans typologize the world in order to understand it" (Singleton and Bograd 2000:3), but it is necessary to understand the implications for archaeological interpretation.

In chapter 3 I went to great lengths to justify my calling Below Cliff a poor white tenantry. As chapter 5 highlighted, however, such a label grossly over-simplifies the racial complexities of the plantation landscape. Where does that leave the typologies, categories, and taxonomies that we so heavily rely on to order our world? Regardless of cognitive predispositions, there is an under-lying danger in the practice of assuming group cohesiveness and collective identity. In associating particular material assemblages to specific ethnic or racial groups, archaeologists run the risk of reifying cultural differences that served as the basis for practices of discrimination or oppression. As Christopher Matthews warns, "There is a fine line between recognizing and reifying difference" (2001:72). In his critique of anthropology's past and suggestions for its future, Michel-Rolph Trouillot raises a similar point, arguing that "the physical and symbolic violence exerted to create and enforce these categories [those that delineate Others as seen in his concept of the 'savage slot'] in specific times and places, and the identities tied to them, were always and remain both different and incommensurable. The needs and the means to redress the inequalities so produced cannot be the same" (Trouillot 2003:72).

Trouillot is making a critical point about the study of marginalized or Other groups that have traditionally been the focus of anthropological study. It is certainly the case that anthropology and archaeology continue to come to grips with their colonial past and their own role in the overarching projects of modernity (see Thomas 2004; Lydon and Rizvi 2010), but Trouillot warns that good-intentioned scholarly attempts to rectify these disciplinary pasts unconsciously do the work of reproducing the categories that were essential for Othering and discrimination in the first place. He contends that the result is the persistence of restrictive identities "that give most Others few choices in defining themselves or in changing the terms of their relations with the unmarked" (Trouillot 2003:74). I take issue with the last part of this statement in which Trouillot largely refers to whites as the unmarked norm; the ever-growing body of literature associated with critical whiteness studies has convincingly argued that whiteness had to be created, remade, and reified along with other racial categories. Trouillot does, however, raise a poignant critique that speaks to underlying archaeological practices.

Typologizing artifacts is a useful and age-old archaeological practice that has provided immeasurable insight into artifact manufacture, form, style, function, use, reuse, discard, and deposition. Such methods, however, are not without their limitations and dangers. In commenting on the borrowing of biological concepts by archaeologists, Anna Agbe-Davies notes the ways in which the archaeological usage of typologies of material culture has seeped into a taxonomic system of peoples to whom we relate these artifacts (Agbe-Davies 2015:68). Using a modal method of analysis rather than one that relies on typologies, her approach demonstrates the diversity of questions that can be asked and addressed when multiple attributes of material culture are investigated on their own terms. Espousing an anarchistic approach to archaeology, Edward Henry and colleagues (2017) highlight similar problems with relying on normative, colonial classifications of things and entire societies. They make clear that critiques of typologies need not eschew the use of types as an analytical tool but can instead decolonize archaeological epistemologies by challenging the salience of categories (see also Gnecco and Langebaek 2014).

These approaches have trenchant lessons beyond how we analyze and group artifacts; they can assist in destabilizing reductive racial, class, gender, or other categories that have reified how the Other is defined. What I suggest here is that taxonomic systems, like racial categories, for instance, need to be critically interrogated to discern the work that they do in the past and the present. Black-feminist-inspired archaeologies (Franklin 2001; Battle-Baptiste 2011) are a powerful example of how the disenfranchising dimensions of racial and gender categories can be reappropriated to embolden new narratives that have been traditionally silenced. At the same time, considerations must be made for what kind of work these categories hinder. Their destabilization affords potential for exploring those people and things that operate in, through, between, and outside of these categories—it affords the potential for alternatives.

This discussion is intended to push archaeological method and theory to more critically engage with the breadth of relationships—among people, structures, institutions, ideologies, and material things—that facilitate the production, reproduction, and transformation of individual and/or group identity. I am certainly not suggesting that we abandon specific analyses of particular nationalistic, racial, class, gender, religious, or political groups. Rather, it is essential to engage with the heterogeneous people, structures, ideologies, and things that individuals confront on a daily basis in order to interpret their place in the world. In relation to my discussion of African American or African diaspora archaeology, despite institutional and ideological segregation on multiple levels of society, it is essential to acknowledge the implications of the fact that Africans and people of African descent were not alone on the streets of Annapolis, in the public markets of New York City, on the plantations of Jamaica, or in the maroon communities of Brazil. Rather, their relationships with those that were considered to be insiders and outsiders to their groups affected their personal identities and position in socioeconomic power structures.

Similarly, poor whites were not alone in their tenantry below the cliff. Their relationships with planters, management, enslaved and free Afro-Barbadians, local merchants, parochial officials, and their community members were crucial factors in how they fit into, were excluded from, or knowingly avoided local economic processes. These relationships also affected how they identified themselves, which included their thoughts on their complex racial identity and genealogy. This interpretation, however, stands in marked contrast to the dominant narrative of Barbadian history. The poor whites were portrayed as being a people set apart from plantation society. Represented in the metanarrative of Caribbean modernity, they were physically situated on the margins of the plantation and irrelevant in terms of plantation production processes; categorized as purely white, they were also seen to be ostracized from black socioeconomic realms. The alternative being proposed here is that explicitly modern circumstances in which the poor whites of Below Cliff lived influenced and gave rise to their formulation of modernity based on dynamic relationships with other diverse plantation residents and the economic systems that they molded to suit their needs.

This revelation does little to contradict the arguments presented throughout this book. To suggest that these final thoughts on the ambiguities of poor white identity discredits any interpretation put forth about the poor whites in general is to miss the point. My point is to show that these categories were created under specific circumstances and held political, social, and economic weight. Additionally, ambiguities can be productive (Richard and MacDonald 2015). This project, therefore, is an attempt to undo the work that has been done by these categories in the past and present. Archaeological assemblages are the result of complex and dynamic negotiations between people and things as they confront the heterogeneous individuals around them in addition to the material conditions in which they are situated. While particular ideologies provide notions of prescribed roles and positions for individuals and groups, evidence suggests that there were alternatives. Rather than the racially arrogant and idle degenerates that they were portrayed as being, poor whites living in Below Cliff adhered to a politics of work whereby they participated in informal and intimate economies in which their labor was only loosely harnessed by capitalist processes. Additionally, despite stereotypes casting them as racially pure and isolated, they had complex relationships with the Afro-Barbadian neighbors, friends, and family members with whom they worked, traded, socialized, procreated, married, battled, disassociated from, and identified. Like most Barbadians, if not most Caribbean peoples, these relations forged their personal identities in the past and present. Those living below the cliff were inextricably affected by the processes of modernity, but how they responded to encounters with those around them and the forces acting on them constituted an alternative all their own.

NOTES

Introduction

1. According the 2010 national census, the island's population stands at 277,821. Data on ethnicity, however, are only provided for 226,193 residents (Barbados Statistical Service 2013).

2. Throughout this volume racial identities and markers will not be capitalized, unless used in a proper noun. This formatting decision is not meant to diminish the power that such markers hold. Rather, these labels are the subject of scrutiny and argued to be unstable. The use of lowercase letters for white and black demonstrates that these identities, despite the social, legal, and economic power they wielded, were often fragile and contested.

3. Surnames of Barbadian families are used throughout this study, including when referencing specific house sites and kinship networks. These names are true to the historical and oral record found in Barbados. At the same time, I purposely avoid using first names to protect the identities of specific community members. All individuals consented to participate in the research process, but many members of the Below Cliff community have experienced unwanted attention from occasionally intrusive journalists and photographers.

4. Theresa Singleton's (2015) recent discussion of how archaeologists can employ the master-slave dialectic is particularly demonstrative of how archaeological approaches to the plantation landscape have understandably focused on this quintessential relationship.

5. This was made possible thanks to the dynamic community interested in island history and heritage. I am grateful to the Barbados Museum and Historical Society, the Barbados National Trust, and the University of the West Indies for these opportunities and for the thoughtful feedback from attendees.

6. Multiple racial categories are used colloquially on the island, including white, black, brown, colored, red, high brown, and so forth. Although often omitted from official records, these categories reveal the social significance and intersection of race and class identities.

7. Bajan can refer to the distinct island accent and dialect in addition to being a nationalistic identity marker.

8. The "colonial period" in Barbados is an extensive era comprising the period from 1627 to 1966. Throughout these centuries Barbados underwent several significant socioeconomic transformations including the sugar revolution, the establishment of a sugar and slave society, plantation amelioration, rebellion, emancipation, social unrest, and independence (see Beckles 2007).

9. Population figures and racial demographics are discussed in more detail in chapter 2, but for a brief overview of early population figures, see Dunn 1969; Handler and Lange 1978:14–15, 20–29.

Chapter 1

1. A second factory, Andrews, is said to be reopening after improvements and technological upgrades are made.

2. However, during the initial settlement of the island in 1627, Amerindians from Guiana were brought to assist the English in establishing the colony (see Handler 1969).

3. For this reason, among others that will become clear throughout this book, I have intentionally softened direct comparisons between the Redlegs of Barbados and poor whites in other locales, particularly the United States. The literature on poor whites in the United States, however rich and nuanced, dwarfs that of similar populations in other world regions, which can have the effect of making American poor whites the measuring stick for analyses. A comparative approach should, of course, be encouraged, and it is my hope that this study will inspire such work. This study, however, will be firmly situated in the Barbadian context.

4. The figure given here is a median based on historical estimations. Seventeenth-century population figures are approximations and often unreliable. Additionally, even in later centuries when figures are more reliable, socioeconomic breakdowns of the white population are not provided. Therefore, Jill Sheppard has estimated that at any given time the population of the poor whites was likely three-fourths of the total white population. Within these parameters, the population fluctuated from an estimated 12,000 in 1715 to about 8,000 at the time of emancipation (Sheppard 1977:34, 43).

5. Mills argues that the racial contract is the ideological and epistemological foundation on which modern notions of governmentality, economy, society, geography, and philosophy are built, superseding other contractarian agreements such as the social contract (1997).

6. In Barbados, planters took juridical action in the mid-seventeenth century to ensure that no enslaved person could leave the plantation without written permission from their master (Jennings 1654:16–21). Additionally, a 1657 proclamation by Governor Searle mandated similar written permission for Irish servants (see Gwynn 1932:236–237).

7. In Barbados, despite the fact that the island is only 166 square miles, densely populated, and relatively flat, marronage was still a common problem for planters (see Handler 1997).

Chapter 2

1. Despite threats from the Dutch, who landed in the Bridgetown harbor in the 1660s, imperial forces never invaded the island.

2. Evidence also suggests that there were smaller numbers of Portuguese, Spanish, French, and German indentured servants (see, for example, Gunkel and Handler 1970).

3. A category for "white" individuals was used in official records and unofficial population estimates. It is unclear how each author or record keeper understood the term *white* in this early modern context.

4. This practice became less common as the sugar revolution took over and arable land was at a premium. If land was awarded at all, it was usually "rab" land that was undesirable for agricultural production (Beckles 1989).

5. The law in question is described by Richard Dunn (1969:8), but his source is unclear. Laws concerning militia requirements were frequently altered throughout the seventeenth century; for instance, a 1697 act required that one servant serve in the militia for every 20 acres of land owned (Hall 1764:138–155; see also Handler 1984).

6. For connections between Barbados and South Carolina, see Greene et al. 2001; Alleyne and Fraser 1989; and Hoffius 2011.

7. Pedro Welch has warned against overestimating the population of Irish servants (2012), but, unfortunately, reliable figures are lacking from which to draw any accurate estimates on the ethnic origins of servants.

8. For instance, a deed from 1653 for Clifton Hall Plantation (the estate home to Below Cliff) indicates that 40 acres below the cliff was "leased land" (BDA RB3/3:11). The specifics of this arrangement are discussed in more detail in the following chapter.

9. This is a marked difference from the landscape of the antebellum US South in which archaeologists have observed overseers' dwellings at a distance of one mile from the great house. This is more typical of plantations with a dispersed rather than centralized settlement (Otto and Burns 1983:194–195).

10. Another rebellion conspiracy that was entirely attributed to enslaved Africans took place in 1675 (Handler 1982).

11. For the conceptual and ideological implications of the age of revolution in the Caribbean context, see Fischer 2004.

12. It remains unclear how the racial identities of the study participants were determined.

Chapter 4

1. Poor relief has a long history in England, and such practices would be transported to and transformed in Caribbean colonies (for England see Slack 1995; for Jamaica see Roper 2012).

2. Debates surrounding who was deemed deserving of poor relief throughout the English colonial sphere would span the Atlantic with the likes of John Locke weighing in on the issue in 1697. Locke was a proponent of scarce poor relief that should be meted out only in the rare circumstances when someone was physically unable to work. In his formulation, poor relief for those deemed able to work would take the form of employment that would benefit the community at large (see Bourne 1876:377–391).

3. Local registries (as well as vestry minutes) often provide more detailed information than national censuses, and in Barbados, historians and anthropologists have thoroughly mined both forms of documentation (see, for example, Dunn 1969; Handler 1974; Gragg 2000; Shaw 2013; Jones 2007; Newton 2008; Stafford 2003; Marshall 2003; Watson 2003).

4. Baptismal, marriage, and burial records were consulted for the parish of St. John for the years 1825–1848, while the records from St. Margaret's were consulted from the time of its opening in 1863 to the abandonment of Below Cliff in the early 1960s.

5. In the postemancipation era (after 1838) it is possible that those listed as residents of Clifton Hall were residing on top of the cliff in the newly established tenantry. However, given that St. John's parish church is in close proximity to the postemancipation tenantry, it is likely that those residing on Clifton Hall lands and being baptized at St. Margaret's were living below the cliff. This was confirmed by former Below Cliff residents.

6. The breakdown of occupations provided for Below Cliff residents from these registries is as follows: 48% laborers, 15.6% planters, 8.4% fisherman, 4.3% carpenters, 3.9% shoemakers, and 19.8% mix of skilled professions such as police officers, shopkeepers, bookkeepers, plumbers, domestics, and distillers.

7. Despite an economic boom in the island's sugar industry due to the Haitian Revolution, in general, the profits seen by Anglo sugar producers in the Caribbean began to dwindle as the Cuban and Brazilian market expanded. Additionally, Barbadian sugar took an added hit due to the growth of the beet sugar industry in eastern Europe.

8. There is, of course, a fundamental irony in using ceramic typologies in a study that seeks to unsettle other forms of categorization, like race, which is the topic of the following chapter. The reliance on ceramic categorizations is used here to demonstrate how place and method of production can affect cost and, by extension, consumption options. The categorization of material culture is not without inherent problems (Agbe-Davies 2015), but the differences between imported ceramics present provide valuable evidence of the realities of economic hardship.

9. This count includes 58 shards that were collected from STPs. While discrete stratigraphic layers were not easily discernable within STPs, the overwhelming majority of shards collected were on the surface or just below the surface and are, therefore, included in the count.

10. The size and undiagnostic nature of many of the shards made it difficult to identify bottle type with any certainty, but color and shape, in conjunction with diagnostic shards, suggest that alcohol bottles were the most common vessels represented.

11. There is gender bias in the historical record and in the oral histories collected. The overwhelming majority of the records consulted only provided the occupations for male heads of household or fathers of baptized children. At the time of research, few female former residents, due to old age, were able to make the trip into the woods. They had similar recollections about labor and occupations to those expressed by the male former residents discussed here, but many of their stories are not directly related to the households that are discussed in this context.

Chapter 5

1. Unlike other English Caribbean territories such as Montserrat, expanded

demographics for individuals of European origins were unrecorded. For instance, it is unclear how many Irish, English, or Scottish individuals made up the white population throughout the seventeenth century (for Montserrat see Akenson 1997).

2. There were also exceptions to this rule. For instance, dozens of Scottish rebels were sent to labor in Barbados following a rebellion in 1745.

3. There were also exceptions to this general rule, particularly for free people of color (see Handler 1974). The infamous case of Old Doll at Newton Plantation is also a provocative outlier that challenges this notion of racial identity and status.

4. I use *culture* carefully, in full recognition of its political and uncritical usage in such literature, in addition to its weakened ability to have analytical weight in anthropological literature over the course of the past several decades. In particular, it is now recognized that cultural groups no longer exist within closed, self-evident boundaries (a similar case will be made further on for the concreteness of racial categories). Trouillot has gone so far as to suggest the abandonment of the term (2003:95–116).

5. The broad category of coarse earthenwares is favored here over locally produced or the oft-used Afro-Caribbean wares. Samples have yet to undergo X-ray fluorescence (XRF) and neutron activation analysis (NAA) testing. It is hoped that such methods will be able to conclusively determine whether sherds represent locally made or imported coarse earthenwares. When possible, judgments concerning place of manufacture are made based on vessel form, paste composition, and glaze. In most cases, however, the broader category of coarse earthenware is used instead of assigning a speculative place of production or racial association.

6. The School of Female Industry was a small training facility in the parish designed to instruct young, poor white girls how to conduct domestic chores in preparation for domestic service. At any given time, the school would have housed no more than 10 to 15 young girls, so the allocated space was likely limited to a single pew (for more on the school see Forde-Jones 1998; Reilly 2014).

7. Within this body of literature, the politics and significance of racial inter-mixture are often secondary concerns in favor of the socioeconomic position of free people of color (Handler 1974) or the role of white women in colonial society (Bush 1981; Beckles 1993).

8. There were instances of planters manumitting enslaved women who were pregnant or the progeny of their relationships with enslaved women, but such instances seem to be the exception (for more on manumissions, see Handler 1974; Handler and Pohlmann 1984).

Chapter 6

1. There is no homogeneous way in which all Barbadians conceptualize and talk about race. Understandings and experiences of race on the island can be affected by kinship networks, class positioning, generation, religion, and gender. Discussed here, however, is one particular understanding of race that was encountered during the course of research.

2. For the sake of brevity, it is impossible to engage in an extended discussion of this particular brand of Marxist archaeology, but Randall McGuire's (2002) dialectical Marxism uses power as the pivot on which dialectical relations change. As such, interpretations are grounded in power struggles, running the risk of being reduced to compliance or resistance (see also Spriggs 1984; Paynter 1989; McGuire and Paynter 1991; for a case study on a Caribbean plantation, see Delle 1998, 2014b).

3. This term originated during the French Revolution to refer to radical left-wing members of the working class. In this context, however, it is likely void of political connotations and probably refers to the poor quality or appearance of their garments.

REFERENCES CITED

Archival Resources

BDA   Barbados Department of Archives, Black Rock, St. Michael, Barbados

SMR   St. Margaret's Registries, St. John's Church, St. John, Barbados

HCPP   House of Commons Parliamentary Papers, ProQuest

NM   Newton Manuscripts, MS 523, London University Library, UK

UCL LBS   University College London Legacies of British Slave-Ownership Database, https://www.ucl.ac.uk/lbs/search/

USPGA   United Society for the Propagation of the Gospel Archives, London

Secondary Sources

AGBE-DAVIES, ANNA S.

   2009   Scales of Analysis, Scales of Value: Archaeology at Bush Hill House, Barbados. *International Journal of Historical Archaeology* 13(1):112–126.

   2015   *Tobacco, Pipes, and Race in Colonial Virginia: Little Tubes of Mighty Power.* Left Coast Press, Walnut Creek, California.

AGORSAH, EMMANUEL KOFI

   1994   *Maroon Heritage: Archaeological, Ethnographic, and Historical Perspectives.* University of the West Indies Press, Mona, Jamaica.

   1999   Ethnoarchaeological Consideration of Social Relationship and Settlement Patterning among Africans in the Caribbean Diaspora. In *African Sites: Archaeology in the Caribbean,* edited by J. Haviser, pp. 38–64. Markus Wiener Press, Princeton, New Jersey.

   2007   Scars of Brutality: Archaeology of the Maroons in the Caribbean. In *Archaeology of Atlantic Africa and the African Diaspora,* edited by A. Ogundiran and T. Falola, pp. 332–354. Indiana University Press, Bloomington.

AKAMATSU, RHETTA

   2010   *The Irish Slaves: Slavery, Indenture, and Contract Labor among Irish Immigrants.* CreateSpace Independent Publishing Platform.

AKENSON, DONALD H.

   1997   *If the Irish Ran the World: Montserrat, 1630–1730.* McGill-Queen's University Press, Montreal.

ALLEYNE, WARREN, AND HENRY FRASER

   1989   *Barbados Carolina Connection.* Macmillan Caribbean, Kingston, Jamaica.

AMUSSEN, SUSAN DWYER

   2007   *Caribbean Exchanges: Slavery and the Transformation of English Society, 1640–1700.* University of North Carolina Press, Chapel Hill.

ANDERSON, JON

   2004   Talking Whilst Walking: A Geographical Archaeology of Knowledge. *Area* 36(3):254–261.

ANONYMOUS

1824   *A Report of a Committee.* Notes courtesy of Jerome S. Handler.

1828   *Sketches and Recollections of the West Indies by a Resident.* London.

ARCANGELI, MYRIAM

2015   *Sherds of History: Domestic Life in Colonial Guadeloupe.* University Press of Florida, Gainesville.

ARMSTRONG, DOUGLAS V.

1990   *The Old Village and the Great House: An Archaeological and Historical Examination of Drax Hall Plantation, St. Ann's Bay, Jamaica.* University of Illinois Press, Urbana.

1998   Cultural Transformation within Enslaved Laborer Communities in the Caribbean. In *Studies in Culture Contact: Interaction, Culture Change, and Archaeology,* edited by J. Cusick, pp. 378–401. Southern Illinois University Press, Carbondale.

2003   *Creole Transformation from Slavery to Freedom: Historical Archaeology of the East End Community, St. John, Virgin Islands.* University Press of Florida, Gainesville.

2008   Excavating African American Heritage: Towards a More Nuanced Understanding of the African Diaspora. *Historical Archaeology* 42(2):123–137.

2015   Cave of Iron and Resistance: A Preliminary Examination. *Journal of the Barbados Museum and Historical Society* 61:178–199.

ARMSTRONG, DOUGLAS V., AND MARK W. HAUSER

2004   An East Indian Laborers' Household in Nineteenth-Century Jamaica: A Case for Understanding Cultural Diversity through Space, Chronology, and Material Analysis. *Historical Archaeology* 38(2):9–21.

ARMSTRONG, DOUGLAS V., AND KENNETH G. KELLY

2000   Settlement Patterns and the Origins of African Jamaican Society: Seville Plantation, St. Ann's Bay, Jamaica. *Ethnohistory* 47(2):369–397.

ARMSTRONG, DOUGLAS V., AND MATTHEW C. REILLY

2014   The Archaeology of Settler Farms and Early Plantation Life in Seventeenth-Century Barbados. *Slavery and Abolition* 35(3):399–417.

ARMSTRONG, DOUGLAS V., KARL S. WATSON, AND MATTHEW C. REILLY

2012   The 1646 Hapcott Map, Fort—(Trents) Plantation, St. James, Barbados: A Significant Resource for Research on Early Colonial Settlement in Barbados. *Journal of the Barbados Museum and Historical Society* 58:137–154.

ATALAY, SONYA

2012   *Community-Based Archaeology: Research with, by, and for Indigenous and Local Communities.* University of California Press, Berkeley.

AUGÉ, MARC

1995   *Non-places: Introduction to an Anthropology of Supermodernity.* Verso, New York.

BABSON, DAVID W.

1990   The Archaeology of Racism and Ethnicity on Southern Plantations. *Historical Archaeology* 24(3):20–28.

BAKER, LEE D.

1998   *From Savage to Negro: Anthropology and the Construction of Race, 1896–1954.* University of California Press, Berkeley.

2010   *Anthropology and the Racial Politics of Culture.* Duke University Press, Durham, North Carolina.

BARBADOS HOTEL AND TOURISM ASSOCIATION

2014   Barbados Hotel and Tourism Association Annual Report 2014. Electronic document, www.bhta.org/index/resources/publications.html, accessed December 14, 2015.

BARBADOS STATISTICAL SERVICE

2013   National Census. Bridgetown, Barbados. Electronic document, www.barstats.gov.bb, accessed November 18, 2014.

BARKER, DAVID

2011   Geographies of Opportunity, Geographies of Constraint. In *The Caribbean: A History of the Region and Its Peoples,* edited by S. Palmié and F. Scarano, pp. 25–38. University of Chicago Press, Chicago.

BATES, LYNSEY A.

2015   "The Landscape Cannot Be Said to Be Really Perfect": A Comparative Investigation of Plantation Spatial Organization on Two British Colonial Sugar Estates. In *The Archaeology of Slavery: A Comparative Approach to Captivity and Coercion,* edited by L. Marshall, pp. 116–142. Southern Illinois University Press, Carbondale.

BATES, LYNSEY A., JOHN M. CHENOWETH, AND JAMES A. DELLE (EDITORS)

2016   *Archaeologies of Slavery and Freedom in the Caribbean: Exploring the Spaces in Between.* University Press of Florida, Gainesville.

BATTLE-BAPTISTE, WHITNEY

2011   *Black Feminist Archaeology.* Left Coast Press, Walnut Creek, California.

2017   Cruise Ships, Community, and Collective Memory at Millars Plantations, Eleuthera, Bahamas. *Historical Archaeology* 51(1):60–70.

BAUGHER, SHERENE, AND SUZANNE M. SPENCER-WOOD

2010   *Archaeology and Preservation of Gendered Landscapes.* Springer, New York.

BAUMAN, RICHARD, AND CHARLES L. BRIGGS

2003   *Voices of Modernity: Language Ideology and the Politics of Inequality.* Cambridge University Press, New York.

BAYLEY, FREDERIC W. N.

1833   *Four Years' Residence in the West Indies.* London.

BEAUDRY, MARY C.

2008   "Above Vulgar Economy": The Intersection of Historical Archaeology and Microhistory in Writing Archaeological Biographies of Two New England Merchants. In *Small Worlds: Method, Meaning, and Narrative in Microhistory,* edited by J. Brooks, C. DeCorse, and J. Walton, pp. 173–198. School for Advanced Research Press, Santa Fe, New Mexico.

BECKLES, HILARY McD.

1982   English Parliamentary Debate on "White Slavery" in Barbados, 1659. *Journal of the Barbados Museum and Historical Society* 36(4):344–352.

1985   Plantation Production and White "Proto-Slavery": White Indentured
        Servants and the Colonisation of the English West Indies, 1624–1625. *The
        Americas* 41(3):21–45.

1988   Black over White: The "Poor-White" Problem in Barbados Slave Society.
        Immigrants and Minorities 7(1):1–15.

1989   *White Servitude and Black Slavery in Barbados, 1627–1715.* University of
        Tennessee Press, Knoxville.

1990   A "Riotous and Unruly Lot": Irish Indentured Servants and Freemen
        in the English West Indies, 1644–1713. *William and Mary Quarterly*
        47(4):503–522.

1993   White Women and Slavery in the Caribbean. *History Workshop Journal*
        36:66–82.

1997   Capitalism, Slavery, and Caribbean Modernity. *Callaloo* 20(4):777–789.

1999   *Centering Women: Gender Discourses in Caribbean Slave Society.* Ian Ran-
        dle, Kingston, Jamaica.

2007   *A History of Barbados: From Amerindian Settlement to Nation-State.* Cam-
        bridge University Press, Cambridge.

2013   *Britain's Black Debt: Reparations for Slavery and Native Genocide.* Univer-
        sity of the West Indies Press, Mona, Jamaica.

BECKLES, HILARY McD., AND ANDREW DOWNES
1987   The Economics of Transition to the Black Labor System in Barbados,
        1630–1680. *Journal of Interdisciplinary Studies* 18(2):225–247.

BENÍTEZ-ROJO, ANTONIO
1996   *The Repeating Island: The Caribbean and the Postmodern Perspective.* Duke
        University Press, Durham, North Carolina.

BERGMAN, STEPHANIE, AND FREDERICK H. SMITH
2014   Blurring Disciplinary Boundaries: The Material Culture of Improve-
        ment during the Age of Abolition in Barbados. *Slavery and Abolition*
        35(3):418–436.

BERLIN, IRA
1998   *Many Thousands Gone: The First Two Centuries of Slavery in North America.*
        Harvard University Press, Cambridge, Massachusetts.

BLACKBURN, ROBIN
1997   The Old World Background to European Colonial Slavery. *William and
        Mary Quarterly* 54(1):65–102.

BLOCH, MAURICE E. F.
1998   *How We Think They Think: Anthropological Approaches to Cognition, Mem-
        ory, and Literacy.* Westview Press, Boulder, Colorado.

BLOCK, KRISTEN, AND JENNY SHAW
2011   Subjects without an Empire: The Irish in the Early Modern Caribbean.
        Past and Present 210:33–60.

BOGUES, ANTHONY
2003   *Black Heretics, Black Prophets: Radical Political Intellectuals.* Routledge,
        New York.

BOLTON, CHARLES C.
1994   *Poor Whites in the Antebellum South: Tenants and Laborers in Central North Carolina and Northeast Mississippi.* Duke University Press, Durham, North Carolina.

BOURNE, HENRY R. F.
1876   *The Life of John Locke in Two Volumes.* Henry S. King, London.

BRANDER RASMUSSEN, BIRGIT, ERIC KLINENBERG, IRENE J. NEXICA, AND MATT WRAY (EDITORS)
2001   *The Making and Unmaking of Whiteness.* Duke University Press, Durham, North Carolina.

BRIDENBAUGH, CARL, AND ROBERTA BRIDENBAUGH
1972   *No Peace beyond the Line: The English in the Caribbean, 1624–90.* Oxford University Press, New York.

BRIGHTON, STEPHEN A.
2001   Prices That Suit the Times: Shopping for Ceramics at the Five Points. *Historical Archaeology* 35(3):16–30.
2009   *Historical Archaeology of the Irish Diaspora: A Transnational Approach.* University of Tennessee Press, Knoxville.

BROWNE, DAVID V. C.
2012   *Race, Class, Politics, and the Struggle for Empowerment in Barbados, 1914–1937.* Ian Randle, Kingston, Jamaica.

BRUBAKER, ROGERS
2004   *Ethnicity without Groups.* Harvard University Press, Cambridge, Massachusetts.

BUCK-MORSS, SUSAN
2009   *Hegel, Haiti, and Universal History.* University of Pittsburgh Press, Pittsburgh, Pennsylvania.

BURROWES, MARCIA P. A.
2000   History and Cultural Identity: Barbadian Space and the Legacy of Empire. PhD dissertation, University of Warwick, Warwick, England.

BUSH, BARBARA
1981   White "Ladies," Coloured "Favorites," and Black "Wenches"; Some Considerations on Sex, Race, and Class Factors in Social Relations in White Creole Society in the British Caribbean. *Slavery and Abolition* 2(3):245–262.

CAMP, STACEY LYNN
2011   The Utility of Comparative Research in Historical Archaeology. In *The Important of Material Things*, Vol. II, edited by J. Schablitsky and M. Leone, pp. 13–28. Society for Historical Archaeology, Rockville, Maryland.

CAMPBELL, PETER F.
1982   *The Church in Barbados in the Seventeenth Century.* Barbados Museum and Historical Society, Bridgetown, Barbados.
1993   *Some Early Barbadian History.* Caribbean Graphics and Letchworth, Bridgetown, Barbados.

Canny, Nicholas
2001 *Making Ireland British: 1580–1650.* Oxford University Press, New York.

Canuto, Marcello A., and Jason Yaeger (editors)
2000 *The Archaeology of Communities: A New World Perspective.* Routledge, New York.

Carter, Henderson
2012 *Labour Pains: Resistance and Protest in Barbados, 1838–1904.* Ian Randle, Kingston, Jamaica.

Caspari, Rachel
2003 From Types to Populations: A Century of Race, Physical Anthropology, and the American Anthropological Association. *American Anthropologist* 105(1):65–76.

Cateau, Heather
2006 Beyond Planters and Plantership. In *Beyond Tradition: Reinterpreting the Caribbean Historical Experience,* edited by H. Cateau and R. Pemberton, pp. 3–21. Ian Randle, Kingston, Jamaica.

Cecil-Fronsman, Bill
1992 *Common Whites: Class and Culture in Antebellum North Carolina.* University Press of Kentucky, Lexington.

Certeau, Michel de
1984 *The Practice of Everyday Life.* University of California Press, Berkeley.

Césaire, Aimé
2000 [1955] *Discourse on Colonialism.* Monthly Review Press, New York.

Chakrabarty, Dipesh
1992 Postcoloniality and the Artifice of History: Who Speaks for "Indian" Pasts? *Representations* 37:1–26.
2000 *Provincializing Europe: Postcolonial Thought and Historical Difference.* Princeton University Press, Princeton, New Jersey.

Chapman, Matthew J.
1833 *Barbadoes, and Other Poems.* J. Fraser, London.

Chenoweth, John M.
2017 *Simplicity, Equality, and Slavery: An Archaeology of Quakerism in the British Virgin Islands, 1740–1780.* University Press of Florida, Gainesville.

Cipolla, Craig N., and Katherine H. Hayes (editors)
2015 *Rethinking Colonialism: Comparative Archaeological Approaches.* University Press of Florida, Gainesville.

Cobb, Charles R., and Stephanie Sapp
2014 Imperial Anxiety and the Dissolution of Colonial Space and Practice at Fort Moore, South Carolina. In *Rethinking Colonial Pasts through Archaeology,* edited by N. Ferris, R. Harrison, and M. Wilcox, pp. 212–231. Oxford University Press, New York.

COHN, BERNARD S., AND NICHOLAS B. DIRKS
   1988   Beyond the Fringe: The Nation State, Colonialism, and the Technologies
           of Power. *Journal of Historical Sociology* 1(2):224–229.
COLERIDGE, HENRY NELSON
   1826   *Six Months in the West Indies in 1825.* London.
COMAROFF, JEAN, AND JOHN COMAROFF
   1991   *Of Revelation and Revolution: Christianity, Colonialism, and Consciousness
           in South Africa.* University of Chicago Press, Chicago.
COOK, LAUREN J., REBECCA YAMIN, AND JOHN P. MCCARTHY
   1996   Shopping as Meaningful Action: Toward a Redefinition of Consumption
           in Historical Archaeology. *Historical Archaeology* 30(4):50–65.
COOPER, FREDERICK, AND ANN LAURA STOLER
   1997   Between Metropole and Colony: Rethinking a Research Agenda. In *Tensions
           of Empire: Colonial Cultures in a Bourgeois World,* edited by F. Cooper and A.
           Stoler, pp. 1–56. University of California Press, Berkeley.
COOPER, FREDERICK, AND ANN LAURA STOLER (EDITORS)
   1997   *Tensions of Empire: Colonial Cultures in a Bourgeois World.* University of
           California Press, Berkeley.
CRATON, MICHAEL
   2009   *Testing the Chains: Resistance to Slavery in the British West Indies.* Cornell
           University Press, Ithaca, New York.
CRUICKSHANK, GRAEME
   2005   *Scottish Pottery.* Shire Publications, Buckinghamshire, England.
CURET, L. ANTONIO, AND MARK W. HAUSER (EDITORS)
   2011   *Islands at the Crossroads: Migration, Seafaring, and Interaction in the Carib-
           bean.* University of Alabama Press, Tuscaloosa.
DAVIS, KAREN FRANCES
   1978   The Position of Poor Whites in a Color-Class Hierarchy: A Diachronic
           Study of Ethnic Boundaries in Barbados. PhD dissertation, Wayne State
           University, Detroit, Michigan.
DAVY, JOHN
   2010   *The West Indies, before and since Slave Emancipation, Comprising the Wind-
           ward and Leeward Islands' Military Command.* Cambridge University
           Press, New York.
DAWDY, SHANNON LEE
   2006a   The Taphonomy of Disaster and the (Re)formation of New Orleans.
           American Anthropologist 108(4):719–730.
   2006b   Thinker-Tinkers, Race and the Archaeological Critique of Modernity.
           Archaeological Dialogues 12(2):143–164.
   2008   *Building the Devil's Empire: French Colonial New Orleans.* University of
           Chicago Press, Chicago.
   2010   Clockpunk Anthropology and the Ruins of Modernity. *Current Anthro-
           pology* 51(6):761–793.

DeCorse, Christopher R.

2008   Varied Pasts: History, Oral Tradition, and Archaeology on the Mina
        Coast. In *Small Worlds: Method, Meaning, and Narrative in Microhistory*,
        edited by J. Brooks, C. DeCorse, and J. Walton, pp. 77–95. School for
        Advanced Research Press, Santa Fe, New Mexico.

2013   *Postcolonial or Not? West Africa in the Pre-Atlantic and Atlantic Worlds.*
        Collection Afriques Transnationales, IFRA Nigeria.

DeCorse, Christopher R., and Gerard L. Chouin

2003   Trouble with Siblings: Archaeological and Historical Interpretation of
        the West African Past. In *Sources and Methods in African History: Spoken,
        Written, Unearthed*, edited by T. Falola and C. Jennings, pp. 7–15. Uni-
        versity of Rochester Press, Rochester, New York.

Deetz, James

1996   *In Small Things Forgotten: An Archaeology of Early American Life.* Anchor
[1977] Books, New York.

Delle, James A.

1998   *An Archaeology of Social Space: Analyzing Coffee Plantations in Jamaica's
        Blue Mountains.* Plenum Press, New York.

2000   Gender, Power, and Space: Negotiating Social Relations under Slavery on
        Coffee Plantations in Jamaica, 1790–1834. In *Lines That Divide: Historical
        Archaeologies of Race, Class, and Gender*, edited by J. Delle, S. Mrozowski,
        and R. Paynter, pp. 168–201. University of Tennessee Press, Knoxville.

2014a   Archaeology and the "Tensions of Empire." In *Rethinking Colonial Pasts
        through Archaeology*, edited by N. Ferris, R. Harrison, and M. V. Wilcox,
        pp. 333–347. Oxford University Press, New York.

2014b   *The Colonial Caribbean: Landscapes of Power in the Plantation System.*
        Cambridge University Press, New York.

Delle, James A., Stephen A. Mrozowski, and Robert Paynter (editors)

2000   *Lines That Divide: Historical Archaeologies of Race, Class, and Gender.*
        University of Tennessee Press, Knoxville.

Díaz-Andreu, Margarita

2007   *A World History of Nineteenth-Century Archaeology: Nationalism, Colonial-
        ism, and the Past.* Cambridge University Press, New York.

Dickson, William

1789   *Letters on Slavery.* J. Phillips, London.

1814   *Mitigation of Slavery in Two Parts.* R. and A. Taylor, London.

Dolan, Chris

2012   *Redlegs.* Vagabond Voices, Glasgow, Scotland.

Douglass, Frederick

2008   The Effect of Circumstances upon the Physical Man. In *The Nature of
[1854] Difference: Sciences of Race in the United States from Jefferson to Genomics*,
        edited by E. Hammonds and R. Herzig, pp. 37–41. MIT Press, Cam-
        bridge, Massachusetts.

DOWNES-ALLEYNE, GILLIAN
2017   Black Radial Consciousness in Barbados, 1951–2001. *Journal of the Barbados Museum and Historical Society* 63:133–155.

DUNN, RICHARD
1969   The Barbados Census of 1680: Profile of the Richest Colony in English America. *William and Mary Quarterly* 26(1):3–30.
2000   *Sugar and Slaves: The Rise of the Planter Class in the English West Indies,*
[1972] *1624–1713.* University of North Carolina Press, Chapel Hill.

DYER, RICHARD
1997   *White.* Routledge, New York.

EDGAR, HEATHER J., AND KEITH L. HUNLEY (EDITORS)
2009   Race Reconciled: How Biological Anthropologists View Human Variation. *American Journal of Physical Anthropology* 139(1):1–107.

ELIOT, EDWARD
1833   *Christianity and Slavery.* London.

ENGERMAN, STANLEY, SEYMOUR DRESCHER, AND ROBERT PAQUETTE (EDITORS)
2001   *Slavery.* Oxford University Press, New York.

EPPERSON, TERRENCE W.
1990   Race and Disciplines of the Plantation. *Historical Archaeology* 24(4):29–36.
2004   Critical Race Theory and the Archaeology of the African Diaspora. *Historical Archaeology* 38(1):101–108.

ESPERSEN, RYAN
2018   From Hell's Gate to the Promised Land: Perspectives on Poverty in Saba, Dutch Caribbean, 1780 to the Mid-Twentieth Century. *Historical Archaeology* 52(4):773–797.

FAFCHAMPS, MARCEL
1984   The Plantation Archaeology of the Southeastern Coast. *Historical Archaeology* 18(1):1–14.
1992   Solidarity Networks in Preindustrial Societies: Rational Peasants with a Moral Economy. *Economic Development and Cultural Change* 41(1):147–174.

FAIRBANKS, CHARLES H.
1984   The Plantation Archaeology of the Southeastern Coast. *Historical Archaeology* 18(1):1–14.

FANON, FRANTZ
2004   *The Wretched of the Earth.* Grove Press, New York.
[1961]
2008   *Black Skin, White Masks.* Grove Press, New York.
[1952]

FARMER, KEVIN
2011   Women Potters? A Preliminary Examination of Documentary and Material Culture Evidence from Barbados. *History in Action* 2(1):1–8.

FARNSWORTH, PAUL
1999   From the Past to the Present: An Exploration of the Formation of African-Bahamian Identity during Enslavement. In *African Sites: Archaeology in the Caribbean*, edited by J. B. Haviser, pp. 94–130. Marcus Wiener, Princeton, New Jersey.

FARNSWORTH, PAUL (EDITOR)
2001   *Island Lives: Historical Archaeologies of the Caribbean*. University of Alabama Press, Tuscaloosa.

FELLOWS, KRISTEN R., AND JAMES A. DELLE
2015   Marronage and the Dialectics of Spatial Sovereignty in Colonial Jamaica. In *Current Perspectives on the Archaeology of African Slavery in Latin America*, edited by P. Funari and C. E. Orser Jr., pp. 117–132. Springer, New York.

FINCH, JONATHAN
2013   Inside the Pot House: Diaspora, Identity, and Locale in Barbadian Ceramics. *Journal of African Diaspora Archaeology and Heritage* 2(2):115–130.
2015   Atlantic Landscapes: Connecting Place and People in the Modern World. *Journal of African Diaspora Archaeology and Heritage* 4(3):195–213.

FINCH, JONATHAN, DOUGLAS V. ARMSTRONG, EDWARD BLINKHORN, AND DAVID BARKER
2013   Surveying Caribbean Cultural Landscapes: Mount Plantation, Barbados, and Its Global Connections. *Internet Archaeology* 35.

FISCHER, SIBYLLE
2004   *Modernity Disavowed: Haiti and the Cultures of Slavery in the Age of Revolution*. Duke University Press, Durham, North Carolina.

FOGLE, KEVIN R., JAMES A. NYMAN, AND MARY C. BEAUDRY (EDITORS)
2015   *Beyond the Walls: New Perspectives on the Archaeology of Historical Households*. University Press of Florida, Gainesville.

FORDE-JONES, CECILY
1998   Mapping Racial Boundaries: Gender, Race, and Poor Relief in Barbadian Plantation Society. *Journal of Women's History* 10(3):9–31.

FORRET, JEFF
2006   *Race Relations at the Margins: Slaves and Poor Whites in the Antebellum Countryside*. Louisiana State University Press, Baton Rouge.

FORTESCUE, J. W. (EDITOR)
1903   *Calendar of State Papers, Colonial Series, America and West Indies, January, 1693–14 May, 1696*. Mackie, London.

FOSTER, KEVIN MICHAEL
1997   Vindicationist Politics: A Foundation and Point of Departure for an African American Studies Paradigm. *Transforming Anthropology* 6(1and2):2–9.

FOWLES, SEVERIN
2010   People without Things. In *An Anthropology of Absence: Materialization*

of Transcendence and Loss, edited by M. Bille, F. Hastrup, and T. Flohr Sørensen, pp. 23–41. Springer, New York.

FRANKENBERG, RUTH

1993   *White Women, Race Matters: The Social Construction of Whiteness*. University of Minnesota Press, Minneapolis.

FRANKENBERG, RUTH (EDITOR)

1997   *Displacing Whiteness: Essays in Social and Cultural Criticism*. Duke University Press, Durham, North Carolina.

FRANKLIN, MARIA

1997   "Power to the People": Sociopolitics and the Archaeology of Black Americans. *Historical Archaeology* 31(3):36–50.

2001   A Black Feminist Inspired Archaeology? *Journal of Social Archaeology* 1(1):108–125.

FRASER, HENRY, AND BOB KISS

2011   *Barbados Chattel Houses*. Toute Bagai, Port of Spain, Trinidad.

FREEMAN, CARLA

2000   *High Tech and High Heels in the Global Economy: Women, Work, and Pink-Collar Identities in the Caribbean*. Duke University Press, Durham, North Carolina.

FUENTES, MARISA J.

2016   *Dispossessed Lives: Enslaved Women, Violence, and the Archive*. University of Pennsylvania Press, Philadelphia.

GALENSON, DAVID W.

1981   *White Servitude in Colonial America: An Economic Analysis*. Cambridge University Press, Cambridge, England.

GALLE, JILLIAN E.

2004   Designing Women: Measuring Acquisition and Access at the Hermitage Plantation. In *Engendering African American Archaeology: A Southern Perspective*, edited by J. Galle and A. Young, pp. 39–72. University of Tennessee Press, Knoxville.

2010   Costly Signaling and Gendered Social Strategies among Slaves in the Eighteenth-Century Chesapeake: An Archaeological Perspective. *American Antiquity* 75(1):19–43.

GAONKAR, DILIP PARAMESHWAR

2001   On Alternative Modernities. In *Alternative Modernities*, edited by D. Gaonkar, pp. 1–23. Duke University Press, Durham, North Carolina.

GAONKAR, DILIP PARAMESHWAR (EDITOR)

2001   *Alternative Modernities*. Duke University Press, Durham, North Carolina.

GIBSON, HEATHER R.

2009   Domestic Economy and Daily Practice in Guadeloupe: Historical Archaeology at La Mahaudière Plantation. *International Journal of Historical Archaeology* 13(1):27–44.

GIDWANI, VINAY

2008   *Capital, Interrupted: Agrarian Development and the Politics of Work in India.* University of Minnesota Press, Minneapolis.

GILCHRIST, ROBERTA

1999   *Gender and Archaeology: Contest the Past.* Routledge, New York.

GILROY, PAUL

1993   *The Black Atlantic: Modernity and Double Consciousness.* Harvard University Press, Cambridge, Massachusetts.

GLENNIE, PAUL, AND NIGEL THRIFT

1996   Reworking E. P. Thompson's "Time, Work-Discipline and Industrial Capitalism." *Time and Society* 5(3):275–299.

GMELCH, GEORGE

2012   *Behind the Smile: The Working Lives of Caribbean Tourism.* Indiana University Press, Bloomington.

GNECCO, CRISTÓBAL, AND CARL LANGEBAEK (EDITORS)

2014   *Against Typological Tyranny in Archaeology: A South American Perspective.* Springer, New York.

GODWYN, MORGAN

1680   *The Negro's and Indians Advocate, Suing for Their Admission into the Church.* Printed for the author, London.

GONZÁLEZ-RUIBAL, ALFREDO

2006   The Dream of Reason: An Archaeology of the Failures of Modernity in Ethiopia. *Journal of Social Archaeology* 6(2):175–201.

2008   Time to Destroy: An Archaeology of Supermodernity. *Current Anthropology* 49(2):247–279.

2013   Reclaiming Archaeology. In *Reclaiming Archaeology: Beyond the Tropes of Modernity,* edited by A. González-Ruibal, pp. 1–29. Routledge, New York.

2014   *An Archaeology of Resistance: Materiality and Time in an African Borderland.* Rowman and Littlefield, Lanham, Maryland.

GONZÁLEZ-RUIBAL, ALFREDO (EDITOR)

2013   *Reclaiming Archaeology: Beyond the Tropes of Modernity.* Routledge, New York.

GONZÁLEZ-TENNANT, EDWARD

2014   The "Color" of Heritage: Decolonizing Collaborative Archaeology in the Caribbean. *Journal of African Diaspora Archaeology and Heritage* 3(1):26–50.

GOODMAN, ALAN H.

2013   Bringing Culture into Human Biology and Biology Back into Anthropology. *American Anthropologist* 115(3):359–373.

GORDILLO, GASTÓN R.

2014   *Rubble: The Afterlife of Destruction.* Duke University Press, Durham, North Carolina.

GOSDEN, CHRIS (EDITOR)

2006   Race, Racism, and Archaeology. *World Archaeology* 38(1).

GOUCHER, CANDICE, AND EMMANUEL KOFI AGORSAH

2011 Excavating the Roots of Resistance: The Significance of Maroons in Jamaican Archaeology. In *Out of Many, One People: The Historical Archaeology of Colonial Jamaica*, edited by J. Delle, M. Hauser, and D. Armstrong, pp. 144–162. University of Alabama Press, Tuscaloosa.

GRAGG, LARRY DALE

2000 The Pious and the Profane: The Religious Life of Early Barbados Planters. *The Historian* 62(2):265–283.

2003 *Englishmen Transplanted: The English Colonization of Barbados, 1627–1660*. Oxford University Press, New York.

GRAVLEE, CLARENCE C.

2009 How Race Becomes Biological: Embodiment of Social Inequality. *American Journal of Physical Anthropology* 139:47–57.

2013 Race, Biology, and Culture: Rethinking the Connections. In *Anthropology of Race: Genes, Biology, and Culture*, edited by J. Hartigan Jr., pp. 21–42. School for Advanced Research Press, Santa Fe, New Mexico.

GRAY, D. RYAN

2011 Incorrigible Vagabonds and Suspicious Spaces in Nineteenth-Century New Orleans. *Historical Archaeology* 45(3):55–73.

GREENE, JACK P., ROSEMARY BRANA-SHUTE, AND RANDY J. SPARKS (EDITORS)

2001 *Money, Trade, and Power: The Evolution of South Carolina's Plantation Society*. University of South Carolina Press, Columbia.

GREENE, JACK P., AND PHILIP D. MORGAN (EDITORS)

2009 *Atlantic History: A Critical Appraisal*. Oxford University Press, New York.

GUNKEL, ALEXANDER, AND JEROME S. HANDLER

1970 A German Indentured Servant in Barbados in 1652: The Account of Heinrich von Uchteritz. *Journal of the Barbados Museum and Historical Society* 33:91–100.

GWYNN, AUBREY

1932 Documents Relating to the Irish in the West Indies. *Analecta Hibernica* 4:139–286.

HALL, MARTIN

2000 *Archaeology and the Modern World: Colonial Transcripts in South Africa and the Chesapeake*. Routledge, New York.

HALL, RICHARD

1764 *Acts Passed in the Island of Barbados, from 1643 to 1762*. Printed for Richard Hall, London.

HALL, STUART

1977 Pluralism, Race, and Class in Caribbean Society. In *Race and Class in Post-Colonial Society*, edited by UNESCO. UNESCO, Paris.

1980 Race, Articulation, and Societies Structured in Dominance. In *Sociological Theories: Race and Colonialism*, edited by UNESCO. UNESCO, Paris.

1986 Gramsci's Relevance for the Study of Race and Ethnicity. Reprinted in

Stuart Hall: Critical Dialogues in Cultural Studies, edited by D. Morley and K. Chen, pp. 411–440. Routledge, New York.

1991   What Is This "Black" in Black Popular Culture? Reprinted in *Black Popular Culture*, edited by G. Dent. Bay Press, Seattle.

1997   Subjects in History: Making Diasporic Identities. In *The House That Race Built: Black Americans*, edited by W. Lubiano. Pantheon, New York.

2017   *Familiar Stranger: A Life between Two Islands*. Duke University Press, Durham.

HAMILAKIS, YANNIS

2007   *The Nation and Its Ruins: Antiquity, Archaeology, and National Imagination in Greece*. Oxford University Press, New York.

HANCOCK, ANGE-MARIE

2016   *Intersectionality: An Intellectual History*. Oxford University Press, New York.

HANDLER, JEROME S.

1963a A Historical Sketch of Pottery Manufacture in Barbados. *Journal of the Barbados Museum and Historical Society* 30:129–153.

1963b Pottery Making in Rural Barbados. *Southwestern Journal of Anthropology* 19(3):314–334.

1965   Land Exploitative Activities and Economic Patterns in a Barbados Village. PhD dissertation, Brandeis University, Waltham, Massachusetts.

1966   Small-Scale Sugar Cane Farming in Barbados. *Ethnology* 5(3):264–283.

1967   Father Antoine Biet's Visit to Barbados in 1654. *Journal of the Barbados Museum and Historical Society* 32:56–76.

1969   The Amerindian Slave Population in Barbados in the Seventeenth and Early Eighteenth Centuries. *Caribbean Studies* 8:38–64.

1971a *A Guide to Source Materials for the Study of Barbados History, 1627–1834*. Southern Illinois University Press, Carbondale.

1971b The History of Arrowroot and the Origin of Peasantries in the British West Indies. *Journal of Caribbean History* 2:46–93.

1974   *The Unappropriated People: Freedmen in the Slave Society of Barbados*. Johns Hopkins University Press, Baltimore.

1977   Amerindians and Their Contributions to Barbadian Life in the Seventeenth Century. *Journal of the Barbados Museum and Historical Society* 35:189–210.

1982   Slave Revolts and Conspiracies in Seventeenth-Century Barbados. *New West India Guide* 56(1and2):5–42.

1984   Freedmen and Slaves in the Barbados Militia. *Journal of Caribbean History* 19:1–25.

1997   Escaping Slavery in a Caribbean Plantation Society: Marronage in Barbados, 1650s–1830s. *New West Indian Guide* 71(3and4):183–225.

2002   Plantation Slave Settlements in Barbados, 1650s to 1834. In *In the Shadow of the Plantation: Caribbean History and Legacy*, edited by A. Thompson and W. Marshall, pp. 123–161. Ian Randle, Kingston, Jamaica.

HANDLER, JEROME S., AND STEPHANIE BERGMAN

2009   Vernacular Houses and Domestic Material Culture on Barbadian Sugar Plantations, 1640–1838. *Journal of Caribbean History* 43(1):1–36.

HANDLER, JEROME S., AND FREDERICK W. LANGE

1978   *Plantation Slavery in Barbados: An Archaeological and Historical Investigation.* Harvard University Press, Cambridge, Massachusetts.

HANDLER, JEROME S., AND JOHN T. POHLMANN

1984   Slave Manumissions and Freedmen in Seventeenth-Century Barbados. *William and Mary Quarterly* 41(3):390–408.

HANDLER, JEROME S., AND MATTHEW C. REILLY

2015   Father Antoine Biet's Account Revisited: Perspectives on Irish Catholics in Mid-Seventeenth Century Barbados. In *Caribbean Irish Connections*, edited by A. Donnell, M. McGarrity, and E. O'Callaghan, pp. 33–46. University of the West Indies Press, Mona, Jamaica.

2017   Contesting "White Slavery" in the Caribbean: Enslaved Africans and European Indentured Servants in Seventeenth-Century Barbados. *New West Indian Guide* 91:30–55.

HANDLER, JEROME S., AND LON SHELBY

1973   A Seventeenth Century Commentary on Labor and Military Problems in Barbados. *Journal of the Barbados Museum and Historical Society* 34:117–121.

HANDLER, JEROME S., AND DIANE WALLMAN

2014   Production Activities in the Household Economies of Plantation Slaves: Barbados and Martinique, Mid-1600s to Mid-1800s. *International Journal of Historical Archaeology* 18(3):441–466.

HARLOW, VINCENT T.

1926   *A History of Barbados: 1625–1685.* Negro Universities Press, New York.

HARRIS, OLIVER J. T., AND JOHN ROBB

2012   Multiple Ontologies and the Problem of the Body in History. *American Anthropologist* 114(4):668–679.

HARRISON, RODNEY, AND JOHN SCHOFIELD

2010   *After Modernity: Archaeological Approaches to the Contemporary Past.* Oxford University Press, New York.

HARTIGAN, JOHN, JR.

1999   *Racial Situations: Class Predicaments of Whiteness in Detroit.* Princeton University Press, Princeton, New Jersey.

2005   *Odd Tribes: Toward a Cultural Analysis of White People.* Duke University Press, Durham, North Carolina.

HARTIGAN, JOHN, JR. (EDITOR)

2013   *Anthropology of Race: Genes, Biology, and Culture.* School for Advanced Research Press, Santa Fe, New Mexico.

HARVEY, DAVID
  1990   *The Condition of Postmodernity*. Blackwell, Oxford, England.
  2006   *The Limits to Capital*. Verso, New York.
  [1982]

HAUSER, MARK W.
  2008   *An Archaeology of Black Markets: Local Ceramics and Economies in Eighteenth-Century Jamaica*. University Press of Florida, Gainesville.
  2011   Routes and Roots of Empire: Pots, Power, and Slavery in the 18th-Century British Caribbean. *American Anthropologist* 113(3):431–447.
  2015   Blind Spots in Empire: Plantation Landscapes in Early Colonial Dominica (1763–1807). In *The Archaeology of Slavery: A Comparative Approach to Captivity and Coercion*, edited by L. Marshall, pp. 143–165. Southern Illinois University Press, Carbondale.

HAUSER, MARK W., AND DOUGLAS V. ARMSTRONG
  2012   The Archaeology of Not Being Governed: A Counterpoint to a History of Settlement of Two Colonies in the Eastern Caribbean. *Journal of Social Archaeology* 12(3):310–333.

HAUSER, MARK W., AND KENNETH G. KELLY (EDITORS)
  2009   Centering the Caribbean: Landscapes and Scale in Caribbean Historical Archaeology. *International Journal of Historical Archaeology* 13(1):1–126.

HAVISER, JAY B.
  2015a   Community Archaeology as an Essential Element for Successful Heritage Management. In *Managing Our Past into the Future: Archaeological Heritage Management in the Dutch Caribbean*, edited by C. L. Hofman and J. B. Haviser, pp. 133–151. Sidestone Press, Leiden, Netherlands.
  2015b   Truth and Reconciliation: Transforming Public Archaeology with African Descendant Voices in the Dutch Caribbean. *Journal of African Diaspora Archaeology and Heritage* 4(3):243–259.

HAVISER, JAY B. (EDITOR)
  1999   *African Sites: Archaeology in the Caribbean*. Markus Wiener, Princeton, New Jersey.

HAYES, KATHERINE HOWLETT
  2013   *Slavery before Race: Europeans, Africans, and Indians at Long Island's Sylvester Manor Plantation, 1651–1884*. New York University Press, New York.

HEATH, BARBARA J.
  1999   Buttons, Beads, and Buckles: Contextualizing Adornment within the Bounds of Slavery. In *Historical Archaeology, Identity Formation, and the Interpretation of Ethnicity*, edited by M. Franklin and G. Fesler. Colonial Williamsburg Research Publications, Williamsburg, Virginia.

HENRY, EDWARD R., BILL ANGELBECK, AND UZMA Z. RIZVI
  2017   Against Typology: A Critical Approach to Archaeological Order. *SAA Archaeological Record* 17(1):28–32.

HENRY, PADGETT

2004   The Caribbean Plantation: Its Contemporary Significance. In *Sugar, Slavery, and Society: Perspectives on the Caribbean, India, the Mascarenes, and the United States*, edited by B. Moitt, pp. 157–185. University Press of Florida, Gainesville.

HERSKOVITS, MELVILLE J.

1990   *The Myth of the Negro Past.* Beacon Press, Boston, Massachusetts.
[1941]

HICKS, DAN

2007   *"The Garden of the World": An Historical Archaeology of Sugar Landscapes in the Eastern Caribbean.* British Archaeological Reports Series 1632, Oxford, England.

HIGMAN, BARRY W.

2000   The Sugar Revolution. *Economic History Review* 53(2):213–236.

2011   *A Concise History of the Caribbean.* Cambridge University Press, New York.

HODGSON, STUDHOLME

1838   *Truths from the West Indies.* William Ball, London.

HOFFIUS, STEPHEN G. (EDITOR)

2011   *South Carolina and Barbados Connections: Selections from the South Carolina Historical Magazine.* Home House Press, Charleston, South Carolina.

HOFFMAN, MICHAEL A.

1993   *They Were White and They Were Slaves: The Untold History of the Enslavement of Whites in Early America.* Wiswell Ruffin House, Dresden, New York.

HOGAN, LIAM, LAURA McATACKNEY, AND MATTHEW C. REILLY

2016   The Irish in the Anglo-Caribbean: Servants or Slaves? *History Ireland* 24(2). Electronic document, https://www.historyireland.com/volume-24/the-irish-in-the-anglo-caribbean-servants-or-slaves/.

HOLSTON, JAMES

1999   Alternative Modernities: Statecraft and Religious Imagination in the Valley of the Dawn. *America Ethnologist* 26(3):605–631.

HOYOS, F. A.

1978   *Barbados: A History from Amerindians to Independence.* Macmillan, London.

HUGHES, GRIFFITH

1750   *The Natural History of Barbados: In Ten Books.* Printed for the author, London.

HUGHES, RONALD G.

1979   St. Elizabeth's Village, St. John. *Journal of the Barbados Museum and Historical Society* 36:66–71.

HUTTON, CHRISTOPHER M.

2005   *Race and the Third Reich: Linguistics, Racial Anthropology, and Genetics in the Dialectic of Volk.* Polity Books, Cambridge, England.

ISENBERG, NANCY

2016   *White Trash: The 400-Year Untold History of Class in America.* Viking, New York.

JABLONSKI, NINA G.

2012   *Living Color: The Biological and Social Meaning of Skin Color.* University of California Press, Berkeley.

JACKSON, JOHN B.

1984   *Discovering the Vernacular Landscape.* Yale University Press, New Haven, Connecticut.

JACKSON, JOHN L., JR.

2001   *Harlem World: Doing Race and Class in Contemporary Black America.* University of Chicago Press, Chicago.

JACOBSON, MATTHEW FRYE

1998   *Whiteness of a Different Color.* Harvard University Press, Cambridge, Massachusetts.

JAMES, C. L. R.

1963   *The Black Jacobins: Toussaint L'Ouverture and the San Domingo Revolution.*
[1938] Random House, New York.

JAMESON, FREDRIC

1991   *Postmodernism; or, The Cultural Logic of Late Capitalism.* Duke University Press, Durham, North Carolina.

JENNINGS, JOHN (EDITOR)

1654   *Acts and Statutes of the Island of Barbados.* Printed by Will. Bentley, London.

JOHNSON, GAYE THERESA, AND ALEX LUBIN (EDITORS)

2017   *Futures of Black Radicalism.* Verso, New York.

JOHNSON, HOWARD

1998   Introduction. In *The White Minority in the Caribbean,* edited by H. Johnson and K. Watson, pp. ix–xvi. Ian Randle, Kingston, Jamaica.

JONES, CECILY

2007   *Engendering Whiteness: White Women and Colonialism in Barbados and North Carolina, 1627–1865.* Manchester University Press, Manchester, England.

JONES, SIÂN, AND LYNETTE RUSSELL

2012   Archaeology, Memory, and Oral Tradition: An Introduction. *International Journal of Historical Archaeology* 16(2):267–283.

JONES, SIÂN, AND LYNETTE RUSSELL (EDITORS)

2012   Archaeology, Memory, and Oral Tradition. *International Journal of Historical Archaeology* 16(2).

JORDAN, DON, AND MICHAEL WALSH

2008   *White Cargo: The Forgotten History of Britain's White Slaves in America.* New York University Press, New York.

JORDAN, ELIZABETH G.
2005 "Unrelenting Toil": Expanding Archaeological Interpretations of the Female Slave Experience. *Slavery and Abolition* 26(2):217–232.

JORDAN, WINTHROP D.
1962 American Chiaroscuro: The Status and Definition of Mulattoes in the British Colonies. *William and Mary Quarterly* 19(2):183–200.
1968 *White over Black: American Attitudes toward the Negro, 1550–1812.* University of North Carolina Press, Chapel Hill.

KEAGY, THOMAS J.
1972 The Poor Whites of Barbados. *Revista de historia de América* 73/74:9–52.
1975 The "Redlegs" of Barbados. *Américas* 27(1):14–21.

KELLEHER, LAWRENCE R.
2001 *To Shed a Tear: A Story of Irish Slavery in the British West Indies.* Writers Club Press, iUniverse.

KELLY, HENRY E.
1999 *Scottish Sponge-Printed Pottery: Traditional Patterns, Their Manufacturers and History.* Lomonside, Glasgow, Scotland.

KELLY, JOHN D.
2002 Alternative Modernities or an Alternative to "Modernity": Getting Out of the Modernity Sublime. In *Critically Modern: Alternatives, Alterities, Anthropologies*, edited by B. Knauft, pp. 258–286. Indiana University Press, Bloomington.

KELLY, KENNETH G., AND BENOÎT BÉRARD (EDITORS)
2014 *Bitasion: Archéologie des Habitations—Plantations des Petites Antilles.* Sidestone Press, Leiden, Netherlands.

KELLY, KENNETH G., AND MEREDITH D. HARDY (EDITORS)
2009 *French Colonial Archaeology in the Southeast and the Caribbean.* University Press of Florida, Gainesville.

KELSO, WILLIAM M.
1997 *Archaeology at Monticello: Artifacts of Everyday Life in the Plantation Community.* Thomas Jefferson Memorial Foundation, Charlottesville, Virginia.

KIDDEY, RACHEL
2017 *Homeless Heritage: Collaborative Social Archaeology as Therapeutic Practice.* Oxford University Press, New York.

KNAUFT, BRUCE M.
2002 Critically Modern: An Introduction. In *Critically Modern: Alternatives, Alterities, Anthropologies*, edited by B. Knauft, pp. 1–54. Indiana University Press, Bloomington.

KNAUFT, BRUCE M. (EDITOR)
2002 *Critically Modern: Alternatives, Alterities, Anthropologies.* Indiana University Press, Bloomington.

KOSELLECK, REINHART
1985 *Futures Past: On the Semantics of Historical Time.* MIT Press, Cambridge, Massachusetts.

KUPPERMAN, KAREN O.

2012   *The Atlantic in World History.* Oxford University Press, New York.

KUSENBACH, MARGARETHE

2003   Street Phenomenology: The Go-Along as Ethnographic Research Tool. *Ethnography* 4(3):455–485.

LAMBERT, DAVID

2001   Liminal Figures: Poor Whites, Freedmen, and Racial Reinscription in Colonial Barbados. *Environment and Planning D: Society and Space* 19(3):335–350.

2005   *White Creole Culture, Politics and Identity during the Age of Abolition.* Cambridge University Press, Cambridge, England.

LANGE, FREDERICK W., AND JEROME S. HANDLER

1980   The Archaeology of Mapp's Cave: A Contribution to the Prehistory of Barbados. *Journal of the Virgin Islands Archaeological Society* 9:3–17.

LENIK, STEPHAN

2011   Mission Plantations, Space, and Social Control: Jesuits as Planters in French Caribbean Colonies and Frontiers. *Journal of Social Archaeology* 12(1):51–71.

LEONE, MARK P.

1999   Ceramics from Annapolis, Maryland: A Measure of Time Routines and Work Discipline. In *Historical Archaeologies of Capitalism,* edited by M. Leone and P. Potter Jr., pp. 195–216. Springer, New York.

2005   *The Archaeology of Liberty in an American Capital: Excavations in Annapolis.* University of California Press, Berkeley.

2010   *Critical Historical Archaeology.* Left Coast Press, Walnut Creek, California.

LEWIS, GARY

1999   *White Rebel: The Life and Times of TT Lewis.* University of the West Indies Press, Mona, Jamaica.

LIEBMANN, MATTHEW

2008   Introduction: The Intersections of Archaeology and Postcolonial Studies. In *Archaeology and the Postcolonial Critique,* edited by M. Liebmann and U. Rizvi, pp. 1–20. AltaMira Press, Lanham, Maryland.

2012   *Revolt: An Archaeological History of Pueblo Resistance and Revitalization in 17th Century New Mexico.* University of Arizona Press, Tucson.

LIEBMANN, MATTHEW, AND UZMA Z. RIZVI (EDITORS)

2008   *Archaeology and the Postcolonial Critique.* AltaMira Press, Lanham, Maryland.

LIGON, RICHARD

2013   *A True and Exact History of the Island of Barbados.* Edited by David Smith. E-text, 4th ed. Hackett, New York.

LINEBAUGH, PETER, AND MARCUS REDIKER

2000   *The Many-Headed Hydra: Sailors, Slaves, Commoners, and the Hidden History of the Revolutionary Atlantic.* Beacon Press, Boston.

LITTLE, BARBARA J., AND PAUL A. SHACKEL

2007   *Archaeology as a Tool of Civic Engagement*. AltaMira Press, Lanham, Maryland.

LOFTFIELD, THOMAS C.

2001   Creolization in Seventeenth-Century Barbados: Two Case Studies. In *Island Lives: Historical Archaeologies of the Caribbean*, edited by P. Farnsworth, pp. 207–233. University of Alabama Press, Tuscaloosa.

LONG, EDWARD

1774   *The History of Jamaica; or, General Survey of the Antient and Modern State of That Island: II*. Printed for T. Lowndes, London.

LOREN, DIANA D.

2012   Fear, Desire, and Material Strategies in Colonial Louisiana. In *The Archaeology of Colonialism: Intimate Encounters and Sexual Effects*, edited by B. Voss and E. Casella, pp. 105–121. Cambridge University Press, New York.

LYDON, JANE, AND UZMA Z. RIZVI (EDITORS)

2010   *Handbook of Postcolonial Archaeology*. Left Coast Press, Walnut Creek, California.

McCAFFERTY, KATE

2002   *Testimony of an Irish Slave Girl*. Penguin, New York.

McCLINTOCK, ANNE

1995   *Imperial Leather: Race, Gender, and Sexuality in the Colonial Contest*. Routledge, New York.

McDAVID, CAROL

2011   When Is "Gone" Gone? Archaeology, Gentrification, and Competing Narratives about Freedmen's Town, Houston. *Historical Archaeology* 45(3):74–88.

McDAVID, CAROL, AND DAVID W. BABSON (EDITORS)

1997   In the Realm of Politics: Prospects for Public Participation in African-American and Plantation Archaeology. *Historical Archaeology* 31(3):1–152.

McGUIRE, RANDALL H.

2002   *A Marxist Archaeology*. Percheron Press, Clifton Corners, New York.

2008   *Archaeology as Political Action*. University of California Press, Berkeley.

McGUIRE, RANDALL H., AND ROBERT PAYNTER

1991   *The Archaeology of Inequality*. Basil Blackwell, Oxford, England.

McGUIRE, RANDALL H., AND PAUL RECKNER

2005   Building a Working Class Archaeology. In *Industrial Archaeology: Future Directions*, edited by E. Casella and J. Symonds, pp. 217–241. Springer, New York.

MACK, RAYMOND W.

1965   Race, Class, and Power in Barbados: A Study of Stratification as an Integrating Force in a Democratic Revolution. In *Social Change in Developing Areas: A Reinterpretation of Evolutionary Theory*, edited by H. Barringer, G. Blanksten, and R. Mack, pp. 131–154. Schenkman, Cambridge, Massachusetts.

MacPherson, John

1963 *Caribbean Lands: A Geography of the West Indies*. Longman Caribbean, Kingston, Jamaica.

Maghbouleh, Neda

2017 *Limits of Whiteness: Iranian Americans and the Everyday Politics of Race*. Stanford University Press, Stanford.

Maisano, Chris

2017 The New "Culture of Poverty." *Catalyst* 1(2). Electronic document, https://catalyst-journal.com/vol1/no2/new-culture-of-poverty-maisano.

Marshall, Trevor, Peggy McGeary, and Grace Thompson (editors)

1981 *Folk Songs of Barbados*. Macmarson Associates, Bridgetown, Barbados.

Marshall, Woodville

1988 Villages and Plantation Sub-Division. In *Emancipation III: A Series of Lectures to Commemorate the 150th Anniversary of Emancipation*, edited by W. Marshall, pp. 1–19. University of the West Indies, Cave Hill and the National Cultural Foundation, Bridgetown, Barbados.

2003 Charity for the Undeserving? The Carpenter Trust and the Creation of the Parish Land Tenantry in St. Philip. *Journal of the Barbados Museum and Historical Society* 49:167–191.

Marshall, Woodville (editor)

1977 *The Colthurst Journal: Journal of a Special Magistrate in the Islands of Barbados and St. Vincent, July 1835–September 1838*. KTO Press, New York.

Marshall, Yvonne

2002 What Is Community Archaeology? *World Archaeology* 34(2) 211–219.

Martínez, Samuel

2007 *Decency and Excess: Global Aspirations and Material Deprivation on a Caribbean Sugar Plantation*. Paradigm, Boulder, Colorado.

Marx, Karl

1973 *Grundrisse: Foundations of the Critique of Political Economy*. Penguin, New York.

Matthews, Christopher N.

2001 Political Economy and Race: Comparative Archaeologies of Annapolis and New Orleans in the Eighteenth Century. In *Race and the Archaeology of Identity*, edited by C. Orser Jr., pp. 71–87. University of Utah Press, Salt Lake City.

2010 *The Archaeology of American Capitalism*. University Press of Florida, Gainesville.

Matthews, Christopher N., and Allison M. McGovern (editors)

2015 *The Archaeology of Race in the Northeast*. University Press of Florida, Gainesville.

Mayne, Alan, and Tim Murray (editors)

2001 *The Archaeology of Urban Landscapes: Explorations in Slumland*. Cambridge University Press, New York.

M'CHAREK, AMADE

2013   Beyond Fact or Fiction: On the Materiality of Race in Practice. *Cultural Anthropology* 28(3):420–442.

MELVILLE, HERMAN

1922   *The Apple-Tree Table and Other Sketches*. Princeton University Press,
[1854] Princeton, New Jersey.

MENARD, RUSSELL R.

2006   *Sweet Negotiations: Sugar, Slavery, and Plantation Agriculture in Early Barbados*. University of Virginia Press, Charlottesville.

MENIKETTI, MARCO G.

2015   *Sugar Cane Capitalism and Environmental Transformation: An Archaeology of Colonial Nevis, West Indies*. University of Alabama Press, Tuscaloosa.

MERRIMAN, NICK (EDITOR)

2004   *Public Archaeology*. Routledge, New York.

MERRITT, KERI LEIGH

2017   *Masterless Men: Poor Whites and Slavery in the Antebellum South*. Cambridge University Press, New York.

MILLER, GEORGE L.

1980   Classification and Economic Scaling of 19th-Century Ceramics. *Historical Archaeology* 14:1–40.

1991   A Revised Set of CC Index Values for Classification and Economic Scaling of English Ceramics from 1787 to 1880. *Historical Archaeology* 25(1):1–25.

MILLS, CHARLES W.

1997   *The Racial Contract*. Cornell University Press, Ithaca, New York.

2010   *Radical Theory, Caribbean Reality: Race, Class, and Social Domination*. University of the West Indies Press, Mona, Jamaica.

MINTZ, SIDNEY W.

1974   *Caribbean Transformations*. Columbia University Press, New York.

1985   *Sweetness and Power: The Place of Sugar in Modern History*. Penguin, New York.

MINTZ, SIDNEY W., AND RICHARD PRICE

1992   *The Birth of African-American Culture: An Anthropological Perspective*.
[1976] Beacon Press, Boston.

MOLEN, PATRICIA A.

1971   Population and Social Patterns in Barbados in the Early Eighteenth Century. *William and Mary Quarterly* 28(2):287–300.

MONAHAN, MICHAEL J.

2011   *The Creolizing Subject: Race, Reason, and the Politics of Purity*. Fordham University Press, New York.

MOREAU DE SAINT-MÉRY, M. L. E.

1797   *Description topographique, physique, civile, politique et historique de la partie francaise de l'isle Saint-Domingue*. A Philadelphie.

MORRISON, KAREN Y.

2010   Slave Mothers and White Fathers: Defining Family and Status in Late
       Colonial Cuba. *Slavery and Abolition* 31(1):29–55.

MROZOWSKI, STEPHEN A.

2006   *The Archaeology of Class in Urban America.* Cambridge University Press,
       New York.

MROZOWSKI, STEPHEN A., JAMES A. DELLE, AND ROBERT PAYNTER

2000   Introduction. In *Lines That Divide: Historical Archaeologies of Race, Class,
       and Gender,* edited by J. Delle, S. Mrozowski, and R. Paynter, pp. xi–xxxi.
       University of Tennessee Press, Knoxville.

MULLINS, PAUL R.

2008   Excavating America's Metaphor: Race, Diaspora, and Vindicationist
       Archaeologies. *Historical Archaeology* 42(2):104–122.

2012   *The Archaeology of Consumer Culture.* University Press of Florida, Gaines-
       ville.

NELSON, ALONDRA

2016   *The Social Life of DNA: Race, Reparations, and Reconciliation after the
       Genome.* Beacon Press, Boston.

NETTLEFORD, REX M.

2003   *Caribbean Cultural Identity: The Case of Jamaica.* Markus Wiener, Prince-
       ton, New Jersey.

NEWELL, SASHA

2012   *The Modernity Bluff: Crime, Consumption, and Citizenship in Côte d'Ivoire.*
       University of Chicago Press, Chicago.

NEWMAN, SIMON P.

2013   *A New World of Labor: The Development of Plantation Slavery in the British
       Atlantic.* University of Pennsylvania Press, Philadelphia.

NEWTON, MELANIE J.

2008   *The Children of Africa in the Colonies: Free People of Color in Barbados in
       the Age of Emancipation.* Louisiana State University Press, Baton Rouge.

NORTON, HOLLY K.

2013   Estate by Estate: The Landscape of the 1733 St. Jan Slave Rebellion. PhD
       dissertation, Syracuse University, Syracuse, New York.

O'CALLAGHAN, SEAN

2000   *To Hell or Barbados: The Ethnic Cleansing of Ireland.* Brandon Books, Dub-
       lin.

OKAMURA, KATSUYUKI, AND AKIRA MATSUDA (EDITORS)

2011   *New Perspectives in Global Public Archaeology.* Springer, New York.

OLDMIXON, JOHN

1708   *The British Empire in America, Containing the History of the Discovery,
       Settlement, Progress, and Present State of All the British Colonies, on the
       Continent and Islands of America.* John Nicholson at the King's Arm Press,
       London.

Olivier, Laurent

2011   *The Dark Abyss of Time: Archaeology and Memory.* Rowman and Littlefield, Lanham, Maryland.

2013   The Business of Archaeology Is the Present. In *Reclaiming Archaeology: Beyond the Tropes of Modernity,* edited by A. González-Ruibal, pp. 117–129. Routledge, New York.

Omi, Michael, and Howard Winant

2015   *Racial Formation in the United States.* 3rd ed. Routledge, New York.

O'Neill, Peter D., and David Lloyd

2009   *The Black and Green Atlantic: Cross-Currents of the African and Irish Diasporas.* Palgrave Macmillan, New York.

Opitz, Rachel S., Krysta Ryzewski, John F. Cherry, and Brenna Moloney

2015   Using Airborne LiDAR Survey to Explore Historic-Era Archaeological Landscapes on Montserrat in the Eastern Caribbean. *Journal of Field Archaeology* 40(5):523–541.

Orser, Charles E., Jr.

1988   The Archaeological Analysis of Plantation Society: Replacing Status and Caste with Economics and Power. *American Antiquity* 53(4):735–751.

1990   Archaeological Approaches to New World Plantation Slavery. *Archaeological Method and Theory* 2:111–154.

2007   *The Archaeology of Race and Racialization in Historic America.* University Press of Florida, Gainesville.

2011   The Archaeology of Poverty and the Poverty of Archaeology. *International Journal of Historical Archaeology* 15(4):533–543.

Orser, Charles E., Jr. (editor)

2001   *Race and the Archaeology of Identity.* University of Utah Press, Salt Lake City.

2004   *Race and Practice in Archaeological Interpretation.* University of Pennsylvania Press, Philadelphia.

Orser, Charles E., Jr., and Pedro A. Funari

2001   Archaeology and Slave Resistance and Rebellion. *World Archaeology* 33(1):61–72.

Ortiz, Fernando

1995   *Cuban Counterpoint: Tobacco and Sugar.* Duke University Press, Durham, North Carolina.

Otto, John Solomon, and Augustus Marion Burns III

1983   Black Folks and Poor Buckras: Archaeological Evidence of Slave and Overseer Living Conditions on an Antebellum Plantation. *Journal of Black Studies* 14(2):185–200.

Owen, Tim

2015   An Archaeology of Absence (or the Archaeology of Nothing). *Historic Environment* 27(2):70–83.

PALMIÉ, STEPHAN

2002   *Wizards and Scientists: Explorations in Afro-Cuban Modernity and Tradi-tion*. Duke University Press, Durham, North Carolina.

PALMIÉ, STEPHAN, AND FRANCISCO A. SCARANO (EDITORS)

2011   *The Caribbean: A History of the Region and Its Peoples*. University of Chi-cago Press, Chicago.

PARKER, MATTHEW

2011   *The Sugar Barons: Family, Corruption, Empire, and War in the West Indies*. Walker, New York.

PATTERSON, ORLANDO

1982   *Slavery and Social Death: A Comparative Study*. Harvard University Press, Cambridge, Massachusetts.

PAYNTER, ROBERT

1989   The Archaeology of Equality and Inequality. *Annual Review of Anthropol-ogy* 18(1):369–399.

PIERRE, JEMIMA

2013   *The Predicament of Blackness: Postcolonial Ghana and the Politics of Race*. University of Chicago Press, Chicago.

PINCKARD, GEORGE

1806   *Notes on the West Indies: Vol II*. Baldwin, Cradock, and Joy, London.

PLUMMER, MAGGIE

2012   *Spirited Away: A Novel of the Stolen Irish*. CreateSpace Independent Pub-lishing Platform.

POLANCO, MIEKA BRAND

2014   *Historically Black: Imagining Community in a Black Historic District*. New York University Press, New York.

POTTER, PARKER B., JR.

1991   What Is the Use of Plantation Archaeology? *Historical Archaeology* 25(3):94–107.

POYER, JOHN

1808   *The History of Barbados, from the First Discover of the Island, in the Year 1605, till the Accession of Lord Seaforth, 1801*. J. G. Barnard, London.

1941   Letter to Lord Seaforth. *Journal of the Barbados Museum and Historical Society* 8:150–165.

PRICE, EDWARD T.

1957   The Redlegs of Barbados. *Yearbook of the Association of Pacific Coast Geog-raphers* 10:35–39.

PUCKREIN, GARY A.

1984   *Little England: Plantation Society and Anglo-Barbadian Politics, 1627–1700*. New York University Press, New York.

RABINOW, PAUL

1989   *French Modern: Norms and Forms of the Social Environment*. University of Chicago Press, Chicago.

REEVES, MATTHEW

2011   Household Market Activities among Early Nineteenth-Century Jamaican
        Slaves: An Archaeological Case Study from Two Slave Settlements. In *Out
        of Many, One People: The Historical Archaeology of Colonial Jamaica*, edited
        by J. Delle, M. Hauser, and D. Armstrong, pp. 183–210. University of
        Alabama Press, Tuscaloosa.

REILLY, MATTHEW C.

2013   Archaeological Approaches to the "Poor Whites" of Barbados: Tired Ste-
        reotypes and New Directions. *Journal of the Barbados Museum and Histor-
        ical Society* 59:1–27.

2014   The School of Female Industry: "Poor White" Education in the Era of
        Slavery. *Journal of the Barbados Museum and Historical Society* 60:94–118.

2015a   The Irish in Barbados: Labour, Landscape, and Legacy. In *Caribbean Irish
        Connections*, edited by A. Donnell, M. McGarrity, and E. O'Callaghan, pp.
        47–63. University of the West Indies Press, Mona, Jamaica.

2015b   The Politics of Work, "Poor Whites," and Plantation Capitalism in Barba-
        dos. In *Historical Archaeologies of Capitalism,* edited by M. P. Leone and J.
        E. Knauf, pp. 375–397. Springer, New York.

2016a   Archaeologies of Instability: Order and Disorder in Colonial Barbados.
        Journal of Social Archaeology 16(2):216–237.

2016b   "Poor White" Recollections and Artifact Reuse in Barbados: Consid-
        erations for Archaeologies of Poverty. *International Journal of Historical
        Archaeology* 20(2):318–340.

2016c   "Poor Whites" on the Peripheries: "Poor White" and Afro-Barbadian Inter-
        action on the Plantation. In *Roots of Empire: Archaeologies of Freedom and
        Slavery in the Caribbean*, edited by L. Bates, J. Delle, and J. Chenoweth, pp.
        49–78. University Press of Florida, Gainesville.

RICHARD, FRANÇOIS G.

2010   Recharting Atlantic Encounters: Object Trajectories and Histories of
        Value in the Siin (Senegal) and Senegambia. *Archaeological Dialogues*
        17(1):1–27.

2011   Materializing Poverty: Archaeological Reflections from the Postcolony.
        Historical Archaeology 45(3):166–182.

RICHARD, FRANÇOIS G., AND KEVIN C. MACDONALD (EDITORS)

2015   *Ethnic Ambiguity in the African Past: Materiality, History, and the Shaping of
        Cultural Identities*. Left Coast Press, Walnut Creek, California.

RICHARDSON, BONHAM C.

1985   *Panama Money in Barbados, 1900–1920*. University of Tennessee Press,
        Knoxville.

RIMMER, JAYNE, PETER CONNELLY, SARAH R. JONES, AND JOHN WALKER (EDITORS)

2011   Poverty in Depth: New International Perspectives. *International Journal of
        Historical Archaeology* 15(4).

RIVERS, MARCELLUS, AND OXENBRIDGE FOYLE
1659   *England's Slavery, or Barbados Merchandize*. London.

RIVOAL, ISABELLE, AND NOEL B. SALAZAR
2013   Introduction: Contemporary Ethnographic Practice and the Value of Ser-
        endipity. *Social Anthropology* 21(2):178–185.

RIZVI, UZMA Z.
2016   Decolonization as Care. In *Slow Reader: A Resource for Design Thinking
        and Practice*, edited by C. F. Strauss and A. P. Pais, pp. 85–95. Valiz,
        Amsterdam.

ROBIN, CYNTHIA
2002   Outside of Houses: The Practices of Everyday Life at Chan Nòohol,
        Belize. *Journal of Social Archaeology* 2(2):245–268.

ROBIN, CYNTHIA, AND NAN A. ROTHSCHILD
2002   Archaeological Ethnographies: Social Dynamics of Outdoor Space. *Jour-
        nal of Social Archaeology* 2(2):159–172.

ROBINSON, CEDRIC J.
1983   *Black Marxism: The Making of the Black Radical Tradition*. University of
        North Carolina Press, Chapel Hill.

ROEDIGER, DAVID R.
2007   *The Wages of Whiteness: Race and the Making of the American Working
        Class*. New ed. Verso, New York.
2017   *Class, Race, and Marxism*. Verso, New York.

ROPER, SHANI
2012   "A Almshouse Ting Dat": Development in Poor Relief and Child Welfare
        in Jamaica during the Interwar Years. PhD dissertation, Rice University,
        Houston.

ROSENBERG, HARRY
1962   Social Mobility among the Rural White Population of Barbados. Master's
        thesis, Brandeis University, Waltham, Massachusetts.

RUGEMER, EDWARD B.
2013   The Development of Mastery and Race in the Comprehensive Slave Codes
        of the Greater Caribbean during the Seventeenth Century. *William and
        Mary Quarterly* 70(3):429–458.

RYZEWSKI, KRYSTA, AND JOHN F. CHERRY
2015   Struggles of a Sugar Society: Surveying Plantation-Era Montserrat, 1650–
        1850. *International Journal of Historical Archaeology* 19(2):356–383.

RYZEWSKI, KRYSTA, AND LAURA MCATACKNEY
2015   Historic and Contemporary Irish Identity on Montserrat: The "Emerald
        Isle of the Caribbean." In *Caribbean Irish Connections*, edited by A. Don-
        nell, M. McGarrity, and E. O'Callaghan, pp. 119–139. University of the
        West Indies Press, Mona, Jamaica.

SAID, EDWARD
1978   *Orientalism*. Vintage, New York.

SAINSBURY, W. NOEL

1893   *Calendar of State Papers, Colonial Series, America and West Indies, 1675–1676.* Mackie, London.

SAYERS, DANIEL O.

2014   *A Desolate Place for a Defiant People: The Archaeology of Maroons, Indigenous Americans, and Enslaved Laborers in the Great Dismal Swamp.* University Press of Florida and the Society for Historical Archaeology, Gainesville.

SCARAMELLI, KAY TARBLE DE

2012   Effects of Empire: Gendered Transformations on the Orinoco Frontier. In *The Archaeology of Colonialism: Intimate Encounters and Sexual Effects,* edited by B. Voss and E. Casella, pp. 138–155. Cambridge University Press, New York.

SCHEID, DWAYNE L.

2015   The Political Economy of Ceramic Production in Barbados: From Ceramic Industry to Craft Production. PhD dissertation, Syracuse University, Syracuse, New York.

SCHMIDT, PETER R., AND THOMAS C. PATTERSON (EDITORS)

1995   *Making Alternative Histories: The Practice of Archaeology and History in Non-western Settings.* School for Advanced Research Press, Santa Fe, New Mexico.

SCHWARTZ, STUART B.

1997   Spaniards, "Pardos," and the Missing Mestizos: Identities and Racial Categories in the Early Hispanic Caribbean. *New West Indian Guide* 71(1and2):5–19.

SCOTT, DAVID

2004   *Conscripts of Modernity: The Tragedy of Colonial Enlightenment.* Duke University Press, Durham, North Carolina.

2013   *Omens of Adversity: Tragedy, Time, Memory, Justice.* Duke University Press, Durham, North Carolina.

SCOTT, JAMES C.

1976   *The Moral Economy of the Peasant: Subsistence and Rebellion in Southeast Asia.* Yale University Press, New Haven, Connecticut.

1988   *Seeing Like a State: How Certain Schemes to Improve the Human Condition Have Failed.* Yale University Press, New Haven, Connecticut.

2009   *The Art of Not Being Governed: An Anarchist History of Upland Southeast Asia.* Yale University Press, New Haven, Connecticut.

SHACKEL, PAUL A.

2009   *The Archaeology of American Labor and Working-Class Life.* University Press of Florida, Gainesville.

2011   *New Philadelphia: An Archaeology of Race in the Heartland.* University of California Press, Berkeley.

2013   Changing the Past for the Present and the Future. *Historical Archaeology* 47(3):1–11.

SHACKEL, PAUL A., AND ERVE J. CHAMBERS (EDITORS)

2004   *Places in Mind: Public Archaeology as Applied Anthropology.* Routledge, New York.

SHACKEL, PAUL A., AND MICHAEL P. ROLLER (GUEST EDITORS)

2013   Reversing the Narrative. *Historical Archaeology* 47(3).

SHAW, JENNY

2013   *Everyday Life in the Early English Caribbean: Irish, Africans, and the Construction of Difference.* University of Georgia Press, Athens.

SHEPPARD, JILL

1977   *The "Redlegs" of Barbados: Their Origins and History.* KTO Press, New York.

SHILSTONE, E. M.

1933   A List of Persons Who Left Barbados in the Year 1679. *Journal of the Barbados Museum and Historical Society* 1:155–180.

SIEDOW, ERIK

2014   Reconfiguring Redware: Typological and Analytical Considerations of Barbadian Red Earthenware. *Journal of the Barbados Museum and Historical Society* 60:152–180.

SILLIMAN, STEPHEN W.

2014   Archaeologies of Indigenous Survivance and Residence: Navigating Colonial and Scholarly Dualities. In *Rethinking Colonial Pasts through Archaeology,* edited by N. Ferris, R. Harrison, and M. V. Wilcox, pp. 57–75. Oxford University Press, New York.

SILLIMAN, STEPHEN W. (EDITOR)

2008   *Collaborating at the Trowel's Edge: Teaching and Learning in Indigenous Archaeology.* University of Arizona Press, Tucson.

SIMMONS, PETER

1976   "Red Legs": Class and Color Contradictions in Barbados. *Studies in Comparative International Development* 11(1):3–24.

SINGLETON, THERESA A.

1999   An Introduction to African-American Archaeology. In *I, Too, Am America: Archaeological Studies of African-American Life,* edited by T. Singleton, pp. 1–20. University of Virginia Press, Charlottesville.

2015   *Slavery behind the Wall: An Archaeology of a Cuban Coffee Plantation.* University Press of Florida, Gainesville.

SINGLETON, THERESA A. (EDITOR)

1999   *I, Too, Am America: Archaeological Studies of African-American Life.* University of Virginia Press, Charlottesville.

2009   *The Archaeology of Slavery and Plantation Life.* Left Coast Press, Walnut Creek, California.

SINGLETON, THERESA A., AND MARK BOGRAD

2000   Breaking Typological Barriers: Looking for the Colono in Colonoware. In *Lines That Divide: Historical Archaeologies of Race, Class, and Gender,* edited by J. Delle, S. Mrozowski, and R. Paynter, pp. 3–21. University of Tennessee Press, Knoxville.

SLACK, PAUL
1995   *The English Poor Law, 1531–1782.* Cambridge University Press, New York.

SLOCUM, KAREN
2017   Caribbean Free Villages: Toward an Anthropology of Blackness, Place, and Freedom. *American Ethnologist* 44(3):425–434.

SMEDLEY, AUDREY, AND DRIAN D. SMEDLEY
2012   *Race in North America: Origin and Evolution of a Worldview.* Westview Press, Boulder, Colorado.

SMITH, ABBOT EMERSON
1947   *Colonists in Bondage: White Servitude and Convict Labor in America, 1607–1776.* University of North Carolina Press, Chapel Hill.

SMITH, FREDERICK H.
2008   *The Archaeology of Alcohol and Drinking.* University Press of Florida, Gainesville.

SMITH, FREDERICK H., AND KARL S. WATSON
2009   Urbanity, Sociability, and Commercial Exchange in the Barbados Sugar Trade: A Comparative Colonial Archaeological Perspective on Bridgetown, Barbados in the Seventeenth Century. *International Journal of Historical Archaeology* 13(1):63–79.

SMITH, M. G.
1965   *The Plural Society in the British West Indies.* University of California Press, Berkeley.

SMITH, MARK M.
1994   Counting Clocks, Owning Time: Detailing and Interpreting Clock and Watch Ownership in the American South, 1739–1865. *Time and Society* 3(3):321–339.

SPENCER-WOOD, SUZANNE M. (EDITOR)
1987   *Consumer Choice in Historical Archaeology.* Plenum Press, New York.

SPENCER-WOOD, SUZANNE M., AND CHRISTOPHER N. MATTHEWS
2011   Impoverishment, Criminalization, and the Culture of Poverty. *Historical Archaeology* 45(3):1–10.

SPENCER-WOOD, SUZANNE M., AND CHRISTOPHER N. MATTHEWS (EDITORS)
2011   Archaeologies of Poverty. *Historical Archaeology* 45(3).

SPRIGGS, MATTHEW (EDITOR)
1984   *Marxist Perspectives in Archaeology.* Cambridge University Press, New York.

STAFFORD, PAT
2003   Death of a Plantation, Growth of a Community: Goodland, St. Michael, 1900–1960. *Journal of the Barbados Museum and Historical Society* 49:204–218.

STOLER, ANN LAURA
1995   *Race and the Education of Desire: Foucault's* History of Sexuality *and the*

Colonial Order of Things. Duke University Press, Durham, North Carolina.

2002   *Carnal Knowledge and Imperial Power: Race and the Intimate in Colonial Rule.* University of California Press, Berkeley.

2009   *Along the Archival Grain: Epistemic Anxieties and Colonial Common Sense.* Princeton University Press, Princeton, New Jersey.

STOLER, ANN LAURA (EDITOR)

2013   *Imperial Debris: On Ruins and Ruination.* Duke University Press, Durham, North Carolina.

STONER, MICHAEL J.

2000   Codrington Plantation: A History of a Barbadian Ceramic Industry. Master's thesis, Armstrong Atlantic State University, Savannah, Georgia.

STUART, ANDREA

2012   *Sugar in the Blood: A Family's Story of Slavery and Empire.* Knopf, New York.

SUSSMAN, ROBERT W.

2014   *The Myth of Race: The Troubling Persistence of an Unscientific Idea.* Harvard University Press, Cambridge, Massachusetts.

TAYLOR, CHARLES

1999   Two Theories of Modernity. *Public Culture* 11(1):153–174.

TAYLOR, ERIN B.

2013   *Materializing Poverty: How the Poor Transform Their Lives.* Rowman and Littlefield, Lanham, Maryland.

THOMAS, JULIAN

2004   *Archaeology and Modernity.* Routledge, New York.

THOME, JAMES ARMSTRONG, AND JOSEPH HORACE KIMBALL

1838   Emancipation in the West Indies: A Six Months' Tour in Antigua, Barbados, and Jamaica, in the Year 1837. American Anti-Slavery Society, New York.

THOMPSON, ALVIN O. (EDITOR)

2002   *In the Shadow of the Plantation: Caribbean History and Legacy.* Ian Randle, Kingston, Jamaica.

THOMPSON, E. P.

1967   Time, Work-Discipline, and Industrial Capitalism. *Past and Present* 38:56–97.

THOMPSON, PETER

2009   Henry Drax's Instructions on the Management of a Seventeenth-Century Barbadian Sugar Plantation. *William and Mary Quarterly* 66(3):565–604.

TOMLINS, CHRISTOPHER

2010   *Freedom Bound: Law, Labor, and Civic Identity in Colonizing English America, 1580–1865.* Cambridge University Press, New York.

TRIGGER, BRUCE G.

2006   *A History of Archaeological Thought.* 2nd ed. Cambridge University Press, New York.

TROUILLOT, MICHEL-ROLPH

1988   *Peasants and Capitalism: Dominica in the World Economy.* Johns Hopkins
        University Press, Baltimore.

1992   The Caribbean Region: An Open Frontier in Anthropological Theory.
        Annual Review of Anthropology 21:19–42.

1995   *Silencing the Past: Power and the Production of History.* Beacon Press, Bos-
        ton.

2003   *Global Transformations: Anthropology and the Modern World.* Palgrave
        Macmillan, New York.

TYLER, KATHARINE

2012   *Whiteness, Class, and the Legacies of Empire: On Home Ground.* Palgrave
        Macmillan, New York.

VOSS, BARBARA L.

2008   *The Archaeology of Ethnogenesis: Race and Sexuality in Colonial San Fran-
        cisco.* University of California Press, Berkeley.

2012   Sexual Effects: Postcolonial and Queer Perspectives on the Archaeology of
        Sexuality and Empire. In *The Archaeology of Colonialism: Intimate Encoun-
        ters and Sexual Effects*, edited by B. Voss and E. Casella, pp. 11–28. Cam-
        bridge University Press, New York.

VOSS, BARBARA L., AND ELEANOR CONLIN CASELLA (EDITORS)

2012   *The Archaeology of Colonialism: Intimate Encounters and Sexual Effects.*
        Cambridge University Press, New York.

WATSON, KARL STEWART

1970   The Redlegs of Barbados. Master's thesis, University of Florida, Gaines-
        ville.

2000a   *A King of Right to Be Idle: Old Doll, Matriarch of Newton Plantation.*
        Rewriting History: Number Three. Department of History, University of
        the West Indies, Cave Hill Campus and the Barbados Museum and His-
        torical Society.

2000b   "Walk and Nyam Buckras": Poor-White Emigration from Barbados,
        1834–1900. *Journal of Caribbean History* 34(1and2):130–156.

2003   Bridgetown Expands in the Late Nineteenth Century: The Creation of the
        Suburbs of Belleville and Strathclyde. *Journal of the Barbados Museum and
        Historical Society* 49:192–203.

WATSON, MARK R., AND ROBERT B. POTTER

1993   Housing and Housing Policy in Barbados: The Relevance of the Chattel
        House. *Third World Planning Review* 15(4):373–395.

2001   *Low-Cost Housing in Barbados: Evolution or Social Revolution?* University
        of the West Indies Press, Mona, Jamaica.

WEBSTER, JANE

1999   Resisting Traditions: Ceramics, Identity, and Consumer Choice in the
        Outer Hebrides from 1800 to the Present. *International Journal of Histori-
        cal Archaeology* 3(1):53–73.

WEIK, TERRANCE M.

2012   *The Archaeology of Anti-Slavery Resistance.* University Press of Florida, Gainesville.

WELCH, PEDRO L. V.

2003   *Slave Society in the City: Bridgetown, Barbados, 1680–1834.* Ian Randle, Kingston, Jamaica.

2005   Exploring the Marine Plantation: An Historical Investigation of the Barbados Fishing Industry. *Journal of Caribbean History* 39(1):19–37.

2012   Poor Whites in Barbadian History. In *Narratives of the Occluded Irish Diaspora*, edited by M. Ó hAodha and J. O'Callaghan, pp. 125–148. Peter Lang, Oxford, England.

2013   Family Structures/Living in Sin. Lecture presented as part of *The Emancipation Project, 1838–1937* lecture series. April 25, 2013, Barbados Museum and Historical Society, Bridgetown.

WHITE, CHERYL

2010   Kumako: A Place of Convergence for Maroons and Amerindians in Suriname, SA. *Antiquity* 84(324):467–479.

WILKIE, LAURIE A., AND PAUL FARNSWORTH

2005   *Sampling Many Pots: An Archaeology of Memory and Tradition at a Bahamian Plantation.* University Press of Florida, Gainesville.

WILLIAMS, ERIC

1984   *From Columbus to Castro: The History of the Caribbean.* Vintage, New York.

1994   *Capitalism and Slavery.* University of North Carolina Press, Chapel
[1944] Hill.

WILLIAMSON, JOHN

1817   *Medical and Miscellaneous Observations Relative to the West India Islands.* Alex Smellie, Edinburgh.

WOLF, ERIC

1982   *Europe and the People without History.* University of California Press, Berkeley.

WOODERSON, CARTER G.

1930   The Negro Washerwoman, a Vanishing Figure. *Journal of Negro History* 15(3):269–277.

WOODWARD, ROBYN P.

2011   Feudalism or Agrarian Capitalism? The Archaeology of the Early Sixteenth-Century Spanish Sugar Industry. In *Out of Many, One People: The Historical Archaeology of Colonial Jamaica*, edited by J. A. Delle, M. W. Hauser, and D. V. Armstrong, pp. 23–40. University of Alabama Press, Tuscaloosa.

WRAY, MATT

2006   *Not Quite White: White Trash and the Boundaries of Whiteness.* Duke University Press, Durham, North Carolina.

WRAY, MATT, AND ANNALEE NEWITZ (EDITORS)

2013   *White Trash: Race and Class in America*. Routledge, New York.

WURST, LOUANN, AND ROBERT K. FITTS

1999   Introduction: Why Confront Class? *Historical Archaeology* 33(1):1–6.

WYNTER, SYLVIA

2003   Unsettling the Coloniality of Being/Power/Truth/Freedom: Towards the Human, After Man, Its Overrepresentation—An Argument. *CR: The New Centennial Review* 3(3):257–337.

ZIMMERMAN, LARRY J., AND JESSICA WELCH

2011   Displaced and Barely Visible: Archaeology and the Material Culture of Homelessness. *Historical Archaeology* 45(1):67–85.

INDEX

Page numbers in italics refer to illustrations.

84–85; official records concerning, 88–90; origins of, 86–87; pathways of, 85, 92, 106–8, 153–54, 183; as poor white tenantry, 86–90; population of, 90, 107; postemancipation changes in, 165–66; racial identities in, 85, 93, 98, 107, 191; research on, 11–12, 16–18, 20–21; socioeconomic interactions of, 106–9; spatial organization of, 151–55; surviving residents of, 84; as vernacular landscape, 150–55, 183

Bequia, 77

Bhabha, Homi, 73

Black Radical Tradition, 49

Bloch, Maurice, 37–38

Block, Kristen, 65

breadfruit, 159

Bridenbaugh, Carl, 60

Bridenbaugh, Roberta, 60

Bridgetown, 5, 18, 20, 46, 55, 66, 67, 76, 78, 79, 91, 132, 156, 182

Brighton, Stephen, 131

Browne, David, 148

Brubaker, Rogers, 44

Buck-Morss, Susan, 49

burial records, 171, *171*

Bussa's Rebellion, 134

buttons, 135–38, *137*

Canny, Nicholas, 59

capitalism: architectural practices affected by, 141–42; Barbadian labor and, 180–83; Below Cliff in relation to, 180–83; and Caribbean modernity, 28; moral economies compared with, 139, 142; plantations as instance of, 34, 35, 180; resistance to, 178, 181–83

Caribbean: cultural identities in, 149–50, 201n4; modernity in, 27–30, 33, 50–51, 179; race in, 146–47

CARICOM (Caribbean coalition), 12–13

Carlisle, Earl of, 57

Carpenter, Richard, 170

Carpenter Trust, 170

Carter (doctor), 91

Cateau, Heather, 66, 67

CC index, 127

ceramics, 104, 119, 124–25, *126*, 127–31, *129*, *130*, 161–63, *162*. *See also* earthenware

Certeau, Michel de, 48

Chakrabarty, Dipesh, 180

Chalky Mount, 157–59

Chapman, Matthew, 113

chattel houses, 2, 80, 99, 103, 121–25, *122*, 140

Chenoweth, John, 134

children: of enslaved Africans/ Afro-Barbadians, 60; of indentured servants, 60; mixed-race, 168–72; of Redlegs, 115

church seating regulations, 164–65

Church View, 78, 165

class: in Barbados, 33; plantation life and, 40; in plantation society, 21; race in relation to, 33–34, 40–45; Redlegs and, 40–41. *See also* poor relief; poverty; Redlegs (poor whites): economic circumstances of

Clifton Hall Plantation, 38, 84–85, 86–87, 90, 107, 134, 139, 150, 154, 165, 184

Clifton Hall tenantry, 165

Codrington Plantation, 74

Coleridge, Henry Nelson, 75, 113, 135, 148

Colleton Plantation, 90

Colt, Henry, 67–68

Colthurst, John, 71–72, 168

Columbus, Christopher, 27

community archaeology, 82–84

Contract Law, 88

Cooper, Thomas, 86

cotton, 61

Craton, Michael, 168

servant versus slave, 62, 64; spatial organization of, on plantations, 151; for sugar production, 61–62; types of, 62; of whites on plantations, 66–67; women and, 45–46, 74, 135–36; work versus, 181–83
Ladders (pathway), 107, 153–54
Lambert, David, 8, 73
Lange, Frederick W., 91, 146
Layne, Leslie, 140
laziness. *See* idleness
Lewis, Gary, 67
Liebmann, Matthew, 12, 39
Ligon, Richard, 61, 63
limestone, 1, 2, 55, 101–7, 121, 123–25, 134, 160, 189
liminality, 73
Linebaugh, Peter, 49, 178
Locke, John, 199n2
Long, Edward, 147

McClintock, Anne, 45
McGuire, Randall, 202n2
manumission, 47, 74, 201n8
Mapps Cave, 134
marginal spaces: Below Cliff as instance of, 175; Redlegs in, 38–39, 51, 54, 81, 112, 194; significance of, 38–39, 110; tenantries as, 20, 66–67, 154; transgressive behaviors in, 167
market activity, 108, 155–56
marriage. *See* intermarriage
Marshall, Edward, 157
Marshall, Woodville, 91, 170
Marshall's Pen, 161
Martin, George, 86
Marx, Karl, 180, 181
Marxism, 33–34, 35, 180, 182, 202n2
Masters and Servants Act (1838), 165
Masters and Servants Act (1840), 122
material culture: in Below Cliff, 95–97, 100, 103–6, *105*, 124, 126–38, 157–63, 188–91; capitalism in relation to, 45; consumption patterns

linked to, 112, 128–29, 131, 160–61; economic circumstances revealed by, 127–38; interpretation of, 10, 21, 80, 97, 100, 104, 112, 191; social interactions suggested by, 155–63. *See also* artifact reuse; ceramics
Matthews, Christopher N., 41, 141–42, 192
Mayers, Lucretia, 157
Melville, Herman, 111
Menard, Russell, 57, 60
metal artifacts. *See* nails; tin cans
militia, 67, 69–72, *72*, 77, 165
Miller, George, 127
Mills, Charles, 32–33, 167
Mintz, Sidney, 146, 154–55
miscegenation. *See* intermarriage
modernity/modernities: alternative, 19, 22, 48–51, 174–80, 182, 188; archaeology in relation to, 27, 30, 48; Caribbean, 19, 27–30, 33, 50–51, 179; conceptualizations of, 26–27, 29, 175–77; cultural, 28, 177; legacy of, 174–75; race and, 22; resistance to, 48–49, 176–79
modernization, 19, 28–29, 177, 179
Monahan, Michael, 16, 43, 147
Monkey Jump (pathway), 107, 153–54
Monticello, 151
Montserrat, 57
Moondance Productions, 4
moral economies, 139, 142, 181. *See also* informal economies
Moreau de Saint-Méry, M. L. E., 146
Mount Plantation, 131
Mrozowski, Stephen A., 45
Mullins, Paul, 31

nails, 140, *141*
Negro Yard, 153
Nettleford, Rex, 34
Newcastle, 78, 165
Newcastle Plantation, 90, 108
Newell, Sasha, 139